THE REAL WORLD GUIDE TO H... MENT

THE REAL WORLD GUIDE TO FASHION SELLING AND MANAGEMENT

Gerald J. Sherman

Sar Perlman

Fairchild Publications, Inc.

New York

Executive Editor: Olga T. Kontzias
Acquisitions Editor: Joseph Miranda
Art Director: Adam B. Bohannon
Production Manager: Ginger Hillman
Production Editor: Elizabeth Marotta
Production Intern: Michael Noto
Senior Development Editor: Jennifer Crane
Development Editor: Jason Moring
Copy Editor: Vivian Gomez
Interior Design and Layout: Ron Reeves
Cover Design: Adam B. Bohannon

Library of Congress Catalog Card Number: 2006925282
ISBN-13: 978-1-56367-421-1
ISBN-10: 1-56367-421-1
GST R 133004424

Printed in Canada
TP14

CONTENTS

PREFACE

Fashion is an exciting industry, in particular because it is ever-changing and volatile. What remains constant, however, is the demand for skilled and knowledgeable salespeople and managers who understand the market needs and adapt to them. The ability to adjust to this fast-paced business is more important now than ever before. In writing *The Real World Guide to Fashion Selling and Management*, we adopted a nuts-and-bolts approach to the world of fashion selling because it will give college graduates a better opportunity to achieve successful careers in this field.

The act of personal selling in the fashion industry is quickly becoming lost in a sea of flashy advertisements, websites, and other technological noise. Students increasingly believe that selling is something that magically happens. Future salespeople and sales executives must have a thorough understanding of the real-world basics of selling before they enter the job market. There are possibly as many sales workshops as there are stars in the sky—an effort by businesses to educate their staffs on how to sell. With more than 25 years of experience, my (Jerry Sherman) background includes owning a successful fashion apparel company and serving as VP for several multi-million-dollar apparel corporations. I've also been a consultant in the industry and taught seminars and classes both nationally and internationally. After working in the industry and as a professor at the Fashion Institute of Technology, New York; Lynn University, Boca Raton, FL; AI Miami International University of Art and Design; and Johnson & Wales University, College of Business, North Miami, FL, I've learned that students need to understand real-world, practical approaches to selling, rather than by trial and error once they are working. When my co-author, Sar Perlman—a veteran journalist, copywriter, web producer, and lecturer—and I joined together to write this book, one of our main objectives was to make it reader-friendly. Textbooks can be intimidating and deal with subject matters that are unrelated to the real world. Our book allows students to understand the information from an academic perspective and prepares them for success in the business world.

The text's fourteen chapters deal with the aspects of fashion selling and management and place them in context with the real world. Chapters 1–3 offer a general introduction to the field; they dispel common myths about it and delve into the inner workings of fashion sales within the retail and wholesale environments. Chapters 4–8 discuss the fundamentals of selling, including prospecting, conducting sales presentations, closing, and cultivating new and existing business relationships. Chapters 9–11 cover the fundamentals for sales management, from setting seasonal sales goals to delivering training programs to the sales force. Chapters 12–14 address the organizational facets of the industry, the trends toward globalization, and the various strategies to adapt to change.

Each chapter prominently defines the key terms as they are introduced, and all the terms are listed in alphabetical order in the glossary at the end of the text. The sidebars using the heading of RW (Real World) explain the most salient points in the chapters. Of particular interest to students are the RW Principle, RW Concept, RW Figure, and RW Story, which highlight significant concepts and principles and provide real-world examples for these concepts.

At the end of the chapters there are detailed case studies featuring successful, high-caliber fashion salespeople and managers who illustrate how these vital principles apply to the existing job market, while in-class role-play exercises allow students to experience these principles firsthand. There are also RW Exercises, which ask students to apply what they learned in the chapters and really think about how they would handle real-life scenarios.

Sales and sales management within the fashion industry are vital and important roles. The proper use of sales methodology, relationship building strategies, and management approaches is the foundation for a successful career in fashion sales and management, and we hope this book will help set you on your way to achieving that success.

ACKNOWLEDGMENTS

We would like to thank Olga T. Kontzias, executive editor of Fairchild Books, for helping formulate the content of this book and encouraging and placing her confidence in us. A special thanks also goes to Jason Moring, our development editor, and Elizabeth Marotta, our production editor, who were instrumental in the creation of this book and always available for advice. Their sound judgment guided us through the process.

We would also like to extend our thanks to Adam Bohannon, our art director, for his outstanding work and assistance.

Many thanks as well to those who have generously given their time to provide us with real-world information for the case studies: George Feldenkreis, chairman and CEO of Perry Ellis International; Oscar Feldenkreis, president and COO of Perry Ellis International; Ron Ellis, president of MRI Mayberry Group; Peter V. Handal, president and CEO, Dale Carnegie & Associates; Alex Hitz, formerly a menswear sales specialist at Macy's; Joan Kerns Kauffman, executive vice president and general manager of Design Center of the Americas; Chris Kolbe, president of Original Penguin; Erv Magram, managing director, catalog division, CCT Marketing LLC; Thomas J. Schwenk, principal and owner of Jordan Thomas & Associates; George Sharoubin, owner of Girogio's Palm Beach; and Karen Walker, international fashion designer. We wish to also thank the following reviewers, selected by Fairchild Books, who were very helpful in their suggestions: Nathan Fleisig, Renee Foster, Audria Green, Melody LeHew, and Dr. Joanne Leoni.

Finally, we would like to give our heartfelt thanks to our respective wives, Jacqueline Sherman and Shilo Perlman, and families for their confidence in us and continued love, support, and patience, particularly during deadline time.

THE REAL WORLD GUIDE TO FASHION SELLING AND MANAGEMENT

CHAPTER 01

SELLING ISN'T A DIRTY WORD

Overview

The first chapter introduces fashion selling in the real world (what we will refer to hereon as RW). It highlights the profession's importance both in business and life, describes common misconceptions about the field of sales, reviews the vital roles salespeople play within the fashion industry, and examines the importance of ethics in selling.

Introduction

Everybody does it: Students persuade their professors to extend assignment deadlines, daughters persuade their mothers to send them to ballet classes, people persuade friends to go on road trips, grandparents persuade their grandchildren to go to college, and wives persuade their husbands to go on snorkeling vacations. They are all selling something.

The people in the aforementioned examples are not selling products or services, nor are they doing it in exchange for payment. However, they are selling their ideas, solutions, and wishes.

Webster's first definition of the verb *sell* is "to give up, deliver, or exchange (property, goods, services, etc.) for money or its equivalent;" however, selling in its broadest sense can't be limited to this exchange. Webster's lists another definition that gives the word a more universal and pragmatic meaning: "to persuade someone of the value of something."

The persuasion process can be as simple as making a simple request or as complex as conducting research in preparation for an important presentation.

For example, wives who try to persuade their husbands to go on snorkeling vacations may find it an easy task to simply make the request. A wife may describe to her husband how much stress she's been under at work and how the vacation will help relieve it. The husband, who may be feeling the effects of her work-related stress at home, not to mention the effects of stress from his own job, may not need much persuasion to realize the value of agreeing to take the vacation.

On the contrary, students who try to persuade their professors to grant them an extension on an assignment may need to explain why, specifically, it is important for them to receive an extension. They may point out how diligent they've been about attending class and point out excellent classroom performance, such as good participation. They may even make promises to not be late again. In other words, students persuade their professors by highlighting the value of approving an extension and in so doing must be prepared to give supporting evidence to make their cases.

Life is full of nonbusiness sales pitches and negotiations. People who are better at selling often experience more satisfying, successful lives. Indeed, people are constantly making attempts to sell ideas to others not only at work, but also within the familial and social environments.

Selling is a subjective process: Every salesperson has a unique style, but virtually every successful selling approach involves communication, observation, presentation, persuasion, negotiation, and the ability to close, all of which will be discussed in more detail in Chapter 5. By mastering sales skills, people can significantly affect the quality of their relationships with family, friends, and coworkers.

In the 1930s, Arthur "Red" Motley, world-renowned sales trainer and former publisher of *Parade* magazine, coined the expression "nothing happens until somebody sells something." This saying still rings true today. For anything actually to happen in life—not just in a sales environment—people need to persuade others to accept an idea or to do an activity.

This chapter shows that when selling is done correctly and with integrity, it is far from a dirty word. It forms the foundation that allows for relationships—both business and personal—to grow and mutually benefit both parties (Figure 1.1).

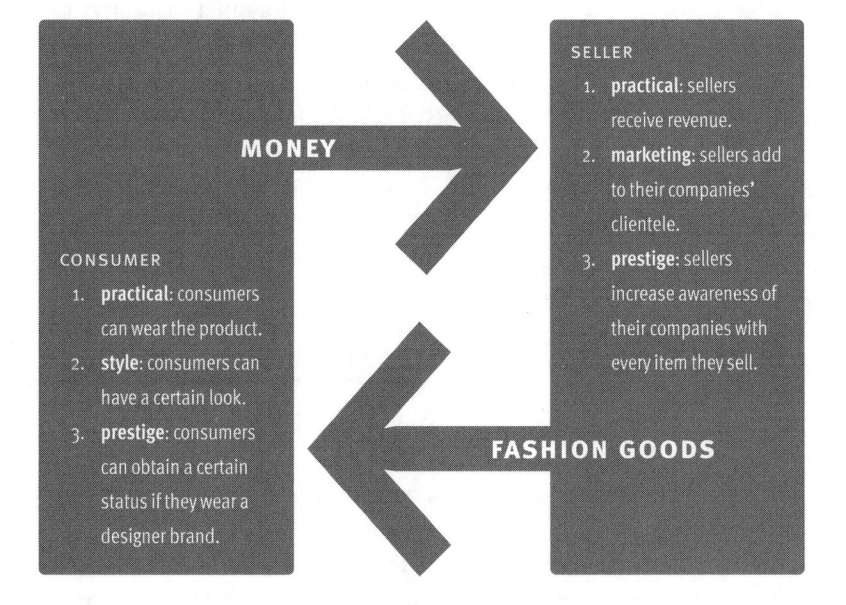

FIGURE 1.1

The Seller and Consumer Relationship

Selling is a mutual and beneficial transaction for both the buyer and seller.

CONSUMER
1. **practical**: consumers can wear the product.
2. **style**: consumers can have a certain look.
3. **prestige**: consumers can obtain a certain status if they wear a designer brand.

MONEY

SELLER
1. **practical**: sellers receive revenue.
2. **marketing**: sellers add to their companies' clientele.
3. **prestige**: sellers increase awareness of their companies with every item they sell.

FASHION GOODS

RW Principle

Every business must have some type of selling vehicle in place so it can promote, record, and process orders for its products or services. Even a mail-order clothing company has a selling vehicle—its glossy catalog.

The Importance of Selling

In the real world, selling is the bedrock of any business. Sales are what enable a business to exchange its products with society for money so it can pay its bills and salaries, fund research and product development, and distribute dividends to stockholders. Without a sufficient sales volume, clothing manufacturers or distributors lack the financial resources to produce existing designs and introduce new lines, and retailers end up with a burgeoning overstock that eats away at profits.

The function of sales is comparable to the body's functions of eating and drinking. For example, a body can have a healthy heart and a sound mind, but without food or water, the body withers away. Likewise, a company's product may be superb and its management team outstanding, but without sales it won't last very long.

Each business formulates its own sales approach and strategy according to the nature of its industry, character of its customers, and economic environment in which it operates. Mastering this formula determines a business's success or failure.

It is now clear that salespeople are important to business, but are they important in the fashion industry? After all, clothing isn't a luxury but a necessity. People need to buy shoes, pants, shirts, winter coats, and underwear periodically throughout their entire lives. But would customers go into a clothing store and make purchases regardless of the presence of a salesperson? Not at all. Without a competent salesperson on the floor, potential customers may lose interest and check out prices and selections at other stores. True, a salesperson does not guarantee that potential customers will never leave to check out the competition, but a competent salesperson will lower this percentage significantly.

Competent salespeople are crucial to all facets of the fashion business. A tie manufacturer must employ a specific selling strategy to persuade distributors and stores to carry its line of ties. A shoe distribution company must sell executives in retail stores on the brands that it distributes.

Why Should You Know How to Sell?

A career in fashion sales and sales management is often exciting, fast-paced, and challenging and therefore carries many rewards. From a financial perspective, salaries for fashion sales positions begin at the low $30,000 range, but with motivation, hard work, and application of sales principles, salaries can reach six figures (Figure 1.2). To a large degree, most salespeople's earnings are determined by their performance. A career in sales offers people the opportunity to maximize their potential.

Beyond monetary compensation, salespeople who obtain outside sales positions can expect a high degree of independence, excellent travel opportunities both nationally and abroad, and flexibility to manage their own productivity. They must still answer to supervisors, make quotas, and follow company policies, of course, but for some people this is as good as it gets without being self-employed.

Furthermore, sales positions are traditionally stepping stones to management and executive positions and offer excellent opportunities for advancement. Salespeople who are familiar with their companies' lines of products, policies, and internal decision makers have an important advantage. Successful salespeople are considered for major promotions not only because their skills and experience but also their relationships with key customers.

A sales career can be extremely fulfilling. Salespeople relish the

RW Concept

Because selling is such a fundamental part of the fashion environment—without it no company could ever exist—it is important that not only fashion salespeople but also managers, executives, and private business owners master the skills associated with it.

FIGURE 1.2

What Salespeople Earn

In its 2003 National Occupational Employment and Wage Estimates Survey,[1] the U.S. Bureau of Labor Statistics reports that there were 13,534,180 sales representatives in the United States, and the earnings were between $31,250 and $40,240 per year. There were 314,180 sales managers in 2003, and the average of their earnings was $91,840. Nordstrom Inc. pays most of their sales associates straight commissions and earnings can reach $75,000 per year or more.[2]

MEDIAN EARNINGS FOR U.S. WHOLESALE FASHION SALES REPRESENTATIVES

$31,250/year

EARNINGS FOR COMMISSIONED SALES ASSOCIATES AT NORDSTROM

$75,000/year

MEDIAN ANNUAL EARNINGS FOR SALES MANAGERS

$91,840/year

opportunity to help others and see it as a perk—many salespeople feel that by helping others through their efforts, they develop new friendships and make a difference. Although the fast-paced nature of a sales career is exciting, it can also be demanding and stressful.

Selling is one of the most critical skills that an entrepreneur can have. If you dream of creating your own fashion label or setting up a distribution company someday, you must know how to make sales. Some of today's most prominent fashion icons began their careers as salespeople.

Even if a sales vocation is not for you, learning the basics of selling will help you develop a solid foundation for the career you are pursuing. Remember that clothing designers sell their designs to product development supervisors, production managers sell assembly-line modifications to their production teams, and accounting departments sell the idea of paying past-due accounts to potentially delinquent account holders before they are sent to collections.

The sales techniques in this book help you to form and improve vital relationships with customers, supervisors, and coworkers. The persuasion methods teach you how to make people cooperate on difficult projects. A better understanding of human interaction improves your personal relationships with your friends and family. Sales skills are fundamental business tools that are very much applicable to virtually every job within the fashion industry.

Behind the Label

Many of today's top fashion brands can trace their success back to their founders' selling skills. An excellent example is the Polo label that Ralph Lauren launched in 1967 with just twenty-six boxes of ties. A men's tie salesman at that time, Lauren recognized that in a fashion world dominated by narrow ties and conventional styles, men yearned for a change. He designed wide, handmade ties using innovative eye-catching patterns and materials. "A tie was the way a man expressed himself," says Lauren. "I believed that men were ready for something new and different. They didn't want to look as if they worked for IBM. A beautiful tie was an expression of quality, taste, style." Aiming to promote a unique lifestyle with his ties, Ralph Lauren named his line after a sport that embodies a world of discreet elegance and classic style: Polo. The ties quickly became a status item. "I never went to fashion school—I was a young guy who had some style. I never imagined Polo would become what it is. I just followed my instincts," he says. Lauren was one of the first designers to merge classic American style with the refinement, tailoring, and sensibility of European fashion, thereby expanding the appeal of consumers in the United States as well as setting the stage for expansion into Europe. Today, the company boasts over $10 billion in worldwide sales of men's, women's, and children's clothing as well home collections and fragrances.[3] (See Table 1.1.)

Donna Karan's career also benefited from her exposure to sales and her sales background. Karan's mother was a showroom sales representative in New York City's garment district, her father was a tailor, and she worked part-time as a salesperson at a local boutique when she was a teenager. After attending Parsons School of Design, she worked as a designer for Anne Klein. It was at Anne Klein that she recognized that female executives needed affordable, yet stylish and comfortable, clothing and launched several unique lines that won her the Coty American Fashion Critics Award and made her famous. In 1984, Karan received seed money from a Japanese textile firm, a major partner in Anne Klein, to launch Donna Karan Co. She made her solo debut in 1988 with the DKNY line. The company now also sells men's and children's clothing, hosiery, and fragrances.

While she was more a designer than a saleswoman, it is evident that she utilized her experience in sales to recognize and capitalize on consumer needs and market trends and satisfy demands.

Tommy Hilfiger started his career in 1969 with a store called the People's Place, which he opened in his hometown in upstate New York. Hilfiger would drive down to New York City, buy jeans and other goods, and resell them to college kids. By the age of twenty-six, Hilfiger owned ten

TABLE 1.1 **Humble Beginnings**	Such top designers as Ralph Lauren and Donna Karan began their careers in fashion sales. Below is a snapshot of where they are today.	
Polo Ralph Lauren Corporation	**Donna Karan International Inc.**	**Tommy Hilfiger Corporation**
650 Madison Avenue New York, NY 10022 Phone: 212-318-7000 Fax: 212-888-5780 www.polo.com Company Type: Public (NYSE: RL) Fiscal Year-end: March 2005 Sales (mil.): $3,305.4 2005 Net Income (mil.): $190.4 2005 Employees: 12,762	550 Seventh Avenue New York, NY 10018 Phone: 212-789-1500 Fax: 212-768-6099 www.donnakaran.com Company Type: Subsidiary of LVMH Fiscal Year-end: December 2000 Sales (mil.): $662.7	9/F Novel Industrial Building 850-870 Lai Chi Kok Road, Cheung Sha Wan Kowloon, Hong Kong Phone: +852-2216-0668 Fax: +852-2312-1368 www.tommy.com Company Type: Public (NYSE: TOM) Fiscal Year-end: March 2004 Sales (mil.): $1,875.8 2004 Net Income (mil.): $132.2 2004 Employees: 5,400

Source: Hoover's.

shops across New York State. Although his business went bankrupt, Hilfiger learned from this experience. Armed with information about what his costumers wanted, he moved to New York City in 1979 and, a few years later, founded Tommy Hilfiger Inc. with the help of two backers. His signature collection made its debut on the catwalk in 1984, and the rest is history.[4]

We can also credit New Zealand's internationally known designer Karen Walker's success to her sales skills. Shortly after graduating fashion college, she launched her label in 1990, personally visiting various retail shops around Auckland to sell her collection. She gradually built a demand for her talent, and five years later, she opened two stores and expanded into Australia. By 1998, she sold her collection to Barney's New York; that year, her collection received attention at the Hong Kong Fashion Week, which brought her name into the international spotlight. After Madonna wore Walker's "Killer Pants" on MTV, her work gained significant media exposure around the world, and it catapulted her into the global design market. Karen Walker's designs are now available in stores worldwide, including New York, London, Hong Kong, and Japan.

It is difficult to predict who will be the next Ralph Lauren, Donna Karan, Tommy Hilfiger, or Karen Walker; however, we can predict that whoever that person is, he or she will likely possess a thorough understanding of sales and use it effectively in the fashion world.

Sales-Related Misconceptions

Unfortunately, some people have a distorted general view of salespeople as dishonest, overbearing, and uncaring and who think solely of making the sale and tell you anything to get your signature on the dotted line. While most of us have encountered such a salesperson at some point or another, they certainly do not reflect the character and behavior of the majority of salespeople—the ones who are successful and have been in business for years. Sales personnel who engage in unethical practices never succeed over the long term, and, in reality, they are a disgrace to the profession. In fact, what these types of people classify as selling isn't really selling at all—it is deceit in disguise.

The association of selling with deceit, lies, sweet-talking, and other underhanded adjectives has long been engrained in our culture, which is a result of the wrong people selling. Individuals who have been improperly trained are not genuinely interested in helping others or are unscrupulous by nature ending up as salespeople invariably produces unsatisfied customers. These customers who have found themselves betrayed would then not only avoid that business or salesperson but may also be inclined to distrust all salespeople in the future.

Thus, the infamous used car salesman who locks the doors, removes the company's sign, and flees out the back door as soon as the customer drives off the lot has given the good, honest, and caring salesperson a bad name over the decades. With enough unqualified people employed in sales and sales management positions, the cumulative effect of bad experiences and misconceptions is often the first obstacle to a true understanding of the field.

Table 1.2 lists some of the myths surrounding the sales profession. Can you identify whether they hold true in the real world? Such myths help promote negative stereotypes of salespeople, but in reality successful salespeople personify the exact opposite of these prevalent misconceptions.

TABLE 1.2 Myth Versus Reality	
Myth	**Reality**
To be successful, salespeople have to exaggerate the benefits of the product they are trying to sell to their would-be customers.	Not true! Salespeople may be able to get away with misleading a few customers, but these unethical tactics will backfire sooner or later. Even if salespeople manage to keep their jobs, they will fail to establish long-term business relationships with their customers, and no customer will ever return. Only honest salespeople succeed and reap the tremendous rewards that business from repeat customers offer.
To get the sale, salespeople have to push their customers.	If customers feel bullied, they may simply find a different salesperson or try another location. While some customers may give into high-pressure tactics, they will do so only once. Nobody likes to be pushed around, and it is highly unlikely that a customer will return after feeling bullied.
Salespeople don't care about their customers; they only care about their compensation.	Successful salespeople are well aware that they can make sales merely by being sensitive to their customers' needs and taking care to resolve their customers' problems. Salespeople who don't listen carefully or simply don't care about issues their customers may have cannot expect to recommend the right products. Compensation is not the sole motive that drives a successful salesperson.

Empathy Listening to another person attentively and understanding their thoughts, emotions, and feelings so you can adjust your own moods and behavior accordingly.

Integrity Behaving in an honest manner and according to social and moral principles.

Drive for Success Having the power and energy to overcome obstacles or rejection and meet the goals that are set.

The Successful Salesperson

To be successful over the long term, salespeople must emulate certain traits and behaviors and possess a keen understanding of the products or services they are selling—it certainly helps when salespeople believe in the quality and value of the products they sell. The following three behavioral characteristics are absolutely crucial in successful salespeople:

+ **empathy**
+ **integrity**
+ **drive for success**

A salesperson who expresses genuine condolences when a client says that his or her father passed away recently and reacts to this situation by

RW Concept

Can a salesperson succeed over the long term if they posses only one or two of the three behavioral characteristics discussed on pages 9–10? Mary is a retail salesperson who is ethical, honest, and strives to succeed in her job, but she lacks empathy. When a customer asks Mary if a particular dress makes the customer look fat, Mary says it does. Instead of sensing the customer's sensitivity to her weight and gently directing her to another item, Mary simply offends the customer. The customer now feels Mary is an uncaring person who doesn't pay attention to her needs and leaves without making a purchase. Now suppose Mary has empathy but no integrity. Mary senses the customer's sensitivity to her weight, but does not care whether the item she sells looks flattering on the customer. She tells the customer that the dress fits her perfectly, and the customer buys the dress; when the customer takes the dress home and realizes that it does not fit her well, she returns it, feeling betrayed by Mary's lies. Last, suppose Mary has empathy and integrity but no drive for success. Mary senses the customer's sensitivity to her weight and gently tells the customer the dress is not for her. However, lacking the drive for success, Mary doesn't direct the customer to another more suitable item. A salesperson must have all three characteristics to succeed.

understanding this may not be the right time for a sales presentation is showing empathy. The opposite would be if a salesperson offers brief sympathies and proceeds with a sales presentation without regard for his or her client.

Salespeople who admit to their customers that they aren't sure when an order will arrive or how long it will take and promise to find out the correct information show integrity. The opposite would be if a salesperson makes up an answer or intentionally avoids the question.

Salespeople who analyze lost sales by trying to pinpoint what they did wrong to correct the errors in the future show a drive to succeed. The opposite would be if salespeople blame lost sales on their customers.

Along with the three behavioral characteristics, product knowledge is also vital to success. If you were shopping for a suit and the salesperson helping you didn't know the benefits of blends versus natural fibers, you would not have confidence in his or her recommendations. When salespeople are familiar with the products or services they are selling and have an understanding of any related intricacies, customers can trust their input to make the right choices. A salesperson who sells suits should be aware of the various fabrics and be ready to explain the benefits and pitfalls to his or her customers.

When salespeople conduct themselves with empathy and integrity and are driven to succeed and when the products they sell are good quality, they find success. There are many elements that are beneficial to successful sales careers, covered later in the book, such as presenting your best image with appropriate attire, using good diction and proper language, and understanding different cultures. However, the three behavioral characteristics discussed in this chapter allow salespeople to form the foundation for long-term sales relationships with all buyers.

History of Selling

The history of sales dates back to the early days of civilization when people started bartering goods. This book focuses on the relatively recent period from the industrial revolution to the present day. For the purposes of clarity, the book divides this particular time frame into five historical periods.

The Production-Oriented Period—1760s to the 1920s

From the onset of the industrial revolution in the 1760s until the 1920s, the Western world was engaged in an intensive production era spurred by the advent of power tools and mechanized assembly lines. The prevalent outlook in those days was that a good product or service would sell itself. Salespeople were considered clerks who simply answered questions and processed sales transactions. The managerial attitude of that time, backed by strong consumer demand for products, was that a customer would buy a product if he or she needed it, and if not then another customer would. Henry Ford epitomized the production-oriented outlook when he quipped that "the customers can have any color Model T Ford they want as long as it's black."

The Great Depression Period—1929 to the mid 1930s

During the Great Depression to the mid 1930s, there was an overproduction of goods and salespeople scrambling to sell them. The desperation that set in often led to fraudulent and dishonest sales practices such as **bait-and-switch**. The zealousness of businesses to increase production, expand facilities, and hire more workers was met not with increased consumer demand, but with heavy investments in the stock market. On Thursday, October 24, 1929, the stock market crashed, bringing down with it the false optimism of the corporate world; many businesses went bankrupt and closed down. Unemployment and **inflation** skyrocketed, and competition for consumer dollars reached a critical stage. Many salespeople used high-pressure and bait-and-switch tactics to make their sales.

The Post-Depression Period—mid 1930s to the early 1950s

Following the brief corporate panic for sales during the Depression, the business world returned to its production-oriented sales pattern. During World War II, production and most manufacturing were devoted to the war effort. Still, the wartime U.S. economy was growing strong, and demand generally exceeded supply. Therefore, manufacturers did not see the importance of expanding their existing sales forces or investing in sales training.

After the end of World War II in 1945, production of consumer goods increased, and thanks to advancements in the field of transportation, goods reached the market faster so they could be consumed quicker. The role of the salesperson was still mostly an administrative one that revolved around processing orders rather than generating new business. In the years that followed, however, consumer demand reached a plateau and slowly dropped, heralding a transformation of the salesperson's role.

The Consumer-Oriented Period—early 1950s to 1990

In the early 1950s, product supply quickly exceeded consumer demand, as consumers refrained from making purchases, and businesses experienced increased pressure from competitors. During this period, businesses began to cater to consumers. Furthermore, the baby boom led

---

RW Dictionary

Bait-and-switch When a salesperson lures a customer with a bargain-priced item and switches the customer's focus to a higher-priced item.

RW Dictionary

Inflation An increase in the volume of money and credit relative to available goods and services resulting in a continuing rise in the general price level.

to every business's ideal: teenagers with disposable incomes. Companies searched for ways to identify and satisfy consumers' needs and wants to succeed. Consumer orientation was more than just a catchy phrase. Salespeople dedicated their efforts to satisfying their consumers' needs.

Managers realized they had to understand what customers wanted, how much customers were willing to pay for products, and how fast customers wanted their products. Companies implemented consumer surveys, focus groups, and other market research tools to answer these and other related questions. Armed with this information, companies then utilized their sales forces, promotions, and advertisements to show customers how their products could satisfy their needs and therefore persuade them to buy.

The shift to consumer orientation prompted a rise in the recruitment, training, and management of sales personnel. Companies analyzed in detail the dynamics of interaction and steps of negotiation between salespeople and customers and formulated numerous methods and techniques to overcome consumer resistance. The forces of supply versus demand played a key role in defining the importance of salespeople. The need to sell (and the subsequent need for effective and successful salespeople) became paramount for a company to increase its market share.

The Relationship Period—1990 to the Present Day

Businesses realized in the early 1990s that while general promotions by way of telemarketing, the Internet, and mass mailings impressed consumers, they still had to rely on competent salespeople to close sales. Without salespeople, there is a risk that consumers will just discard the letters, postcards, brochures, and e-mails they receive.

It is important to understand that although marketing, advertising, direct mail, and other methods of corporate communications do make consumers aware of products, it is the salesperson who persuades the consumer to fulfill the final step and actually buy the product. Marketing's function is to create a want that will become a perceived need, and selling satisfies that need by closing the sale. The fields of marketing and selling serve distinctly different purposes, but together they achieve the prime directive: making the sale.

Marketers and sales managers also recognized that they had to get personal to stand out—after all, salespeople are not only selling a product to customers but also selling themselves. Salespeople began to focus on establishing relationships with would-be customers and keeping those relationships strong. In reality, successful salespeople already knew the importance of building and maintaining relationships with their customers. Still, the need to form long-term relationships has become much more apparent and vital in today's competitive and impersonal environment.

A key element of building relationships with consumers dictates that buyers and sellers must work together to achieve their goals and thus mutually benefit each other. *Personal selling* is the key asset needed to gain such buyer–seller relationships in business-to-consumer and business-to-business marketing. From the 1990s to the present day, personal selling has always played an important role in the mechanics of doing business. Conditions and roles may have changed due to historical events, but the basic ingredient for success in the marketplace—personal selling—has never and will never change.

Sales and Ethics

Arthur Miller's *Death of a Salesman* (1949) tells the tragic story of salesman Willy Loman, who is haunted by his failures as a salesman, husband, and father. Loman eventually takes his own life as a means of escape when he can no longer cope. The play conveys a strong indictment against salespeople and the corporations they represent. It draws heavily on Miller's personal life: Miller's father, who was a successful manufacturer in New York City, lost his business when Miller was thirteen years old, and the family had to move from their posh residence near Central Park to a small house in Brooklyn. Miller worked with his father for a while trying to get the business started again and grew to hate selling.

The play perpetuates the selling myths and misconceptions discussed earlier in this chapter. Loman is a case study of the wrong person selling. At the bottom of Loman's situation, we find a host of ethical and personal issues. Loman cheats on his wife with a potential customer's secretary, obviously overstepping the appropriate boundaries of the personal relationship. He takes advantage of the secretary to get appointments with the decision makers in the company. When his son discovers the affair, Loman tries to make him an accomplice and keep him quiet. Moreover, Loman is more concerned about his reputation and preserving his own image than about helping his customers in earnest. In that respect, the play does an excellent job of describing the problems that result when a salesperson strays from the ethical path.

The importance of understanding ethics and behaving ethically cannot be overstated in the sales field. Ethical conduct is not a guarantee for success; a salesperson must employ selling techniques, actively seek prospects, and properly close on them. However, behaving ethically is a requirement for success nonetheless. In other words, salespeople must do more than behave ethically to sell successfully, but without ethics, they will never succeed in the long term.

Webster's defines ethics as "the study of standards of conduct and moral judgment," or "the system or code of morals of a particular person, religion, group, profession, etc." To behave in an ethical manner, people must first adopt a set of moral standards and follow them. Salespeople who set a moral standard of being open to customer complaints and addressing them properly follow through when they receive complaints. Salespeople who receive complaints and fail to relay it to the proper people for correction despite assuring their customers that they will do so behave in an unethical manner.

John F. Kennedy's Statement of Consumer Rights is a broad-termed, commonsense guide to customer relations; when applied to sales situations, the guide sheds light on ethics in sales. According to the statement, a consumer has

+ the right to choose freely,
+ the right to be informed,
+ the right to be heard, and
+ the right to be safe.

Salespeople should strive to respect these fundamental rights and act in manners that facilitate the fulfillment of these rights.

To fully understand ethics as it relates to sales, we need a more focused view of the subject. The various aspects of sales ethics can be divided into the key behavioral categories that follow.

Being Truthful

Ethical salespeople provide customers with honest, correct information at all times. There are no exceptions. Every facet of sales counts: from accurately describing products or services and their features and benefits to being honest about price, availability, return policies, or any other related issues.

Honesty is equally important after sales are made. If a customer calls because a shipment is late, the salesperson must look into it right away and inform the customer of the real problem and what is being done to remedy it. When the salespeople need to answer questions to which they don't know the answer, they must say so and promise immediate corrective action. In short, they must always keep their customers informed with the truth, no matter how unpleasant it may be.

Truthful salespeople respect their customers and never take advantage of their customer's lack of knowledge or weaknesses. Bait-and-switch tactics, scare tactics, misrepresentation of the facts, and any violation of the law fall

RW Principle

Ultimately, salespeople's loyalties rest with their companies' interests, since this is the source of their livelihood. Such loyalty, however, does not give a salesperson license to lie to the customer. Given a conflict between a company's and a customer's interests, the salesperson's job is to serve the company's interests while striving to maintain a relationship with the customer. For example, suppose that the shipping department decides to ship the orders of a larger account ahead of the salesperson's account, thus delaying the shipping date of the latter. The salesperson should alert the customer right away and encourage him or her to keep the order in place despite the late delivery. This should be done without resorting to lying or casting a negative light on the company, while avoiding conflict as much as possible. Yet, the customer may demand immediate action or cancel the order, in which case the salesperson must respect the customer's wishes and move on. Remember that the fashion business is an extremely volatile environment, and unexpected delays can happen.

under unethical conduct in sales. For a meaningful, long-term business relationship to form, a salesperson must always be 100 percent honest at all times, so the customer is comfortable enough to trust that salesperson.

Salespeople's ethics come into play not only with their customers but also with the companies for which they work. They have access to confidential information, and salespeople who divulge such information to their customers aren't being ethical at all. Informing customers of a company's trade secrets is a violation of that company's trust. Salespeople should politely decline to discuss their companies' internal matters, especially when they do not directly affect customers. Salespeople must maintain a delicate balance between their companies' interests and those of their customers.

Making Commitments Stand

Ethical salespeople always strive to be realistic when making promises to their customers and try to fulfill those promises on or before the agreed upon deadlines. Customers deeply respect and remain loyal to salespeople who are reliable. Salespeople who have good intentions should always be absolutely positive that an order can be fulfilled by a certain time period before saying it can. In the case of custom orders, wise salespeople will go a step further and personally go over items with their production departments or warehouse managers—this way, they can be sure that every detail a job requires can be produced within the deadline.

In the case of rush orders, salespeople should inquire about the fastest production lead times (and shipping schedules, if applicable). If their customers' deadlines cannot be met, they must inform them immediately. For example, the salesperson might tell the customer: "I apologize that there is a delay in the delivery date, and I will make every effort to expedite the order. At this time, the new shipping date is two weeks later, and I will keep you updated as to the progress." When salespeople process rush orders without regard to whether deadlines are feasible or, worse, with the knowledge that it cannot be done in time, it will backfire and their reputations will be damaged. Late deliveries may cause customers to cancel orders, leading to financial losses on deals. Late deliveries may even prompt customers to look around for more reliable vendors. When deadlines can't be met, it is far better to lose a sale than to lose an entire account.

Salespeople should always be familiar enough with the production, warehouse, and shipping departments to know whether they can count on them to meet deadlines. If one of these departments misses delivery dates routinely, a good salesperson takes internal steps to correct the situation. A disorganized, loosely run production department can make even the most ethical salesperson look bad, thus adversely affecting customer relationships.

Assuming One's Social Responsibility

Within a sociological context, salespeople have a certain responsibility to potential customers, current buyers, and the public at large. The primary social responsibility of salespeople is to educate their customers about product-related and technical issues so customers can make better buying decisions. Even if customers do not make a purchase immediately, they will appreciate the salespeople's efforts and remember him or her when the time to buy arrives.

If buyers have an inaccurate understanding of products, or some parts of them, then salespeople must try to explain them. This should be done politely, without disrespecting the customer. Many customers appreciate this added value and repay by placing orders. Additionally, this is an excellent opportunity for salespeople to show customers their knowledge of the field, which, in turn, builds more trust with the customers.

Salespeople who volunteer to be involved in their communities may find that doing so does wonders for their image. Successful salespeople should therefore consider giving back to their communities by volunteering with nonprofit organizations and being involved in community affairs and events. Serving as a local Red Cross volunteer, for example, will give salespeople tremendous satisfaction because they can help others outside the workplace. Customers often prefer to deal with people who take the time to give back.

Ethics in the Sales Environment

In sales, as in life, there are different levels of ethics. A person's ethics can range from complete moral behavior to extreme criminal conduct. Salespeople should always strive to be as ethical as possible because it will dictate their long-term success. But what about buyers? Are buyers ethical, and how does this affect ethical salespeople (Figure 1.3)?

Wise salespeople learn how to recognize and stay away from unethical buyers. When you deal with unethical people, it will adversely affect your reputation and ultimately result in short-term relationships. Salespeople should think twice before blindly recommending credit for their customers and would be wise to leave such decisions to the sales or finance managers.

Ethical customers are easygoing and truthful and make payments on time. When customers and salespeople are honest and adhere to moral principles, their relationships last a long time. Therefore, it behooves salespeople to assess buyers' levels of ethics as early as possible in business relationships. On the contrary, unethical salespeople mostly succeed in forging long-term relationships with unethical customers.

Ethical salespeople should aim to cultivate relationships with ethical

FIGURE 1.3

The Ethics Pyramid

Long-term success is based on the level of
ethics for both the buyer and seller.

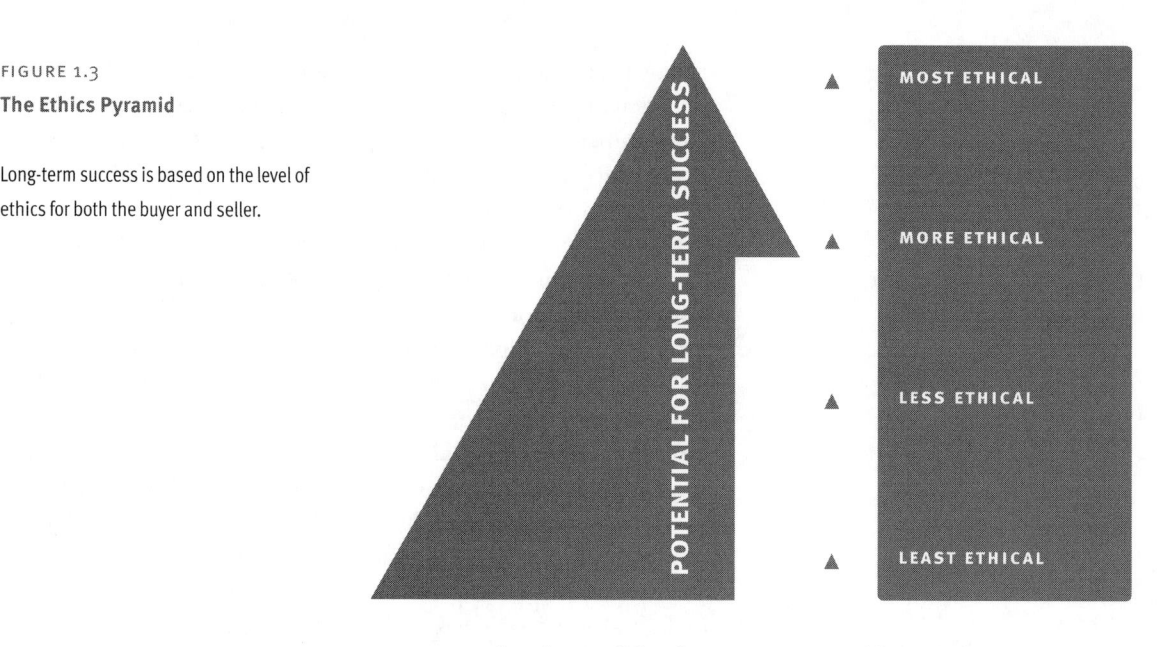

customers, for they will be the most compatible with their own mode
of operation, and, furthermore, a meaningful relationship will most
likely develop. As a corollary, we find that unethical salespeople mostly
succeed in forging long-term relationships with unethical customers.

Another element that the ethical salesperson must confront is superiors and coworkers. When salepeople are faced with corrupt sales managers or when other salespeople behave unethically, it will be hard for
ethical salespeople to remain ethical. At some point or another, the con-
tradicting behavioral patterns will collide, and the resulting argument
may cause a serious strain in the department. Ethical salespeople should
try to identify such potential problems before they turn sour and attempt
to resolve the conflicts as soon as possible, even if it means leaving the
company.

The nature of sales positions is such that it can be very tempting to
behave unethically either as a result of pressure, ambition, and so on.
Only by following ethical principles and resisting such temptation will
salespeople build strong relationships with their customers that will last
many years.

Chapter Summary

+   Everybody sells on a regular basis, whether they are selling an idea,
    a solution, or a way of being. Life is full of nonbusiness sales pitches
    and negotiations. People who are better at selling often experience
    more satisfying, successful lives.

+ Selling isn't a dirty word! The association of selling with deceit, lies, sweet-talking, and other underhandedness has become rooted in our culture thanks to dishonest, untrained, or uncaring salespeople.

+ Successful salespeople must possess three key behavioral characteristics: empathy, integrity, and a drive for success.

+ In recent history, the approach to selling has gone through five distinct periods: the production-oriented period, where production ranked most important; the Great Depression period, where selling turned sour with high-pressure and bait-and-switch tactics as a result of the sharp rise in production versus consumer demand; the post-Depression period, where the production-oriented was reinforced as a result of World War II; the consumer–oriented period, where salespeople catered to consumers' needs; and the present-day relationship period, where the need to establish and maintain long-term relationships with customers has become much more apparent and vital in today's competitive and impersonal environment.

+ In the real world, selling is the bedrock of any business. Sales are what enable a business to exchange its products with society for money so it can pay its bills and salaries, fund research and product development, and distribute dividends to stockholders.

+ Mastering sales skills benefit any person's advancement in every career possible, even if it is not in sales. Sales skills are fundamental business tools; as such, they are applicable to virtually every job within the fashion industry.

+ Ethical salespeople tell the truth, keep promises, and assume social responsibilities.

+ Only by following ethical principles and resisting opportunities to violate them will salespeople build strong relationships with their customers that will last a long time.

RW CASE STUDY

Ralph Lauren's story is a true example of the power that sales skills can have in the fashion industry. One of the authors (Sherman) had the opportunity to see the birth of Lauren's career.

Does a career in sales provide opportunity for growth?

In the late 1960s, I was playing golf with a fellow member at Woodcrest Country Club in Long Island, and we were talking about my favorite subject—selling and salespeople. He was a textile converter who produced men's fabrics for shirtings. He told me about this young tie salesman who went into the men's tie manufacturing business and wanted to expand his product line to men's dress shirts. He said he was giving him a line of credit because he thought that the man was a great salesman with enormous potential. Oh yes!—the salesman's name was Ralph Lauren. I still have one of the original Polo ties.

Seeing how Ralph Lauren has developed into a fashion icon, would you say his sales background was a factor in his success?

While he was engaged in selling ties he was also getting feedback from his customers as to the consumers' wants and needs. Being active in the marketplace as a seller, he was able to find a niche market and, combined with his genius for design and marketing, was able to develop products that the consumer was looking for. While selling ties, he realized that men wanted a change in the look of their ties. . . . Ralph Lauren established the Polo label with a successful line of men's ties. "In direct opposition to the narrow ties and conventional styles of the time, Lauren designs wide, handmade ties using unexpected, flamboyant, opulent materials. The ties quickly became a menswear status item."[5] His wide tie with the Polo logo became a standard for men on the move. His uncanny sense of style and market smarts changed the way many men dressed. Along with the ties came his shirts, which were made with fine tailoring and had a timeless look as most of his designs [had] at that time and even to this day. Being immersed in the marketplace, he soon realized that he was not in the tie [and] shirt business, but he was in the clothing business, so then along came suits, coats, shoes, and other clothing [items]. We all know today the Polo label is part of our lifestyle whether it is clothing or home furnishing[s]. We should point out that selling alone did not make Ralph Lauren successful. However, it did help in putting him in a place where he was able to develop a unique design, marketing, and merchandising strategy. It would seem that Mr. Lauren's creative contributions [have enabled him to go] down in history as one of the most innovative persons in our generation.

Questions to Consider

1. Look up Ralph Lauren's history at the library or on the Internet. What do you think about the role sales skills played in his success?
2. Why do you think sales skills are part of a solid business foundation?

RW EXERCISES

The sales environment is one where ethics are constantly challenged. In any area where transactions involve communication, the temptation to violate the ethical code may be more pronounced because statements and promises are made. For example, if a buyer is ready to sign an order copy and requests an earlier delivery date than the seller is able to confirm, that salesperson's ethics are being challenged. There is a chance that if the salesperson can't deliver the merchandise when the buyer wants it, he or she may lose the order. If that salesperson promises to deliver by the new earlier date, while knowing full well it is impossible, then it is a violation of the ethical code.

Say the order is signed, the salesperson processes the order, and predictably the goods cannot be delivered on time. The salesperson compounds this ethical issue by telling the buyer that there were certain shipping problems, but the order will be given a priority. The bottom line is that the order will be ready for delivery on the original delivery date (not the earlier date requested by the buyer and promised by the salesperson). The buyer perceives this as a late delivery and may cancel the order. In such cases, the salesperson's company is forced to make financial adjustments so the buyer accepts the merchandise.

1. The big question — what would have happened if the salesperson had told the truth?
2. Do you think that the salesperson did the right thing? At least the salesperson was able to generate an order.
3. Do you think this is normal procedure in the RW of selling? Explain why.
4. In your opinion, where do ethics enter the picture?

END NOTES

1. U.S. Department of Labor, Bureau of Labor Statistics. May 2003. *National Occupational Employment and Wage Estimates Sales and Related Occupations.* www.bls.gov/oes/2003/may/oes_41Sa.htm
2. Diamond, Ellen. *Fashion Retailing.* Delmar Publishers, 1993. pp. 181–184.
3. U.S. Census Bureau. www.census.gov/hhes/www/income/earnings/call2usboth.html.
4. The Biography Channel. *Tommy Hilfiger Biography.* www.thebiographychannel.co.uk/new_site/biography.php?id=974&showgroup=.
5. Polo Ralph Lauren. www.polo.com/.

CHAPTER 02

THE CHARACTERISTICS OF SUCCESSFUL SALESPEOPLE AND SALES MANAGERS

+ Review the fundamental characteristics and behavioral patterns that are necessary for salespeople to be successful in fashion sales.
+ See why salespeople must have a passion for their job and must be good listeners.
+ Understand why ethics and integrity in fashion sales are important for salespeople to achieve long-term success.
+ Comprehend a sales manager's role in recruiting salespeople who are ethical and providing them with an environment that encourages such behavior.
+ Look at some of the external forces behind a salesperson's success or failure: For example, salespeople operate best in organized environments. See what managers can do to provide such environments.
+ Learn how careful planning and implementation of office procedures bolsters a salesperson's long-term performance.

Overview

This chapter describes what makes a salesperson or sales manager successful. It details the specific character traits and behavior patterns that are vital to success in sales and reviews whether salespeople and sales managers can predict their sales potential. Lastly, we examine the sales manager's role in selecting salespeople who are likely to succeed and providing an environment where these traits and behaviors are encouraged and rewarded.

Introduction

Not every person is cut out for a top-notch sales position. Some people simply do not have the right combination of personal characteristics that a career in apparel and textile sales management requires and without which a position in sales would produce only frustration, anxiety, and a lack of fulfillment. But for people with the right chemistry, the opportunities for job satisfaction and personal growth in the apparel and textile industries are almost unbounded. From the very first day on the job, many of these people are hooked on the excitement of a business that is fast-paced, the roller-coaster combination of tremendous highs and alternating lows, and the unparalleled opportunity for managerial achievement and financial reward.

To be successful, a salesperson must already have, or be able to genuinely adopt, a set of characteristics and behavioral patterns that are essential to selling successfully, such as compassion, a drive for success, honesty, and confidence. Many of these characteristics may be cultivated and refined on-the-job by conscientious application. Even top-notch salespeople or sales managers are constantly perfecting their techniques, sharpening their sales pitches to razor-sharp accuracy, evaluating their performance in every new selling situation, refining their judgment of each client, and ascertaining their clients' needs.

This chapter does not cover whether people must already possess the already-mentioned characteristics or can acquire them. Rather, it focuses on the importance that having such characteristics bears on successful sales careers. Furthermore, it discusses how external forces encourage and even enhance sales conducive behavior in salespeople. The sales manager has a tremendous responsibility to hire people who already possess most of the characteristics and establish positive training programs and working environments. If sales managers ignore dishonesty in their sales force, then there's a good chance most of their teams, even those with a high degree of ethics, will eventually look at this conduct as acceptable behavior and follow suit. Conversely, sales managers who refuse to tolerate any misrepresentations and unethical behavior encourage their sales force to employ ethical standards.

Office procedures and organization also play a role in a salesperson's success. When offices are disorganized, it eventually affects salespeople's success negatively, even when the salespeople themselves are organized. This chapter makes it evident how internal and external factors determine a salesperson's success. Let's begin by taking a look at the psychological makeup of the successful salesperson.

The Mental Toolbox

What qualities must a sales professional possess? Chapter 1 briefly touched on the basic traits of successful salespeople—empathy, integrity, and a drive for success. This chapter expands on these characteristics and examines some additional characteristics that are vital to success. We also provide a barometer to measure salespeople's potential by inspecting the particular skills that will prepare them for careers in the fashion industry. As you read this chapter, conduct your own self-appraisal as a prospective salesperson. Make notes of your personal strengths and of areas in which you may feel deficient and wish to improve.

Drive for Success

Do you put yourself on the line when you involve yourself in a project, or do you maintain an objective distance from your work? When you are turned down, do you feel frustrated and driven to overcome the obstacle to your success, or do you dismiss failure with a shrug of the shoulder?

The person who is frustrated and motivated to overcome the source of resistance is driven by a high amount of personal self-esteem. This person has a strong drive for success and a need for constant achievement and self-fulfillment. A good salesperson is driven to succeed in a controlled way. When salespeople are turned down by clients, it is natural for them to take the rejection personally. Reasons for not being able to close sales include misdirected sales pitches, insufficient research and preparation, and lack of knowledge about the needs of the customers.

Of course, there are times when a salesperson is not entirely at fault for losing a sale. A product may not be the right fit for a specific client, or a customer may be a difficult and unyielding person who resists the sales presentation. Whatever the obstacles to the sale, trained salespeople do not allow themselves to lash out at buyers for not responding to their sales efforts; such behavior merely serves to destroy relationships that take weeks or months to build in the first place.

Success-driven salespeople bounce back quickly from failure, realizing each sales presentation is another opportunity to restore their self-confidence and make up for past shortcomings. The experience is much like a champion tennis player who's been badly beaten in the first set but bounces back to defeat the opponent in the next two straight sets and win the match. Salespeople who are success-driven accept the blame for their own errors and gain self-gratification from their successes. In fact, remembering a sting of past failures is a chief motivating factor for making all future sales.

How would you rate your own drive for success? If, after rejection, you cannot bounce back stronger and more determined to make the next sale, you may want to train yourself to have greater self-esteem—to see yourself as someone special who has to satisfy personal needs and gain the advantage in the selling process.[1]

Empathy

We define *empathy* as "listening to another attentively; understanding their thoughts, emotions, and feelings; and adjusting your own moods and behavior accordingly." Do you often adjust your mood and behaviors to that of another person and modifying your position to accommodate another's viewpoint, or do you find it difficult to anticipate another person's actions and accept an opinion that conflicts with your own?

Poor sales executives approach each sale as a battle that needs to be won at any cost. The buyer is viewed as the opponent, questions and criticisms are overruled, and an attempt is made to push and bully the buyer into giving the order. To this type of salesperson, the buyer is perceived as a "**big pencil**," someone to be won over for the sake of an order then disregarded. The big pencil attitude may at times produce a sale. However, in the long run, it is sure to induce hostility, mistrust, and the destruction of a harmonious working relationship.

The key to successful selling is empathy, which refers to the ability for one person to understand the moods and behavior patterns of another person, whether they are customers or peers. Empathy enables salespeople to elicit the needs of their customers, both on business and personal levels, and deal with those needs realistically. Professional salespeople adapt themselves to the moods of their customers. In fact, in some instances, salespeople may even find it necessary to put off making sales until more appropriate moments.

Empathetic salespeople understand there is no way to prejudge buyers' states of mind when they first meet them—particularly with buyers who are emotionally overwrought by personal or business problems. It is important for salespeople to properly identify an agitated buyer by learning to listen before even attempting to sell. Having empathy means sending up a receptive antenna and—at least temporarily—ceasing to broadcast.

Empathy also allows salespeople to identify self-centered buyers—good salespeople let such buyers vent their frustrations and praise their own virtues, without feeling personally eclipsed. Salespople who preach when they are expected to be sounding boards quickly terminate any chances to make a sale and endanger good working relationships. Empathetic salespeople can negotiate effectively in the turbulent waters stirred up by hostile

RW Dictionary

Big Pencil A sales slang term denoting the buyer who represents a major account in the marketplace. This buyer signs big orders, either in volume and/or dollar value.

or even hysterical buyers by learning to play a part in a buyer's anger, to assume the sense of outrage as if it were their own, to communicate on a high frequency, and to offer solutions that will quell the excitement and pave the way for a rational business transaction.

Appearance

As further discussed in Chapter 6, neatness, fashion consciousness, and eloquence are essential for success in fashion selling. When a sales manger interviews a job candidate, the first impression usually sets the stage for the interview. Sales managers are interested not only in the way applicants are dressed but also how applicants respond to different situations. They will want to know if applicants are really what they appear to be or if they are just trying to put on a positive front for the job interview.

One of the ways that sales managers can discuss the importance of appearances is to ask applicants to describe their wardrobes. Applicants should answer how to dress for business and why. Their answers will usually give sales managers an idea into how they will dress when left on their own. Do you dress and conduct yourself in a neat, dignified, and controlled manner, or do you dress for maximum effect, calling attention to yourself with flashy, unconventional clothing? In this business of fashion and style, clothes are the instruments by which you make your first contact with buyers and employers alike. The best rule is to dress naturally, if somewhat conservatively, in well-tailored, affordable clothing.

A flashy, overdressed appearance may work against you and exude insecurity instead of confidence. In fact, the big dresser is often regarded as the small businessperson whose ostentatious manner compensates for an inherent lack of talent and ability. For example, a saleswoman should not try to win orders by dressing seductively. Certain customers may get a negative impression and not focus on the business at hand.

As a general rule of thumb, salespeople should match their appearance to the product they are selling. Salespeople who sell higher-priced, well-tailored sportswear should dress similarly. Likewise, salespeople selling moderately priced products often prefer to wear better-made clothing to exhibit their personal sense of good taste. As an example, if a salesperson sells blue jeans and T-shirts, then they will probably be able to dress casually. Wearing a well-tailored denim jacket-and-jeans outfit will enhance the image of the product lines and gain the salespeople credibility.

Generally speaking, sales executives with large textile companies dress more conservatively. These larger companies have established

RW Dictionary

Appearance Refers to a salesperson's choice of wardrobe, accessories, and personal style, as compared with the company he or she represents and the clients with whom he or she meets.

corporate identities and expect their people to conform to a prevailing mode of dress rather than buck the rules. Likewise, retail executives are also likely to conform to the image of their particular stores. They generally dress in a more conservative manner than their counterparts in the apparel industry. Exceptions to these common rules of dressing are salespeople in the West Coast and the Deep South who, due to the balmy climate and relaxed lifestyle, are apt to dress informally. Even so, the standards call for well-made, clean-looking clothing—definitely not the ragged and worn-out nineties youth style.

Assertiveness

Beware of hotshot salespeople who do not care about what they sell. The trick to effective, assertive selling is for salespeople never to seem aggressive and never to let the customer know how hungry they are to make a sale; in other words, they should never let the dollar signs show through. Every good salesperson feels an inward sense of energy that, along with fear of failure, acts as a motivating force. In fact, assertiveness is part of the sales process. It is the need to drum up the maximum amount of business that can be properly handled by a company's manufacturing and distribution setup.

Salespeople should never oversell. Once a customer agrees to make a purchase, a good salesperson doesn't try to push additional merchandise that the customer doesn't want or can't possibly handle. Similarly, a good salesperson who tries to contact a buyer by phone without success, doesn't leave a pile of messages—it's a real turnoff. Additionally, a good salesperson who can't reach a buyer doesn't automatically go over that buyer's head to the immediate superior. Doing so earns that salesperson an enemy. Sellers who are faced with unresponsive buyers who won't return calls or resist making appointments are best off using creative self-assured assertive behavior; it may turn a seemingly impossible situation into a sale.

Salespeople should never give up. The key to contacting a resistant buyer may rest with a friendly assistant. Such an intermediary can communicate a salesperson's message to the buyer and even ascertain the buyer's reaction, becoming, in a sense, an extension of the seller by nurturing the sale. Sometimes finding a buyer's friend who is also in the marketplace or even within the company will help salespeople establish a **center of influence**. Treating others in a genuine, friendly manner may interest them and encourage them to do a favor. These are just a few examples of how salespeople can translate assertiveness into a resourceful sales tool.

Center of Influence A person whose opinion a buyer seeks and respects who is also friendly with the salesperson who is trying to reach that buyer. Typically, it is someone who is involved in industry improvement projects through trade associations and industry organizations and who is well-respected by peers.

Integrity

Integrity carries a very special meaning to a salesperson. It defines a person's character and reputation in the marketplace, forms the backbone of that person's credibility, and is a major factor in gaining the trust and admiration of both superiors in the company and clients.

Integrity is defined as "behaving in an honest manner and according to social and moral principles." What is integrity in the business world? It is, simply, describing things as they are and making commitments stand. What you say is what you do, or you don't say it. Salespeople are judged primarily on their performance, and their accomplishments must live up to their promises. Many inferior salespeople make promises that they can't possibly fulfill, resulting in frequent chaotic situations, undelivered orders, late shipments, and an overproduction of merchandise. They make excuses, covering themselves up against impending disaster. For this reason, salespeople who live up to their promises gain an immense amount of respect.

Salespeople who have integrity operate on a realistic basis. If a company calls to complain about a late shipment, then salespeople should take immediate action rather than procrastinate. If a shipment gets lost, then salespeople should be honest with the buyers and not claim that there's been a work slowdown, a truck was lost en route, or the store's stockroom must have misplaced the merchandise.

Although telling the truth may mean that a seller loses a sale, it doesn't mean that the seller loses the entire account. When a buyer demands a shipment in three days and the seller knows it will take at least three weeks, integrity dictates that the seller be honest and tell the truth. Even if buyers or peers don't have integrity, it is incumbent upon sellers to possess it and be good professionals.

Creativity

Do you tend to blindly follow instructions and accept a course of action because it's the way you've always done so, or do you review a situation and ask yourself how you can improve it? Creative salespeople thoroughly examine the existing sales practices of the companies for which they work and translate them into their own courses of action. They impose their styles on sales relationships and win recognition for instituting changes and improvements.

Many salespeople act simply as conduits between the companies they represent and their buyers. They honor their commitments by their deadlines, but they forget to inject their personal styles into transactions, guide their buyers to make the best possible merchandise selections, or offer advice on how to maximize sales. Every creative salesperson should adopt his or her own approach to selling. They should work closely with clients to help them develop innovative methods of merchandising and display. No longer is it acceptable to simply sell and be done with it.

Similarly, successful textile salespeople understand that the selling process is never complete until goods are moving out of their customers' showrooms. Textile sales executives are responsible for developing tools for merchandising finished clothing and for communicating color, style, and fabric directions that help buyers sell finished products.

Emotional Maturity

Do you let your emotions get the best of you under stress or in the midst of having to make difficult decisions, or are you able to deal with strain and conflict as a normal part of your working day? The buying and selling process is an emotional one. Decisions are made involving tens and hundreds of thousands of dollars' worth of merchandise. Buyers are frequently and understandably insecure about spending large sums of money that are allotted to them.

When buyers say something annoying, salespeople should not take it personally or internalize and react to negative comments; doing so is a sign of immaturity, and there is no room for this in the sales arena. Good salespeople have the ability to keep their cool under pressure, even when customers are emotionally high-pitched or noticeably insecure. Salespeople must always stay in control to exert a reassuring influence on their customers and nudge them toward affirmative decisions.

Testing a Salesperson's Potential

How do the selling characteristics you possess rate against other practicing and prospective salespeople? The following short test to identify the qualifications of candidates for sales positions has been devised by the sales manager of a large company. By rating yourself honestly on each of the criteria discussed in this chapter, you will gain an awareness of how you compare with practicing salespeople in the industry.

In short, you will know if a position in fashion sales is right for you. To the right of each characteristic, place the number you feel best reflects the degree to which you possess each of these characteristics. Use the following scale:

5   possess to an extreme degree
4   possess to own satisfaction
3   possess to some extent
2   possess an insufficient amount
1   don't possess at all

1. Ego drive   (x 4) =
2. Empathy   (x 4) =
3. Appearance   (x 1) =
4. Assertiveness   (x 4) =
5. Integrity   (x 4) =
6. Creativity   (x 2) =
7. Emotional Maturity (x 1) =

                    Total _____

Do the following to determine your score:

+   Multiply your rating for each characteristic by the weighing factor in parentheses alongside it.
+   Add the resulting products to obtain your total score. Apply the following ratings to your score:

90–100 = excellent sales potential
80–89 = good sales potential; some improvement needed
70–79 = satisfactory potential; considerable improvement needed through practice
Under 70 = inadequate potential; great amount of work needed to master the selling process

The Sales Manager's Role in Selecting Salespeople

Sales managers can utilize knowledge of the key characteristics and traits that lead to success in sales to recruit the best salespeople. The selection and hiring process is one of the most difficult responsibilities that a sales manager has. The sales manager must be able to determine if applicants can fit into a company's culture.

Each company has its own personality and its own environment. Therefore, sales managers are charged with finding salespeople who are compatible with the companies that ultimately hire them. Sales managers have to rely on more than just gut feelings. They must look at the current sales staff and the profiles of the most successful salespeople in a company to hire people who fit in with that standard.

The following are just some of the questions that sales managers must answer when determining whether candidates possess the salesperson's personality:

+ Can they handle disappointment and rejection?
+ Can they rebound after defeat?
+ Do they communicate a positive attitude?
+ Do they get along with people?
+ Are they good candidates for the sales training program?
+ Are they compatible with the company's image?
+ Do they like selling?
+ Are they trustworthy?
+ Are they resourceful?
+ Do they seem to be emotionally stable?

To answer these questions, sales managers must observe salespeople's conduct, read body language, and thoroughly check references, and they must accomplish this in about two interviews. Candidates who are looking for sales positions must understand the predicament a manager is in and aim to provide honest answers. Refer to the key concepts in chapter 6—without a doubt, this is the time for candidates to sell themselves.

External Interference

Newly hired salespeople may possess and display all of the required characteristics and work ethics, but they are likely to fail if they are surrounded by a weak administrative structure, lack of demanding leadership, or a slipshod production operation. The best salesperson in the world cannot succeed if order forms are out of date or unavailable, customer files are not maintained, or management is careless and dishonest. If the production department never delivers products on time, a salesperson can't ever expect clients to return with repeat orders.

Management and sales executives have a significant role not only in hiring the most qualified salespeople, but also in setting up an organized sales environment where the positive sales qualities mentioned above are fostered and rewarded. If sales managers demand that sellers be aggressive, then chances are that everyone on the sales force will eventually acquire the bad habit to some degree—even those who realize that pushing clients to buy against their wills is tantamount to business suicide. Conversely, if sales managers set an example for professional and

RW Principle

Without strong administrative support, demanding leadership, and solid production operation, even the best salesperson is likely to fail.

courteous treatment of clients, then this will likely cultivate the same attitude with everyone on the sales force.

It is therefore vital for sales managers to routinely and carefully review their companies' sales management and environments against the characteristics discussed in this chapter, note any areas that need improvement, and implement policy or behavioral changes to rectify problematic areas. Sales managers must also ensure organized office environments and clear-cut procedures since these also play a critical role in a salesperson's success. If finding a needle in a haystack is easier than locating a buyer's most recent order, then the sales manager must take immediate steps to organize office operations.

Paperwork: The Manager's Friend

In the fashion sales world, things happen fast and change often. The sales manager faces delivery deadlines to meet, last-minute order changes to make, and disasters to avert on a daily basis. Successful sales managers recognize that paperwork with a purpose is one of their best friends.

Paperwork with a purpose is any form or written notice that documents an order, a customer change, or an employee action and has a meaningful reason for its existence. Having things in writing prevents errors, avoids confusion, helps sort out conflicts, and serves as a reference for future sales calls and repeat orders. A clearly marked, fully filled out, and signed order form proves highly beneficial when a buyer insists that an order was for a different quantity. A dated fax from a customer requesting last-minute changes can help to explain why delivery was delayed.

Successful salespeople and sales managers must pay attention to details and get any important communications with buyers in writing. In other words, as Table 2.1 shows, sales managers have to be not only people-oriented, but also paperwork-oriented.

Chapter Summary

+ To be successful, salespeople must possess or be able to genuinely adopt a set of characteristics and behavioral patterns that are essential to selling, such as compassion, a drive for success, honesty, and confidence.
+ Many of these characteristics may be cultivated and refined on-the-job by conscientious application.
+ Sales managers have a tremendous responsibility not only in hiring salespeople who already possess most of the characteristics, but

TABLE 2.1
Balancing Act
Sales managers must find a workable balance between the two sides.

People-oriented	Paper-oriented
+ Has a positive attitude—a person who could take two minuses and make them into a plus (positive thinker).	+ Organized—people must have administrative skills to stay on top of things before they become problems.
+ Motivator—a person who can encourage and excite his or her sales personnel in helping them achieve their goals.	+ Monitor salesperson's day-to-day activities—people must determine if they are reaching their goals and have proper systems in place to notify sellers before and during the fact, not afterward.
+ Communicator/teacher—a person who is willing to help the sales team identify their weak spots and offer ways to improve on them.	+ Planners—people who are creative thinkers and come up with solutions using available resources.
+ Supportive/problem solver—a person who is there when needed and when problems arise and has the authority and ability to solve the problem for the salesperson.	
+ Decision maker—a person who knows when to go and when to fold.	

also in establishing positive training programs and conducive working environments where such characteristics are rewarded.

+ Sales professionals must possess a drive for success, empathy, appearance, assertiveness, integrity, creativity, and emotional maturity.

+ Hiring salespeople is one of the most difficult responsibilities of a sales manager's job. The sales manager must be able to determine if applicants can fit into a company's culture.

+ Sales managers must answer key questions by observing a salesperson's conduct, reading body language, or thoroughly checking references.

+ Without strong administrative support, demanding leadership, and a tightly run production operation, even the best salesperson is likely to fail.

+ Paperwork with a purpose is any form or written notice that documents an order, a customer change, or an employee action and has a meaningful reason for its existence.

+ Having things in writing prevents errors, avoids confusion, helps sort out conflicts, and serves as a reference for future sales calls and repeat orders.

RW CASE STUDY

Ron Ellis is the president of MRI The Mayberry Group, a recruitment firm in Mount Airy, North Carolina, that specializes in the fashion, apparel, and retail industries. Some of their clients include Land's End, Nordstrom, Mervyn's, JCPenney, Dick's Sporting Goods, The Children's Place, and Lane Bryant.

What are the characteristics you look for in a candidate when searching for a sales manager or salesperson?

What we look for is a candidate who is—not necessarily in order of importance—confident, articulate business communicators who [have] personal skills and [the] ability to collaborate with others, who [are] effective in convincing others through their enthusiasm, who [are] highly motivated to achieve and surpass past goals, who can balance empathy and professionalism, and who [have] sharp insight into other people's personalities.

How do you determine whether the candidate possesses these characteristics?

To be sure, you cannot determine this from their resume. These days anybody can boost a resume using a preparation service. Resumes are necessary evils, but they are merely a starting point. If the candidate looks good on paper, we arrange for an interview. There we ask a lot of behavior-based questions [that] explore the candidate's past achievement, such as "How did you overcome objections to get this account?" or "How did that project transpire?" rather than theoretical questions [that] ask "How would you do that?" or yes-no questions. Many candidates can sound intelligent when addressing theoretical scenarios, but when they have to recount actual experiences, they must be more accurate and specific since their answers can be analyzed as well as verified with their past employers. The question "Tell me about the last time you had to implement a company policy and the customer did not want to accept the change—how did you handle that?" pins the candidate down and offers invaluable information about [his or her] mode of operation. In addition to the interview, we also verify the facts on the candidate's resume and conduct the Work Behavior Personality Profile—a questionnaire analysis measuring the candidate's dominance, extroversion, urgency, and conformity.

How important is integrity in the case of a candidate applying for a sales position?

Regardless of what occupation you are in, there's no question integrity is extremely important. You must do what you say you'd do and be a candid communicator. To evaluate integrity, we ask related questions as well as check the candidate's answers against their references. In recent times, fashion sales [have] gravitated toward consultative selling rather than "technique" selling. Whereas [twenty] years ago, nearly 80 percent of all apparel was sold to smaller accounts such as specialty stores, today that has changed and department stores do the majority of the selling. The salesperson who calls on Land's End, for example, has to be someone who can develop a meaningful business relationship and who is extremely product knowledgeable. Salespeople with low or no integrity simply cannot survive in this environment.

What advice can you give the sales manager in regards to maximizing their hiring interviews?

Prepare for the interview. One serious mistake many companies make is not preparing for the interview and not checking the facts ahead of time. Then they depend solely on a one-hour interview to make a decision and typically end up hiring based on whether they like the candidate's personality. The other mistake is asking theoretical questions instead of analyzing the candidate's behavioral pattern based on history. Asking such questions cuts through the bluffing and allows you to better know whether the candidate is a good fit.

What advice can you give the student who is aiming to enter the fashion sales field upon graduation?

Our clients are looking for people who can solve complex business and interpersonal problems and who have achieved success in the past. When I previously worked on campus recruiting, we always looked for well-rounded people with good academic achievement but who were also active socially, who were members of student associations or served in student government, for example. For a sales position, I'd rather hire a candidate with [a] 3.2 GPA who has excellent social skills than someone with a 3.9 GPA who can't interact with people or develop relationships well.

Questions to Consider

1. Why do you think Mr. Ellis looks for candidates "who can balance empathy and professionalism" when recruiting for sales positions?
2. What are the advantages of asking a candidate behavioral questions as opposed to theoretical ones? Which question type do you think offers more insight during a hiring interview?
3. Do you think a salesperson with a weak sense of ethics could succeed in a sales position? Why or why not?
4. Why are social skills so important to develop while people are still in school?

RW EXERCISES

1. Using the information and scale on page 29, figure out what your total score is for potential success in fashion sales. Where are you excelling? Where could you stand to improve? What steps could you take to improve them?

2. Think of an instance when you dealt with a successful salesperson. Analyze that salesperson's personality against the seven characteristics discussed in this chapter and note which of the characteristics contributed most to his or her success in your opinion.

3. Pair up with another student so one of you acts as the sales manager and the other acts as a salesperson applying for a job. The salesperson should exhibit a fictitious personality that the manager should aim to identify through conversation and questioning. Using the information in this chapter, the manager must determine whether the salesperson should be hired or not and why. Write down your thoughts and reasons. Switch roles for a different perspective, and note the new responses.

4. Pair up with two other students, so one of you acts as the salesperson, another acts as the buyer, and the third acts as the office administrator, either in retail or B2B. Assume the seller is in a sales meeting and calls up the office with questions. The office administrator should act disorganized and confused. What impact does this situation have on the sale? Write down how the office inefficiency affects the sale and the buyer's perception of the company. Switch roles for a different perspective, and note the new responses.

END NOTES

1. Sherman, Jerry, and Eric Hertz. *Woman Power in Textile & Apparel Sales*. New York: Fairchild Publications, 1979.

CHAPTER 03

RETAIL SALES IN FASHION

Objectives

+ Gain an understanding of low- and high-end fashion retail selling, and discover the career opportunities available in both.

+ Observe where fashion retail stands today, and see typical transaction patterns.

+ Understand the customer–salesperson relationship within the context of retailing.

+ Learn the important retail sales techniques that help you assist customers better and make you a better salesperson.

+ Recognize how store layout, dynamics, and atmosphere can affect customer decisions, and determine how salespeople can contribute to sales-conducive environments.

+ Examine the importance of product knowledge in retail sales.

+ Appreciate why retailers need to understand and be tolerant of and sensitive to different cultures and local retail environments when they work in international markets.

Overview

The third chapter reviews how sales in the fashion industry functions in the real world of retail. Forget the idea of a salesperson asking, "May I help you?"—it doesn't work. Today's fashion retail world is fast-paced and based on quick transactions. Glamorous advertisements and slick commercials are the main selling tools. We explore the anatomy of retail sales today, explain how a retail fashion salesperson fits in today's retail sales context, and describe the career opportunities this field offers. We also recommend customer retention techniques and convey the vital need for salespeople to be knowledgeable about the products they sell or services they offer. Lastly, we discuss the international aspect of fashion retailing.

Introduction

Many of us have experienced something like the hypothetical scenario that follows. A person goes into a store because he or she needs to buy a shirt, and the salesperson immediately approaches and asks, "May I help you?" The salesperson doesn't give up and insists on helping.

Some of the usual replies that follow the dreaded question include: "I'm just looking," "No thanks," "Oh, I'm fine," or even "I don't need help." A person will say just about anything to brush off the annoying intrusion—and it works. The salesperson usually disappears. However, say the person in our hypothetical example resumes his or her search and finally finds the needed item only to discover that it is not the right size and there is no price tag. Now the customer can't find the salesperson. Moreover, say the person is in a hurry. Most likely, the person will convince him or herself that the item is not that great and leave without making a purchase. The result is a lost sale for the salesperson and an unfulfilled desire for the now dissatisfied customer. This example involves only one customer and one salesperson. However, if this type of situation repeats over time by this and the rest of the sales personnel, it can easily cause sales to plummet and shut down a retail store.

Retail employees who are in direct contact with their customers are referred to by various titles, depending on the companies for which they work as well as other factors. For example, Target stores call their retail employees team members, Wal-Mart calls them sales associates, and traditional department stores and boutiques call them either sales associates or salespeople. In some retail stores, all employees who work in sales positions are referred to by the same title. In other retail stores, employees who work in sales positions are referred to by various titles (even within the same store).

Sales associates or team members who work in self-selection retail stores are primarily service-oriented personnel who do not actually sell items and usually don't have commission based programs in place. They do answer questions that customers may have, assist customers in locating items, and check out customers at cash registers. Self-selection retailers depend on their brand names, advertisements, and visual displays to sell their goods. Sales associates in traditional department stores such as Macy's, Nordstrom, and Bloomingdale's assist customers with all items regardless of price; they must be prepared to sell bargain-priced merchandise and high-ticket items such as designer brands, menswear, evening dresses, jewelry, leather, shoes, and home furnishings. Many customers expect salespeople at such stores to provide them with guidance and unbiased information. Retail salespeople work on

RW Dictionary

Retailing The process of selling to the end-user—the person who will be actually using the product.

RW Figure

John Wanamaker Merchant, born in Philadelphia, Pennsylvania. After a few years as secretary of the Philadelphia Young Men's Christian Association, he and his brother-in-law, Nathan Brown, opened a men's clothing store called Oak Hall (1861). In 1869, a year after Brown's death, Wanamaker opened the more fashionable John Wanamaker & Co. He had his brothers manage the store in 1876, in time for the centennial, so he could open the Grand Depot, a huge dry-goods and men's clothing store located in a former Pennsylvania Railroad depot. In 1877, unable to attract other merchants to open shop under his roof, he opened a number of specialty shops that flourished after one year. He expanded into New York City (1896) and continued to enlarge his innovative department stores by advertising effectively in newspapers and implementing a money-back guarantee. He is generally credited as spearheading the advent of the traditional department store concept.

many different compensation plans. They receive hourly wages, annual salaries, salaries plus commissions, or strictly commissions. Macy's, Nordstrom, and Bloomingdale's have incentive programs to compensate their sales associates with commissions on goods sold.

Say a customer enters a clothing store and browses through some expensive suits. This time, the salesperson does not ask, "May I help you?" The trained salesperson observes the customer, notes whether the customer is leaning toward a specific style, and waits for the customer to try something on before approaching. By following this strategy, the salesperson is now armed with product information and can strike up a meaningful conversation with the customer instead of relying on a trite question.

The sales associate position is an important one. A recent consumer habits survey found the following:

> The majority of consumers identified sales floor assistance as an important or very important factor in influencing loyalty to a particular retailer. The most common reason cited for not shopping with a particular retailer again is poor service from store floor sales associates. Today, retailers have the power to increase the time sales associates spend on the sales floor, improve sales volumes and secure customer loyalty, without losing productivity.[1]

Besides helping customers, sales associates learn how to deal with people and have an opportunity to grow within the field of retail sales. Sales associates who put extra effort into learning about the products that they sell and have high transaction volumes have a better chance of being noticed by management and offered sales positions in high-end departments and perhaps even sales management and executive positions.

Career Opportunities

According to the U.S. Department of Labor,[2] there are 3.9 million retail fashion salespeople and sales associates in the United States, with the majority of them employed by department stores. Throughout the next decade, many baby boomers will reach retirement age and leave the workforce. Since baby boomers constitute about 60 percent of today's workforce, this will create a tremendous need for new employees to fill positions in sales and sales management.

Retail selling has great opportunities for college graduates. One reason is that this field is in dire need of salespeople who know how to deal with others and have a good work ethic. College graduates typically have an edge in this respect since they learn about ethics and the importance of good communication skills while they are in school.

Entry-level retail sales positions give recent graduates the opportunity to learn about the companies for which they work, customers, and the marketplace. Retail salespeople are the eyes and ears of the retail business (they are also on the front line!), and being in direct contact with the customers gives them firsthand knowledge of their consumers' wants and needs, which is the very foundation of all business transactions.

Gaining sales experience enables salespeople to acquire the knowledge and skills necessary for promotions. Retailers promote experienced employees to executive positions, which offer higher salaries. Retail managers are constantly looking for competent people who have risen through the ranks and have an intimate knowledge of the workings of the business at all levels. College graduates can use retail sales as a springboard for careers in retail buying, marketing, and management.

The field of retail sales also offers job security—brick-and-mortar retail environments do not outsource jobs, so you can always count on finding sales positions at all levels available in the United States. Certainly, the Internet has encroached on this environment somewhat, but most people want to see, feel, or try on clothing, for example, before buying it, and that's not likely to change soon.

Positions in retail selling also prepare college students for eventual self-employment. Experience in identifying customers' needs and how to satisfy them is essential to starting a new business, be it a small boutique or a larger fashion store. Indeed, many successful retail employees eventually enter the field of fashion manufacturing and open their own businesses.

FIGURE 3.1

Fashion Retail Earnings

A view of median earnings for retail salespeople and management.

✚ ✚ ✚

AVERAGE EARNINGS FOR RETAIL SALESPEOPLE

$24,170

✚ ✚ ✚ ✚ (

TOP EARNINGS FOR RETAIL SALESPEOPLE

$35,860

✚ ✚ ✚ ✚ (

EARNINGS FOR FIRST-LINE SUPERVISORS

$37,500

✚ ✚ ✚ ✚ ✚ ✚ ✚ ✚ ✚ ✚ ✚ ✚ ✚ ✚ ✚

EARNINGS FOR MERCHANDISE MANAGERS

$123,500

In recent years, retail managers have recognized the importance of retail salespeople. Successful retailers have incentive programs in place to reward and compensate retail salespeople for the important work they perform. According to the 2003 U.S. Bureau of Labor Statistics,[3] salaries for retail salespeople who specialize in apparel average around $24,170, with a high of about $35,860 or even higher depending on a salesperson's position and experience, the store, and the department within the store. First-line apparel retail supervisors can expect annual salaries of about $37,500 a year, while retail merchandise managers average about $123,500 (Figure 3.1).

Retail Salespeople's Roles

A fashion retail salesperson's primary objective is to sell; however, salespeople must never forget that their purpose is to serve their customers. There are no sales without customers, and customers will not come back if they are unsatisfied. So, when the retail salesperson treats the customer as the top priority, then sales, repeat sales, commissions, incentives, and profits for the organization will surely follow.

Customers and retailers alike rely on salespeople to offer appropriate advice, provide helpful and honest information about the products that they sell, and assist customers so they can make purchases comfortably. It is absolutely impossible for retail salespeople to succeed if they don't understand their customers' **needs**, aren't familiar with the products they sell, and don't care enough to help their customers feel secure about the purchases they make.

Understanding Needs

What is a customer who is shopping for a pair of new shoes looking for precisely? Is the customer looking for rugged work boots, dress shoes, or evening footwear? These questions may seem obvious, but many salespeople forget to ask. They mistakenly assume they know what their customers want.

Suppose a customer is looking for dress shoes to wear to work. A good salesperson wants to know what the customer does for a living, whether the customer works indoors or outdoors, and what the customer usually wears to work. Salespeople cannot possibly sell successfully without first understanding the specific needs of their customers.

Once retail salespeople define their customers' needs, they must be familiar with the products they sell so they can recommend products that will fulfill those needs. A salesperson who sells shoes, for example, should know the differences between leather and faux leather, the

RW Dictionary

Need The resolution to a problem a customer wishes to solve or something the customer desires.

advantages and disadvantages of rubber soles, and which shoes look best with business attire. When retail salespeople care enough about their customers, they are better equipped to make honest recommendations and help to assuage their customers' doubts.

On the Front Lines

Retail salespeople not only sell but also represent the stores for which they work. It is up to them to communicate the culture and personality of the stores they represent. Retail salespeople are on the front lines because they deal directly with customers, and as such they have the power to determine the success or failure of businesses.

A salesperson's actions have tremendous impact not only on sales but also on the retailer's image. Consumers instinctively equate salespeople with the retailers for which those salespeople work. After all, the salesperson's is the only face that the customer can associate to the retailer's name—to do so is part of human nature, and salespeople must understand and remain aware of this important fact.

When the salesperson is courteous and knowledgeable, projecting a positive and friendly attitude, the customer will in most cases respond to the retailer in the same way. The customer will always remember his or her first impression of the salesperson. Positive impressions are necessary and will make customers want to return for future purchases. Unfortunately, by the same token, if just one salesperson was impolite or uncaring, the customer will now have a negative impression of the retailer as a whole. This demonstrates the importance of the salesperson's role in the organization.

At the Heart of Retail

A salesperson's role in retail can be compared with the human heart's role in the body. Just as the heart pumps new blood into the veins and allows for cells to survive and grow, a salesperson generates income and resources by selling merchandise for the retailer and allows a company to survive.

What would happen if there were no salespeople at a fashion retail store? Self-selection and self-checkout would be imposed upon the customers.

What happens when a customer has a question or concern at a self-selection and self-checkout business? Customers will have absolutely no one to turn to and will not only leave without making a purchase, but also never return.

Retail salespeople are essential to the fashion retail business. They use their product knowledge, presentations, and people skills to move goods, build customer relations, and make sales.

Real-World Retail Sales Approaches

Sales professionals use different methods to approach customers; however, there are certain rules in retail selling that are common to all. Approaching the customer is the most sensitive part of a sale and usually forecasts its outcome. It sets the tone for the transaction and often determines the connection—what some people refer to as *chemistry*—between the salesperson and customer. In the fast-paced and competitive world of retail, chemistry is crucial because salespeople usually don't know customers personally. The **approach** is a salesperson's only chance to win a customer's loyalty.

The beauty of executing a correct sales approach is that it allows a salesperson to improve on the generated chemistry. Remember that preliminary observation is important. Salespeople should always observe their customers' actions and manners, as in whether they seem rushed or relaxed or whether they seem to be looking for a particular item or looking through the racks aimlessly (also called *boredom browsing*).

Based on their preliminary observations, salespeople formulate an unassuming approach that prompts further discussion and allows them to fulfill a customer's needs. Salespeople should never assume they know what a customer is looking for. For example, if a customer is briskly looking through a rack of evening jackets and moves a jacket to its rightful place in a frustrated manner, a salesperson should approach and say, "My apologies for the state of the store. We've had quite a hectic weekend. May I ask what you are looking for so I can find it faster for you?"

Here's another example of a good approach.

Salesperson:	"Hi. Have you shopped in this department before?"
Customer:	"I'm just looking."
Salesperson:	"May I ask what you are looking for?"

At this point, the customer's reaction and response are very important. If the customer answers, then a sale is possible. However, if the customer continues to resist, the salesperson should give the customer space but remember to mention his or her name while maintaining eye contact—this way, if the customer does have a question, the salesperson will be readily available. If possible, salespeople should hand their business cards to customers who are leaving the store and thank them for shopping there. Even if those customers didn't make any purchases, they will leave with a favorable and lasting impression.

RW Dictionary

Approach The actions and words that salespeople use when making contact with their customers for the first time in a retail sales environment.

RW Principle

When a salesperson maintains eye contact with the customer, it establishes empathy, infers honesty on the part of the salesperson, and helps the customer remember the salesperson's face.

The Worst Four Words

"May I help you?" are the worst four words that a retail salesperson can utter because they don't encourage the customer to talk and puts them on the defensive. The four words usually elicit a negative response that stops cold a sales transaction. Examples of better questions to use when approaching customers are "Is there anything in particular that you are looking for?" and "Are you shopping for a gift?"

If a fashion salesperson approached you with "May I help you?," chances are you would feel the salesperson didn't care. This line is a rote approach that is so overused by untrained and uninterested salespeople. In fact, most of us shudder in horror upon hearing these words. The very meaning of the question "May I help you?" implies that the customer is in trouble of some sort and needs rescuing. This almost always puts the customer on the defense. "No, thank you" is usually the immediate response, even if the customer is actually in need of assistance. The subconscious thought by the customer is often "I'm smart enough to figure out what I want, and I don't need your help!"

If customers feel pressured or cornered, then salespeople won't make any sales. The approach has to promote a comfortable environment that makes customers feel there is no rush. Furthermore, if customers just want to look around, they should feel that it is all right to do so. In situations where customers really do want to look around on their own, salespeople should give customers their business cards and keep themselves accessible in case customers have questions or concerns.

It is reasonable for a salesperson to approach customers who go to specific departments or pick up an item. A good approach in this case is to ask if the item is a gift. Again, if the customer resists, then the salesperson should leave the customer alone. One of the worst things a salesperson can do is harass customers with questions and comments after they have clearly indicated they don't need help. This type of **sales stalking** alienates customers. Successful retail salespeople interviewed for this book agree that this practice can be classified as a pressure tactic and should be avoided at all costs.

Salespeople resort to such tactics when they feel pressure from not having made enough sales, but passing the pressure onto their customers is not the answer. Remember that salespeople who rely on pressure tactics may get lucky and make one sale, but they will probably fail to get customers to return for repeat business. At sales meetings and training sessions, management should discourage this short-lived tactic.

Don't Forget to Smile . . . or Frown

Most retail purchases are made emotionally. Good salespeople adjust their behavior and befriend their customers. By being empathic to their

---

RW Principle

Salespeople should approach with comments that encourage customers to have conversations. "May I help you?" usually elicits a negative response, which brings a sale to a grinding halt.

RW Dictionary

Sales Stalking Insisting on "helping" the customer after they have said they do not need help.

customers' frames of mind and moods, salespeople are better able to forge stronger bonds and better levels of communication. Making a customer with a baby, who also seems to be in a hurry, wait is the opposite of empathetic. If the salesperson provides the frazzled customer with efficient, quick service, the customer will no doubt appreciate it and return to the store.

Salespeople should always bear in mind that while some customers may go to a store to browse, many want to buy. In later chapters of the book, we discuss how to get the sale in greater detail.

Building a Customer Base

Interaction with retail customers depends on the skills and training of individual retail salespeople. Although encounters in the retail arena may be brief, there are still ways of establishing and maintaining relationships with retail consumers. One method that is oftentimes neglected is simply to create a customer list and follow through on any new items or events that may be of interest to each.

Many boutiques and high-ticket fashion departments allow salespeople to keep lists of customers with whom they've worked. Lists should include customers' names; addresses, telephone numbers, and e-mail addresses (noting their preferred methods of contact); and the types of merchandise they have bought or may be interested in buying. Employing this technique allows salespeople to generate significant repeat business. The most popular methods to contact customers on such lists are phone calls, e-mails, and cards sent by regular mail.

A successful menswear department store salesperson interviewed for this book says he places his customers' names on an active customer list after he makes his sales. Because he is usually too busy to record everything regarding the sale, he jots down only their names, addresses, and phone numbers. When new items become available, he calls customers on his list and estimates that about one in ten returns to make a purchase. It's growing popular for retailers to train their sales personnel in obtaining not only customers' names and telephone numbers but also to establish profiles that note purchases by prices, sizes, colors, styles, and brand names. Many large and small retailers require their salespeople to notify customers about upcoming sales events and promotions. Smaller independent retailers have been using this technique for years.

Reminding the customer of the salesperson's and store's names through the repeated use of post-sale follow-up is essential to successful fashion selling. It adds a personal touch to a business transaction that puts customers at ease and encourages them to return. The two Rs of

RW Principle

Even though retail transactions are brief, salespeople find ways to follow-up on sales and develop long-lasting relationships with their customers.

fashion selling—relationship and retention—are vital to the health of any retail business. Retail salespeople must understand how the two Rs relate to the successful generation of future sales.

If store policy prohibits compiling customer lists, then salespeople can remind customers to return to them in the future. Business cards come in handy in situations such as these because salespeople can jot down their schedules on the backs of the cards. Satisfied customers will likely remember the good service, keep those cards, and refer to them when they return to make purchases.

After salespeople make a sale, they can highlight for their customers the quality of service they have provided in an unpretentious manner. For example, a salesperson might say, "Thank you so much for shopping with us today. I hope my assistance has exceeded your expectations." Once a sale is made, a salesperson should confirm that customers are satisfied with everything. Normally, a customer's expression will reveal if there is anything wrong. Salespeople should quickly assess if there are any problems and take immediate actions to rectify them.

Salespeople should close their sales transactions by saying, for example, "Please do come back and ask for me in the future. I'll be glad to be of service again." By encouraging customers to remember them, salespeople increase the probability of future business. Undoubtedly, to create a solid customer base, salespeople should deliver consistent excellent service and have professional, courteous manners. Customers remember good salespeople because they can trust them.

Know Thy Product

Know thy product can be easily considered one of the ten commandments of selling. **Product knowledge** and presentation are fundamental to making and increasing sales in retail environments. Imagine going to a boutique that specializes in leather clothing and learning that the salesperson doesn't know how to distinguish between real and faux leather. Suddenly, spending four or five hundred dollars based on the salesperson's recommendations doesn't seem like such a good idea.

Salespeople who have product knowledge inspire confidence and trust—two ingredients that are necessary for making sales. If a salesperson tries to sell a faux leather jacket to a customer who specifically requests the best real leather jacket available in the store, chances are the customer will walk out empty-handed. The salesperson has eroded whatever confidence and trust the customer had when the salesperson failed to fulfill that customer's needs.

Without product knowledge, salespeople cannot maintain dialogues with their customers because they won't be able to give to them any information regarding the products or make recommendations. In

RW Dictionary

Product knowledge Comprehending and being able to explain the features of a product, from its benefits and shortcomings to its compatibility with other products.

fact, one of the most common complaints consumers have regarding their shopping experiences is that salespeople are not knowledgeable. Ironically, salespeople who ask the usual and impersonal "May I help you?" can't actually help because they don't know answers to basic questions about the products they sell. When retail salespeople lack product knowledge, they won't be able to make sales and customers opt to shop at other competing stores. Therefore, it is important for the merchandising department and the retailer's buyers to keep the salespeople at the store level informed of the styles and trends that prompted the store to add a specific line; this type of information can help the salespeople make a more educated presentation to the customers who come in to the store.

Salespeople need to know what products they currently have in stock and if and when anything that is out of stock will be available again. They also need to know of new upcoming merchandise and when they expect it to "hit the floor" (in other words, when it will be available for sale). By being ready to impart such vital information, salespeople will gain credibility. Salespeople who are ready to answer frequently asked questions have the confidence to share their opinions, make recommendations, and convey specialized knowledge, all of which impresses customers and further increases the chances of making a sale.

Getting to Know Fashion

Retail salespeople are responsible for learning everything there is to know about the fashion items they sell; however, management should take an active role in providing training for their sales personnel. It is a grave mistake for managers not to train their salespeople because untrained personnel cause losses in sales and revenue. It is crucial for managers to recognize the importance of salespeople in retail environments.

Most upscale departments and high-ticket item departments have training programs in place for their salespeople. Whether the program is thorough or halfhearted, all salespeople should take these programs seriously. Salespeople who receive inadequate training or none at all should try to gain as much knowledge as possible by critically observing other salespeople (always careful not to pick up bad habits) and conducting their own research about the products they sell.

Bona fide self-training methods for salespeople who work in fashion retail include keeping up-to-date on current fashion trends, subscribing to fashion magazines, and trying on the clothing they are charged with selling (with proper permission, of course). Salespeople are always prepared to give successful presentations to their customers when they have product knowledge.

Sometimes Things Are as They Appear

The way a salesperson handles a garment and presents it to a customer can have a significant effect on whether the customer buys it. If a salesperson treats a $1,000 designer suit as if it were a potato sack, then it may shake a customer's confidence in that salesperson. The customer may interpret the salesperson's actions as disrespectful and even question whether the suit has been handled roughly by others.

Ideally, retail salespeople should be **clotheshorses** who aim to dress in the fashions they sell. Many retail stores such as Ralph Lauren and Gap encourage their employees to wear their brand names to work. Well-dressed salespeople gain immediate respect from customers and effectively advertise the products they sell. Wearing the products they sell is the most effective presentation salespeople can make.

A salesperson who genuinely loves clothing and gets excited when talking about the feel of silk (aka, clotheshorse), for example, will be more successful than a salesperson who could care less about even reading the label. Naturally, there is no way for salespeople to wear the exact outfits customers want to buy. However, by wearing good quality garments that fit well and look smart, salespeople make customers feel that their recommendations are worth following.

Show Time

Store designs greatly affect the buying habits of shoppers. Successful retail salespeople recognize that the retail business is very closely related to show business. Macy's and Bloomingdale's sponsor special events to create excitement and bring in great business—the most obvious example of such an event is Macy's Thanksgiving Day Parade, which gives families something fun to do on a holiday and puts the store's name into the consciousness of these would-be customers. Many people associate Macy's with holiday shopping, as a result. Another example is the special sale events that typically take place on a weekend where customers are offered substantial savings on select items. Such sale events create a buzz with customers, who flock in for the deals but often end up buying additional items at regular price.

Retailers must bear in mind that their business is not only about merchandise but also about merchandising—how retailers present merchandise. Store displays, atmosphere, signage announcing discounts and other sales, and special events help salespeople make sales.

Some people may argue that Wal-Mart and other such stores don't rely on tactics such as throwing special events to promote excitement among their customers; however, such stores do not depend on their salespeople in the same way that department stores depend on them. Stores such as Wal-Mart cater to people who need specific items—in fact, the clothing

---

RW Dictionary

Clotheshorse A person who pays much attention to clothes and fashion trends; also considered a fashion connoisseur.

section of Wal-Mart is only one of many departments, and indeed the clothes are inexpensive items available to the public at bargain prices. Fashion-savvy consumers will likely go elsewhere to shop for clothing—and discount prices are not their sole motivation. Fashion stores must therefore customize their designs and décor to attract customers, and salespeople should make themselves aware of these marketing tactics so they can use it to their advantage. For example, if a store is decorated with neutral colors that exude professionalism, then salespeople should promote that atmosphere and wear beige, brown, olive green, and other such colors.

Store Clutter—Good, Bad, or Ugly?

Under certain circumstances, clutter works. Department stores may create clutter intentionally to lure bargain hunters and encourage them to search for "red-sticker" items that are buried in clearance sections. Clothing of all types in clearance racks are usually assembled by size. Some bargain hunters perceive such disarray as bargains because they believe retailers want to get rid of it.

However, clutter is not beneficial for other stores. Uncluttered fashion departments are usually the most profitable. Consumers are more willing to buy when they are relaxed, and they tend to be relaxed in environments where merchandise is organized and displayed properly and where there are no obstacles to buying.

Retailers should avoid cluttered high-end departments because it likens new merchandise to merchandise on the bargain racks. Although stores have stock personnel who maintain stock and keep it clutter-free, salespeople are responsible for maintaining orderly areas. After all, a department's appearance directly affects the number of sales they may make.

Retailing Away from Home

The rules of retail sales discussed in this chapter include having an effective sales approach, having thorough product knowledge, and delivering a good presentation. Because these rules are based on the principles of human nature, they typically apply to all areas of the world. However, the intricate details of a sales transaction vary from country to country and even from region to region. Etiquette, gestures, speech volume, language, and local fashion styles are examples of such details.

Retail salespeople who have moved to countries different from their own must make themselves aware of the intricate details particular to whatever culture they are now a part of so they can adjust their behavior accordingly. For example, in Europe it is generally considered improper etiquette for a salesperson to ask a customer questions if the customer is just looking. In many cases, if salespeople are even slightly pushy, then they will most likely lose the sale. Gestures are also important; an appropriate greeting in New York may not be an appropriate greeting in Paris or Milan.

Speech volume is particularly important when salespeople are making sales in a country different from their own. In the United States, salespeople have louder speaking voices and are therefore perceived by people from other countries as more aggressive. Japanese salespeople have quieter speaking voices and are therefore considered to have more conservative approaches. Salespeople who move to other countries should be sure to be as fluent as possible not only in the language, but also in the idiomatic nuances of that language. Even if a salesperson moves from the United States to England, he or she should be sure to learn the nuances that make British English different from American English.

Salespeople must also be sensitive to different style, color, and size preferences in countries different from their own. Short miniskirts and casual flip-flops may sell like hotcakes in the United States, but may not sell as well in a more conservative country like Switzerland or in a cold country like Russia.

In short, salespeople should immerse themselves in the cultures in which they work and learn its customs, etiquette, and styles by observing the people around them, flipping through local fashion magazines, and watching fellow salespeople interact with customers.

Salespeople do not need to relocate to other countries to follow the advice given in the preceding paragraphs. A salesperson who moves from New York City to a small town in the Midwest must be mindful that the selling environment is different. The same rules apply: What may be considered acceptable fashion in New York City may not be so readily accepted in the Midwest.

Chapter Summary

+ In retail, salespeople are on the front lines because they deal directly with the end-user—the person who will be using the product. The customer is right there to express their personal needs.
+ The retail environment is fast-paced and highly competitive, and successful retail salespeople must quickly establish meaningful conversations with their customers, identify their customers' needs, and utilize their product knowledge to make recommendations and make sales.

+ Retail salespeople can look forward to promotions to managerial and executive positions, depending on their success and experience.
+ A salesperson's approach often dictates the success or failure of a sales transaction.
+ "May I help you?" are the worst four words a retail salesperson can utter. Instead, salespeople should observe their customers and try to approach with a comment that is appropriate to the situation— this personalized approach puts customers at ease and increases a salesperson's chances of making a sale.
+ Salespeople should compile lists of customers with whom they have worked and contact them regularly by phone, e-mail, or regular mail to inform them of new products. If compiling such lists is impossible, then salespeople can hand to their customers business cards with their schedules jotted down on the backs.
+ Product knowledge and effective presentations are absolutely vital to the success of a sale. Salespeople who don't know about the products they sell cannot give adequate presentations and therefore rarely succeed in retail (or any other type of sales, for that matter).
+ Retail is much like show business. Department stores such as Macy's have events that attract customers, and salespeople must remember to capitalize on the excitement generated by those events.
+ A clean and orderly department makes customers feel at ease and encourages them to buy. Salespeople should maintain their areas, even if it is someone else's job to do so.
+ Retail salespeople who work in countries or regions different from their own should be mindful of the local culture, etiquette, and other acceptable behavior and adjust their selling tactics accordingly.

RW CASE STUDY

Alex Heitz began his career as a clothing retailer but had to sell his small store because of fierce competition from the giant retailers in his area. He decided it was in his best interests to join them rather than fight them and found a job with a well-known department store as a menswear salesperson. Heitz has been with the department store for approximately fifteen years; he won the award as the best salesperson of the year in men's furnishings two years ago. He competed against salespeople from the company's fifty stores. He is happy as a salesperson and is not interested in advancing to a position in management. He explains, "I don't want the pressure of management. I love what I am doing." Heitz loves dealing with and assisting people.

How do you get compensated?

Heitz works strictly on a commission basis. His department pays 5 percent commission. He likes straight commission because of the challenge it presents: "Working on salary alone does not offer me any incentive." He works full-time, which constitutes thirty-five hours per week. The company pays commissions each week and deducts customer returns each week, as well, from his commission statement. He says that salespeople in the store work on straight commission, but a few departments pay an hourly salary to some of their salespeople and pay salary plus commission to others.

What do retail salespeople earn?

Heitz reports that the average full-time, straight-commission retail salesperson in his store earns anywhere from $28,000 to $30,000 per year. He does indicate, however, that salespeople in the shoe department and other high-ticket departments can earn $40,000 per year and even more. Indeed, there are many retail sales associates whose yearly gross sales surpass $1,000,000.

What is your philosophy on customer approach?

Heitz agrees that approaching a customer is the most important part of a retail selling transaction. What annoys him most is when salespeople harass customers by following them around as they browse. He explains that a salesperson must understand that they must respect customers who specifically resist any offer of help and state they rather just look. Heitz reminds salespeople who harass their customers that even if customers prefer to look on their own, they will call salespeople when they see something they want.

When Heitz approaches customers who say they are just looking, he offers his calling card (business card) and tells them he is available if they need assistance. He does not approach with "May I help you?" because he knows this question elicits negative responses. He believes salespeople should always use positive approaches. Heitz suggests the salespeople find out what a customer is looking for by asking if the customer is looking for a gift or something for him or herself. Usually, customers answer the question, and the dialogue and chance for a possible sale begins. He also finds that it helps expedite the sale when he gives his customers choices. Heitz never uses pressures tactics.

Do you receive enough sales training?

Heitz feels that most sales are lost due to insufficient training. He points out that many department stores do not have regularly scheduled sales or product training programs for their sales personnel, including the store for which he works. Most of the product information he receives comes from his own research. He believes salespeople must keep current on the trends regarding the merchandise they sell. He believes that training sessions can lead to a dramatic increase in his sales as well as his colleagues' sales.

What are your thoughts on customer retention?

After he makes a sale, Heitz gives customers his business card and tells them to call if they need any information. He also places his customers' names on an active customer list. He confirms that he is usually too busy to record all the information regarding the actual sale, so he includes their names and contact information. When new merchandise arrives, he calls the customer on his list to let them know. About 10 percent of the people he calls return to the department to make purchases. He would like to increase this percentage because retaining his customer base will help him to increase his income.

What is your opinion regarding visual displays as selling aids?

Heitz feels that visual displays of merchandise are great selling aids, especially since he believes most fashion purchases are impulsive. He likes mannequin displays and would like to see more creative ways of displaying merchandise.

How do you feel about cluttered areas in departments within a store?

He agrees that clutter attracts bargain hunters but feels the most productive departments are those that are organized and clutter-free. He keeps his department looking neat and organized so it is easy for his customers to find the items they need and want.

Questions to Consider
1. What type of compensation would you prefer, and why?
2. What type of sales approach leads to a successful sale? Explain.
3. What methods would you use to retain retail customers?
4. Do you feel that a fashion department can sometimes be too organized? Why?

RW EXERCISES

1. Think of a recent time when you went into a clothing store and were approached by a salesperson. Recall how the salesperson greeted you, your reaction, and whether he or she answered your questions.

Provide a brief analysis of the sales transaction and how you feel the salesperson could improve.

2. Pair up with another student so one of you acts as a salesperson and the other as a customer. The customer should pretend to walk into a department store, and the salesperson should approach by saying, "May I help you?" Note the customer's reaction and whether the approach could have resulted in a sale and why. Switch roles for a different perspective, and note the new responses.

3. Go to a local department store, and visit one of the high-end departments, such as jewelry, leather, suits, or shoes. Browse through the items and wait until a salesperson approaches you. Try to observe the salesperson before he or she approaches, and note how he or she begins the conversation. Does the manner in which the salesperson established a conversation with you encourage you to speak to him or her? Afterward, visit one of the low-end departments and note whether you are approached by a sales associate; if so, note the nature of the conversation. Compare and contrast the two approaches.

4. Discuss in broad terms the specific area within the fashion industry in which you hope to work after you graduate. Would retail sales skills be a part of your job, partially related, helpful, or unrelated? Note whether having some retail sales experience could assist you in your career.

5. Review a recent Sunday classified ads section in your local newspaper. Count the number of available retail jobs. Would you consider applying to any of them? Why? How do the number of ads for retail jobs compare with the number of ads in other fields? How would describe the current condition of the retail sales job market?

6. Pair up with another student so one of you acts as a salesperson and the other acts as a customer. The customer should pretend to walk into a department store, and the salesperson should establish a conversation to discover the customer's need. Note how the discussion proceeds, what the need is, and whether the process (having a conversation and discovering the need) makes the sale possible. Switch roles for a different perspective, and note the new responses.

7. Go to a local department store, and visit one of their low-end departments. Note whether you are approached by a sales associate; if so, note how the salesperson treated you as a customer. Analyze if and how your experience, quality of service, and customer care has changed your perception of the retail store as a whole. For example, would you shop there again? Do you feel differently about the company?

8. Think of a time when you went into a department store and the sales person used language or mannerisms inappropriate to how you were feeling at the time. What effect did this have on you, and how did it affect the transaction?

9. Pair up with another student so one of you acts as a salesperson and the other acts as a customer. The customer should pretend to walk into a department store in a specific mood, and the salesperson should try to behave in a manner appropriate to the situation so as to create a connection with the customer. Note what mood the customer is in, how the salesperson behaved, whether the salesperson's behavior was appropriate, and how everything affected the sale. Switch roles for a different perspective, and note the new responses.

10. Think of a product that you really enjoy and describe it, listing any features that you have found to be advantageous over time. Write a paragraph discussing what you would say to a customer if you were trying to sell this product. Note whether your familiarity with the product helps you make the sale.

12. Pair up with another student so one of you acts as a salesperson and the other acts as a customer. Pick a product that the salesperson knows nothing about and have the salesperson attempt to sell it to the customer. Note the effect of the salesperson's lack of knowledge on the sale. Switch roles for a different perspective, and note the new responses.

13. Go to a local department store, and visit one of the high-end departments. Browse through the items, and wait until a salesperson approaches you. Ask the salesperson complex questions about the product and analyze his or her product knowledge. Analyze how his or her product familiarity or lack thereof affects your decision to buy.

14. Pick a fashion item you know very little about. Using the self-training methods discussed in this chapter, learn more about the product and its features. Note your method of research and what you learned as a result.

15. Think of a recent time you went into a department store. Note the mood and appearance of the staff you dealt with and whether they were consistent with the store's overall atmosphere. Also note how their actions and appearances affected your shopping experience.

16. Visit your local mall, and walk through four different stores. Note each store's atmosphere, design, and dynamics. Note whether any of them were cluttered. Analyze how these aspects affect your reaction as a customer and whether they play a role in your decision to buy.

17. Discuss a retail experience you've had in another country or region, and compare and contrast it with a retail experience you've had at your local store. If you have never traveled outside your area, use the Internet or library research tools to cite cultural differences that may affect retail sales in another country or region.

END NOTES

1. Technology Marketing Corporation. "StorePerform Joins Symbol Technologies' PartnerSelect ISV Partner Program; Mobility Solution Boosts Store Managers and Associates Productivity, and Customer Interaction and Satisfaction." September 26, 2005: Online. www.tmcnet.com/usubmit/2005/Sep/1186113.htm.

2. U.S. Department of Labor, Bureau of Labor Statistics, Occupational Employment Statistics. May 2003. May 2003 National Occupational Employment and Wage Estimates, Sales and Related Occupations. www.bls.gov/oes/2003/may/oes_41Sa.htm.

3. U.S. Department of Labor, Bureau of Labor Statistics, Occupational Employment Statistics. May 2003. National Industry-Specific Occupational Employment and Wage Estimates, NAICS 424300—Apparel, Piece Goods, and Notions Merchant Wholesalers. www.bls.gov/oes/2003/may/naics4_424300.htm.

CHAPTER 04

BUSINESS-TO-BUSINESS SELLING

Overview

The fourth chapter reviews how business-to-business (B2B) selling works within the context of fashion selling in the real world. While transactions in retail sales are primarily quick ones that leave very little time for salespeople to establish relationships, the transactions that occur in B2B sales allow for long-term personal relationships to develop over time. Boutiques and retailers typically work with a small number of trusted suppliers for many years. This chapter explains how salespeople can go about initiating such long-lasting relationships, how they can maintain them, and what opportunities careers in this field offer. Finally, this chapter explores the role of B2B selling in an increasingly global market.

Introduction

B2B selling in the fashion industry occurs, as the name suggests, between businesses. Retail stores such as Macy's, JCPenney, and Nordstrom have to get their merchandise from certain trusted businesses. Likewise, businesses such as McDonald's and the Hilton hotels have to buy their staff uniforms in bulk from trusted businesses. Although many clothing manufacturers and fashion designers sell their merchandise directly to retail stores and boutiques, most have sales forces to do so.

Chapter 3 reviews, among other things, the fast-paced nature of retail sales in the fashion industry. Because businesses in retail sales sell merchandise directly to individuals who will use that merchandise, it can also be called business-to-consumer (**B2C**) selling. For sales relationships to be considered B2B, transactions must occur between fashion manufacturers and retailers or any two businesses.

In B2C sales, salespeople deal with buying decisions that affect individual consumers; they must cater to customers' needs, likes, and dislikes. B2B transactions are more complex because salespeople don't sell to consumers but rather to corporate buyers and individual owners.

Unlike individuals who buy merchandise for their personal use, corporate buyers purchase products that they won't be using personally. Although corporate buyers use their personal tastes to guide them in the purchasing process, they ultimately represent the needs of the businesses for which they work.

Corporate buyers must satisfy their own needs and likes, but they must also fulfill the requests of and take direction from the executives, marketing, and sales staff of their companies. A buyer who is considering a particular line of clothing for purchase, for example, must obviously like it since the buyer needs to be drawn by a line's appeal in the first place. However, the buyer cannot purchase a clothing line solely based on how appealing he or she finds it. Because buyers buy primarily to satisfy the needs and wants of their target customers, they must take into consideration what marketing feels is viable and what sales feels will sell. Buyers must always be aware of the bottom line: Will the product make or save money?

When buyers for Sears are looking to purchase a new line of suits, their concerns are very different from those of consumers who are looking for suits. Consumers tend to purchase one suit at a time, depending on their jobs and the attire preferred or enforced at their places of business. When buying suits, consumers consider how they will incorporate suits into their wardrobes. Conversely, buyers have to envision how a line of suits will appeal to thousands of Sears customers. Buyers for Sheraton hotels aren't concerned about how they will look in new dress shirts that

RW Dictionary

B2B Acronym that stands for business-to-business and involves transactions that take place between fashion manufacturers and retailers or between any two business entities.
B2C Acronym that stands for business-to-consumer and involves sales made by businesses directly to consumers, as occurs in retail sales.

they will purchase for front desk employees, but rather how the shirts will complement the hotel's front desk décor. B2B selling is different from retail selling in many other ways, which are discussed later in the chapter.

Manufacturers Their responsibilities include turning raw materials into finished, sellable products.

Manufacturers' Representatives Individuals who or businesses that bring together manufacturers and buyers in exchange for commissions; they never obtain ownership of goods.

Resellers Their responsibilities include buying goods, typically in volume, and selling smaller quantities to retailers or other businesses; they are also referred to as merchant wholesalers or jobbers.

Who's Who in Fashion Sales

The key players in the B2B fashion industry are **manufacturers**, **manufacturers' representatives**, and **resellers**. Each has a specialty in marketing products or services to other businesses and act as sellers, but each also functions as buyers. Manufacturers buy raw materials, machinery, and equipment, and they design, produce, and assemble raw materials into finished products (whether they do so domestically or outsource it), which they then sell to multiple markets throughout the world. These manufacturers have to be market-oriented and must have salespeople who are able to communicate their message to their target markets.

Successful fashion manufacturers create consumer demand for their products. Designer names are at the forefront of the fashion market. Manufacturers must be skilled at marketing, design, and production and have the necessary resources to reach their markets and maintain their market shares. Advertising plays an integral role in branding, but it is the integration of sales promotions, public relations, and research that keeps products in demand. Fashion names that have persevered throughout the years—such as Tommy Hilfiger, Donna Karan, and Ralph Lauren—utilize every facet of marketing to create brand awareness and a subsequent demand for their products.

Whether manufacturers use direct means to reach retailers or use representatives or resellers as intermediaries, their main objectives are always to satisfy their consumers' needs and establish an effective method of reaching them (Figure 4.1). To reach buyers, manufacturers utilize sales forces; the most prominent fashion manufacturers usually employ captive sales forces (salespeople who represent only them and receive straight salaries, straight commissions, or salaries with commissions and/or bonuses). Other manufacturers also engage the services of independent manufacturers' representatives who are commissioned.

Fashion manufacturers come in all sizes—about 80 percent of businesses in the United States consist of small businesses (fewer than 500 employees)[1] and partnerships,[2] as shown in Table 4.1. In some cases, salespeople who start their career with smaller manufacturers may get a better understanding of the fashion business than those who begin working for larger companies. Fashion manufacturers are burdened with a high risk of failure, especially if they don't properly capitalize on their

The Flow of Goods—A Typical B2B Cycle

Manufacturers receive harvested raw goods so they can turn them into finished goods. They then sell the finished goods directly to retailers or resellers who buy the goods in volume and sell smaller quantities to retail stores and other businesses.

RAW GOODS	→	MANUFACTURER

FINISHED GOODS

RESELLER

SHIPPING/DELIVERY

RETAILER

TABLE 4.1
Small vs. Big Business in the United States

Company Type	Gross Revenues (in 1000s)	Percent of Total U.S. Businesses
Sole Proprietorships	$ 1,020,957,284	72%
Corporations	$17,636,561,349	20%
Partnerships	$ 1,829,568,091	5%
Limited Liability Companies	$ 344,751,557	3%

Source: BizStats.com, Year 2000 Report.

businesses. Sadly, many new companies go under after the first year. Yet, opportunities are greater for small manufacturers because fashion constantly changes, and smaller companies are able to react to change faster than the larger ones.

Many designer brands use outside contractors who have the necessary machinery and labor forces to manufacture their products. In fact, many well-known designer-name products are manufactured overseas by contractors who are given fabrics, designs, patterns, and labels. The resulting lower labor costs have enabled the most well-known brands to offer their customers value and therefore keep a competitive edge in the marketplace. These overseas contractors ship in bulk to the U.S.-based companies, and manufacturers market the final merchandise once it does arrive.

The United States has all but lost the ability to be competitive by manufacturing products domestically, which is a major reason why companies need to manufacture their merchandise abroad. A cursory glance at your own clothing labels will indicate just how many of your fashion products are manufactured abroad. Although they do not do all the manufacturing of products themselves, these companies are still considered manufacturers. Indeed, manufacturers purchase raw materials and other component parts, and in this respect, they also can be considered buyers. They purchase garments, zippers, buttons, and other such items from B2B salespeople. However, manufacturers also sell their merchandise at trade shows—New York, Texas (Dallas), Georgia (Atlanta), and California are some of the markets where they present their products to prospective B2B buyers. Fashion shows during market weeks in New York and other areas give participating manufacturers a chance to expose their products to the marketplace.

Resellers, or wholesalers, do not manufacture products; they purchase finished goods from manufacturers in large quantities, usually with certain discounts. They take title (ownership) of the merchandise and market, warehouse, and ship it to their customers. The resellers' channels are very flexible; their customers can consist of any or all of the following: other resellers, manufacturers, retailers, government agencies, institutions, and other businesses. As a fictitious example, Courtney Company—a wholesaler of zippers, buttons, and trimmings—buys its finished products from Jackie Manufacturing Company; markets its merchandise to Shilo & Company, a wholesaler of notions; and sells directly to Livna Ltd., a small apparel manufacturer.

The resale market is massive in scope. The total reseller sales of all products in the United States, including hard and soft goods, was about 4.3 trillion dollars in 2001, even more than the total retail sales of 3.3 trillion dollars in that same year.

Career Opportunities

B2B fashion selling gives sellers an opportunity to build a business for themselves. This career is for those who are willing to accept responsibility, look forward to a challenge, and are open-minded. People skills along with a high degree of integrity will help neophyte sellers climb the ladder of success in B2B selling. Companies are always looking for sellers who are hardworking and goal-oriented. Many top executives of major companies started their careers as salespeople, demonstrating once again that salespeople have the best opportunities to learn all the aspects of the business. There is always room for success in the industry for dedicated people who like working in reasonably unrestricted environments. The exciting field of B2B fashion selling is for those who like change—it is never boring.

In B2B selling the income level is much greater than it is in retail selling, averaging at $65,360 per year according to U.S. Department of Labor.[3] Obviously the responsibilities are greater, as is the pressure to produce, but to those of you who thrive on challenge and the opportunities to make your marks in life, B2B selling may prove to be a fulfilling career.

B2B salespeople who "bring in the business" are highly regarded by management. In fact, management doesn't consider such successful B2B sellers "overhead" but rather walking "cash registers." Bringing in business is crucial to the future of companies; salespeople who prove they can get new accounts are often assigned to larger accounts or given larger territories and many times promoted to managerial positions.

In terms of job security, successful B2B salespeople who develop strong business relationships with notable clients are indispensable to the businesses for which they work. Management doesn't want to lose prominent customers and will think twice before firing a successful seller. Obviously, salespeople who are reliable and honest are also essential to the companies for which they work, regardless of their client rosters.

Becoming a successful B2B salesperson can lead to not only management positions but also entrepreneurship opportunities. One of the main skills that would-be entrepreneurs need to successfully launch their own businesses is being able to sell fashion. You have already seen examples in Tommy Hilfiger, who started his career as a seller, and Ralph Lauren, who started his as a haberdasher. Will you be the next Tommy Hilfiger or Ralph Lauren? In fact, college graduates are more than ready to successfully enter the fashion sales field because of the education and discipline they have learned in school, including meeting deadlines, completing projects, thinking critically, analyzing problems, and working with others—all of which are relevant in the real world of B2B fashion selling.

Getting Personal

It is important to distinguish sellers' roles in B2B from their roles in B2C, particularly in regards to the relationships they have with their customers. B2B buyers aim to make profits and satisfy the needs of the companies they represent, and B2C buyers aim to consume or obtain goods to satisfy

RW Principle

B2C buyers satisfy their personal needs, but B2B buyers satisfy corporate needs and take risks while keeping in mind potential profits.

RW Concept

Because they involve thousands of dollars in merchandise, the stakes are much higher for B2B transactions than they are for B2C transactions. Buyers and sellers have much to lose if sales go sour.

their own personal needs and wants. Therefore, B2B salespeople deal with a completely different type of customer—they have to make responsible choices that benefit the companies at which they work. The decision process is affected, as is the relationships between buyers and sellers.

In some cases, B2B sellers aren't advising buyers about a single item of clothing or even an entire outfit, but rather on an entire line of clothing. The companies that buyers represent stand to gain or lose thousands of dollars depending on the success of the line. Therefore, a B2B buyer's job performance is highly affected by the choices he or she makes.

Because of the risk factor, B2B buyers must have implicit trust in sellers' product knowledge and recommendations, and sellers must have confidence that buyers will be able to pay for existing and place future orders. They must understand each other's needs and positions to create a mutually beneficial transaction.

B2B sellers typically have fewer customers than retail salespeople, but B2B customers wield a greater purchasing power. It is not uncommon for a single B2B sale to be worth tens of thousands of dollars. B2C salespeople have many more customers, but transactions yield smaller amounts of money.

That said, we must examine the buyer–seller relationship development in both of these areas. Although many sellers in retail stores depend on developing business relationships with their customers, doing so in retail environments is a challenge. As you have already learned, in retail selling the transaction happens quickly, which makes it difficult to establish long-term business relationships. In B2B selling, sellers have fewer clients and transactions so the chances of them fomenting long-term relationships with buyers are not only feasible but also necessary.

Buyers and sellers alike become personally involved in the act of establishing business relationships, which allows them to spend more time solving customer problems and accomplishing objectives and goals. B2B selling is the platform for something that requires old-fashioned personal selling—that is, the following time-tested fundamentals of personal selling that sometimes apply in the world of retail sales and never change:

+ acting with integrity at all times
+ maintaining a positive attitude
+ developing friendly, yet professional, business relationships with buyers
+ being a people person (genuinely liking people)
+ relating to diversified audiences
+ establishing partnerships with buyers

+ staying focused to ensure each transaction mutually benefits sellers and buyers
+ keeping a deep interest in developing profits for a buyer's company
+ having knowledge about your products as well as buyers' products

In the past few years, several new, mostly technology-driven fundamentals have been added to the list. They are as follows:

+ speeding up the decision-making process by using information technology
+ digitally compiling information to analyze market trends better
+ using digitally compiled information to anticipate and adapt to the needs of today's changing markets

In B2B personal selling, it is essential for sellers and buyers to be on the same page. Sellers must act as consultants rather than salespeople who just want to score an order.

B2B selling is a smooth and successful process when both buyers and sellers establish partnerships and share common goals. It is, therefore, integral for a seller to have first a complete understanding of the objectives and problems of a buyer's business. Likewise, a buyer should be acquainted with the current and future products, policies, and credit and delivery terms of a seller's business. Such business relationships can be achieved only when B2B sellers are well versed in product knowledge and company policies and capable of relaying these to buyers properly. Sellers must be proficient in the two PKs (product knowledge and people knowledge) to be successful. The two PKs are discussed in further detail in chapter 8.

Losing a Sale and Gaining a Customer

The main objectives of successful B2B fashion salespeople is to establish and maintain strong and long-term business relationships that lead to multiple sales. To keep relationships intact, sellers in B2B settings must become selective in what they offer to buyers and should refuse to make sales if circumstances prevent an order from being filled. Sellers should always keep in mind that corporate fashion buyers aren't looking for immediate gratification of personal needs, as individual retail customers do; rather, corporate buyers are looking to make long-term profits for their companies. As a result, sellers' performances are contingent on delivering what they promise in a timely and professional manner. When sellers fail to deliver orders—*no matter the reasons or circumstances*—they erode the buyers' trust in them.

Sellers must understand that in B2B the concept of a one-time-only sale doesn't—or at least shouldn't —exist. If a buyer likes a product and trusts the seller, then the buyer will return for more business as long as the seller remains competitive, delivers profitable merchandise, and is customer-oriented. Naturally, buyers like to deal with established, trusted sellers on whom they can depend for quality, reliability, and service. A manufacturer's representative who sells a new line of blouses to a retail store buyer is concerned not only with just making that initial sale, but also fomenting a relationship that yields future business. Maintaining relationships with buyers and the companies these buyers own or represent are facilitated by transactions that benefit both parties.

Consider the following scenario: A manufacturer's representative meets with a buyer to review the upcoming lines for summer. The buyer likes the merchandise but wants it delivered within two months to replace merchandise bought from another company, which the store is phasing out. The buyer stresses that time is of the essence on this order, but the seller hesitates because there is a three-month lead time on this line. The buyer tells the representative that the store really needs delivery in two months and makes a veiled threat that failure to deliver the order in the requested two-month period may affect the future of the entire account. The seller gives into the pressure and reluctantly takes the order, knowing full well that the deadline cannot be met. Two months later, the buyer calls the seller inquiring why the order hasn't shipped to the stores. The representative offers a weak excuse, and regardless of whether the buyer accepts the excuse (or whether the buyer has it coming because he or she was being unreasonable about the deadline), the damage is done: The buyer will not trust the seller again. Now the account is in peril since the buyer's confidence in the seller has deteriorated as a result of the missed deadline.

Even a low-ranking buyer is normally quite sophisticated and far from being a fool. Typical buyers have many alternative suppliers knocking on their doors, and once a seller fails to deliver, a buyer has a network of other sellers from which to choose. Sellers must never let the pressures of making sales drive them to lose a customer. Walking away from sales that are impossible to fulfill often gains sellers respect and trust—in this manner, relationships are strengthened because buyers recognize and appreciate honest sellers more than ones who are solely driven by making sales no matter what the consequences.

Sellers must have a great deal of flexibility in the name of service. When buyers approach with urgent orders, sellers should first consult with their production departments to see if such rush orders are feasible. They should do everything possible to accommodate buyers' requests. It is only when all possibilities are exhausted and it is determined to be impossible to deliver a rush order within the necessary deadline that sellers should refuse to make a sale. Sellers learn how to

RW Concept

It is better for sellers to walk away from a sale than to close an order that is *impossible* to fulfill.

tow this line by identifying a buyer's needs, goals, budget limits, and schedules and figuring out the products and delivery methods that will satisfy all of these parameters. Problem-solving skills are therefore one of the most important skills a B2B salesperson can possess.

Say a buyer is a local boutique that caters to middle-aged women and is trying to expand its business by attracting new customers in their twenties and thirties. As a seller, you learn that the buyer expects to tap into this new market in about three months. The retail prices for this merchandise should range between $25 and $100. The company for which you work has opened a new division called "twenty-to-thirty somethings." In fact, you have been showing the collection to other buyers, so you recognize that it is a natural choice for your potential buyer. The price range and delivery dates are compatible with the buyer's needs. You feel comfortable that the new line will fit into this boutique's merchandising plan based on the reaction from similar boutiques. You call the buyer and make an appointment to present the collection.

You arrive at the store prepared to show the merchandise. The collection consists of about fifteen styles. Because you have superior product knowledge, gained in part because you've shown this line to other boutiques, you know the styles that are selling and the ones that are not. However, the company you represent insists you show all styles and you do. The buyer selects eight items, three of which aren't selling very well— in fact, none of the boutiques to which you have sold the line have ever selected these styles. You know that the boutique is not going to be able to move the items at the retail level. Since your main goal is to build a business relationship with this boutique (and not just make the sale), you opt to maintain the boutique's best interests at heart so it can profit from what it buys from you. In a diplomatic manner so as not to undermine the line or the company you represent, you inform the buyer that you have not had a positive reaction to the three problem styles. The buyer has reason to trust you because you've demonstrated genuine concern for the boutique's success.

Integrity and Problem-Solving Skills Are Necessities

B2B buyers expect the sellers with whom they work to have high degrees of integrity and ethics. They want the sellers to be team players, take proactive roles in product development and planning in the sellers' companies, obtain values, and maintain profit-focused relationships. Buyers recognize that successful business relationships are attainable by having excellent communication skills, friendly atmospheres, and trust. Buyers expect sellers to solve problems; therefore, sellers who seriously meet and exceed these expectations become major players in buyers' rosters of sellers.

B2B sellers aim for buyers to have confidence in them. They look to maintain long-term relationships and do not necessarily expect to get an order every time they meet with buyers. Sellers want to provide buyers with good service and be of assistance in "growing a buyer's business."

Suppose a fashion clothing company that is currently marketing to baby boomers has seen a decline in their market share of certain items they are manufacturing. They notice that they are not selling as many pants and shorts as they did in past years. That buyer must be able to trust the seller with that confidential information so the seller can research the marketplace and resolve the buyer's problem. In fact, the seller discovers that the sizing of the product must be adjusted. The boomers still want a younger look but have to deal with their expanding waistlines. The seller and buyer resolve this problem by designing a hidden elasticized waist-band for shorts and pants. This development enables expanding boomers to keep the same younger looks but get more comfort from the elastic waistbands. Without trust, the buyer and seller could never have addressed the problem, discovered the cause, or resolved it with a new product.

Understanding the Corporate Buyer

Corporate buyers have certain responsibilities that affect their buying decisions, as do other factors, such as how involved they are in the management areas of the companies for which they work. This section examines what a corporate buyer's responsibilities are and what he or she must assess before signing on the dotted line.

In the 1980s, Harvard professor Michael Porter[4] shared his theory of the **value chain**. The basic idea of Porter's value chain is that companies and suppliers compete for a buyer's business, and buyers choose from the competing companies and suppliers based on their perceptions of value—when buyers get value, they are able to pass it to their companies' customers (end users). Porter says each vendor (supplier) who is competing for a buyer's business tries to do so by offering more value—as perceived by the buyer—than is offered by the other suppliers. The value chain then is the vehicle that originates from the customer's perceived value and travels through the channels of distribution, namely the manufacturer, suppliers, and raw material resources.

When making purchasing decisions, buyers are concerned with their **preconceived values**. The priorities of these preconceived values change according to each individual buyer's needs. For example, one buyer may rank high fashion as a top concern while another buyer may rank the cost as the most important. Corporate buyers have to wear many

RW Figure

Michael Porter is the fourth member of the Harvard Business School ever to be honored with the title of university professor in all of its ninety-four years.

Porter's 1980 book *Competitive Strategy* is now in its fifty-third printing and has been translated into seventeen languages. It changed the way CEOs thought of their firms and industries and is still the authoritative text for any strategically minded manager.

In 1985 Porter was named to President Ronald Reagan's Commission on Industrial Competitiveness. The appointment launched his study of national, state, and local competitiveness, findings that were first published in his book *The Competitive Advantage of Nations* in 1990, in which he applied his ideas to whole economies.

With his research group, Porter, fifty-three, operates from a suite of offices tucked into a corner of Harvard Business School's main classroom building. He is no less passionate about his pursuit or ability.

hats. First, they are tasked with making major decisions keeping in mind not only the purchasing framework but also the marketing and research activities and other inner workings (such as sales promotion and marketing) at the companies for which they work. To make informed purchasing decisions, buyers must be familiar with and understand the marketing strategies and trends of the companies they represent.

A buyer's role also includes being a diplomat—developing a collaborative relationship with suppliers as well as with other members of his or her company (production, finance, marketing, and sales). Buyers must work in harmony with a countless number of people to successfully adapt to the ever-changing demands of the job. Buyers must partner with their resellers and keep them informed as to their goals and current priorities. Buyers must motivate the people with whom they work and encourage them to work with suppliers to achieve the goals essential for success. Buyers depend on their suppliers to be flexible and accommodate changing needs.

Buyers must act as logistical experts—keeping the **supply chain** working in unison so that final products are delivered on time. Buyers must also act as managers, directing their own departments' personnel and interacting with accounting, disbursements, and other areas of the company's financial management team to ensure the bottom line of profits is achieved.

Buyers are like jugglers—keeping things in constant motion by satisfying the needs of their companies, customers, and suppliers, while making sure to accomplish their goals.

Juggling Made Easy

Sellers must never interrupt a buyer's juggling act. They must observe and learn so they can join and simplify the act by offering their assistance. Buyers have so many things to keep track of: demands from the sales department, orders from superiors, marketing plans, densely tabulated statistics, inventories, balance sheets, and (most important) fashion styles that will sell. In an ideal business relationship, a seller can help a buyer by providing information, keeping track of orders and delivery dates, and smoothing the supply line.

Clearly, sellers are not the only ones who are interested in forming long-term relationships: Buyers have a vested interest in forming such business relationships with sellers as well. The more a buyer can trust and rely on a supplier and the longer such a relationship lasts, the smoother operations become, leveraging profits for the company and savings for its customers. As you can see, a buyer's choice of suppliers can significantly affect the company's bottom line. The buyer is not buying a product; he's buying a relationship. Smart buyers do their research on potential suppliers by checking with colleagues in the industry. They also do their research on the products these suppliers sell.

This is not to say that buyers have already made up their minds before a sales pitch even takes place. Quite simply, buyers typically take preliminary steps to qualify the company and product they are considering—remember that the sale still has to be made! Buyers only are trying to determine whether sellers know their product and logistics, will deliver on time, and can be trusted. Sellers can assuage such concerns by delivering excellent service and making good on all of their promises.

The Customer's Customers

Being customer-oriented and ethical are not a salesperson's only concerns. There are several important questions salespeople must consider before they can truly help their buyers, the first and foremost being *Who are my buyer's customers?* When salespeople understand their buyers' target market, they can truly grasp their buyers' needs and therefore make much more meaningful and profitable recommendations. After all, buyers' customers are the ones who keep buyers, and therefore salespeople who sell to the buyers, in business.

For example, a high-end shoe boutique has a different clientele from a moderate price one. The high-end boutique's customers are likely much more concerned about a product's look or the designer's name rather than its cost, while moderate-price boutique's consumers are satisfied with popular brand names that are affordable. Some additional questions that salespeople should consider revolve around the buyer's company.

What is the company's mission and business philosophy? It is crucial for salespeople to be aware of what the buyer's company is trying to achieve and the type of service it offers to its customers. Additionally, it helps to know how the company approaches business practices in general and what the company deems appropriate and ethical.

What is the company's structure? A family-owned business operates differently from a company that's part of a conglomerate; a franchise must adhere to rules that an independently owned store may ignore. When salespeople know how their buyers' companies are structured, they can better adapt their services to fit their clients' modes of operation.

What is the company's background? Salespeople should find out how long their buyers have been in business and whether their companies are new to the area, since this can impact their sales, marketing, and purchasing decisions to a large degree. When salespeople familiarize themselves with a company's background, they can better customize the information they provide a buyer and be more likely to guess the direction in which a buyer will go.

It is also useful for salespeople to get to know their buyers personally—listen to their problems and learn their life stories. The more salespeople relate to their buyers, and vice versa, the easier it will be for salespeople to care about them and the stronger business relationships will become. Note that this text is not suggesting that salespeople should go out drinking or dancing with their buyers or spend time with them outside work. If that type of personal friendship does develop, it does so over time. Salespeople should never pretend to be a buyer's best friend just because he or she bought their product—it is offensive and dishonest. This text advises that salespeople try to develop a certain bond with their buyers. Salespeople should talk about topics both can enjoy, take their buyers out to lunch or a sporting event once in a while, and make an effort to remember their buyers' birthdays. Such gestures, when done genuinely, improve rapport and gradually strengthen relationships. Some salespeople take this too far and skirt the line of bribery, which can backfire and cost salespeople their jobs. It is best to follow company policy (and common sense) regarding gifts and entertainment.

B2B in a Global Market

Throughout the past decade, overnight shipping and the Internet, among other things, have created an international B2B environment. True, economists may argue that free-trade zones are responsible for the trend, while political scientists may point to the fall of the Soviet Union or similar political events. Regardless of the reason, most companies can no longer ignore the global market and the opportunities and competition that such a market presents. Increasingly, U.S. companies are looking overseas to develop new markets and augment profits. U.S. exports continue to grow at 7 percent rate per year.[5] Indeed, U.S. fashion is extremely popular around the globe, and brands such as Polo, Calvin Klein, and Nike enjoy superior name recognition and acceptance from London to Hong Kong. However, the United States is still the largest importer of finished goods in the world, followed by Germany and China.[6] As today's B2B salespeople increasingly deal with either suppliers or customers who are based abroad, it is becoming more crucial for them to understand the global B2B market and the roles they play within it.

When preparing to do business overseas, B2B salespeople should do as much research as possible about the culture, customs, and buying habits of the target country. Reliable sources for such information can be coworkers or friends who have lived or worked in the target country or international business and cultural studies books and magazines, many of which can be found at the local library or bookstore. Fashion magazines and publications published in the target country may be harder to find, but efforts to obtain copies can be well worth the time, since these give a sense of the styles and trends currently popular as well as an overall idea of the retail market conditions. The Internet is a good source as well, but always bear in mind that some Web sites may contain misleading and even false information. Salespeople should always check to make sure they are on legitimate sites, such as official or institutional Web sites like those belonging to universities or chambers of commerce, especially before relying on data found on them.

Research should yield factual information about the following:

+ overall market conditions
+ market scope and potential
+ demography
+ average body size and shape and clothing sizes
+ weather (seasons, average temperatures by month, and so on)
+ fashion trends
+ general and business etiquette
+ import taxes, incentives, laws, and restrictions

Salespeople should consider something as simple as dress sizes in other countries as compared with sizing in the United States. For example, U.S. dress sizes are practically incompatible with those of Japan. Japanese women are typically more petite than U.S. women, so sizes considered small in Tennessee can easily qualify as extra large in Tokyo. Sellers who try to sell a line of dresses ranging from sizes 12 to 18 in Japan likely will find it impossible to make a sale because the market for these sizes is virtually nonexistent there.

Salespeople should also consider general and business etiquette when doing business abroad. For example, in many Mediterranean countries, it is perfectly acceptable to be fifteen minutes late to meetings and other business appointments. Sellers who are unaware of this fact may take offense to a buyer's lateness, which will get the relationship off to a bad start. Taking the time to know and understand a buyer's culture, the market conditions in a buyer's home country, and the etiquette followed there will reap a positive outcome for sales and the establishment and development of long-term business relationships across borders.

Chapter Summary

+ Retail is considered business-to-consumer (B2C) because a salesperson sells directly to an individual customer who is likely the end user of a product. Sales that take place between two or more businesses (manufacturers, resellers, retailers, and other businesses) are considered business-to-business (B2B).

+ The fashion manufacturer designs and creates the finished product, either by producing it or by outsourcing it. A manufacturer's representative arranges for the sale between a manufacturer and buyer in exchange for a commission but doesn't ever obtain ownership of the product. A reseller buys finished products in large volume and sells them to retailers and other businesses.

+ The fashion B2B sales field offers college graduates excellent opportunities for career development and advancement, with average annual salaries of more than $60,000.

+ Initiating and maintaining long-term business relationships with buyers is essential to B2B sales.

+ When salespeople act ethically, make deadlines, relay information accurately, and are interested and involved in a buyer's success, it contributes to successful business relationships.

+ Corporate buyers have to wear many hats; they make purchasing decisions for the companies they represent, serve as managers of personnel, coordinate sales and production, and play executive roles in regards to marketing and research activities.

+ Salespeople who know and understand who their buyers' customers are and what their buyers' companies' goals, policies, and business philosophies are will be in better positions to assist their buyers.

+ Because of trends such as overnight shipping and tools such as the Internet, B2B sales increasingly stretch across the globe; as a result, B2B salespeople must adjust to new environments. Sellers must do their research before entering a new market and learn about the culture, business customs, and legal aspects of target countries.

RW CASE STUDY

Thomas J. Schwenk is the principal and owner of Jordan Thomas & Associates, a Galveston, Texas–based strategic sales consulting firm for the fashion and interior design industries. He is also the co-owner of Houston-based Seminars By Designs, which offers a variety of sales training, business and professional development, and health safety and welfare seminars for interior designers and architects.

Are relationships important for B2B salespeople in the interior design field?

Yes, extremely important in fact. Many sales reps are so trained to close the sale, they forget to open the sale. By that I mean forming a meaningful relationship with the buyer. In today's market, selling is really about providing solutions to your customers and being a member of their team. We as salespeople need to see what the customer needs, what solutions we can offer to make their [lives] easier and business more profitable. You can't adopt a simple "out of sight, out of mind" policy; you have to be heard but softly. You can send postcards, e-mails, drop by with a product showing. Your bag of tricks is more specialized, more customized for each customer.

How do you gain an edge in the B2B fashion sales field?

Frankly, there are so many products out there, so many types of shirts, suits, et cetera, that the salesperson cannot compete with everyone. But when the seller is constantly there for the customer, it gives the seller a step-up over the competition. Taking your customer for granted is fatal. Coming up with innovative solutions for the buyer's issues is important, not only in interior design but also in fashion. Attitude in sales is extremely important—you can't go in there as if you know everything. Chances are the designer knows the product better from a technical aspect than the rep; the rep may know better where the fabrics are made or how long it takes to ship, but technically the buyer may be more informed.

Which characteristics typify a successful B2B salesperson in the fashion industry?

I'd say that first and foremost, you must be personally interested in fashion or interior design and love what you sell. The old adage "If you can sell widgets, you can sell anything" isn't true anymore. Today, you have to have passion for your product. You also have to learn quickly about your products and industry, maybe take classes, listen and learn to speak the lingo. Communication skills must be superb, and you have to be assertive but not aggressive.

What are some of the pitfalls when selling to customers overseas?

Generally the sale is still the same, but there are some significant differences. The first being logistics, [for example,] measurements [in the United States] are in yards whereas most of the world uses the metric system, what are the duty taxes, and so on—all of that has to be factored in. It is hard for the designer to figure this out; they count on the seller to take care of all of that. Then you also need to know about their customs and culture. We in America are an impatient society—we want everything done perfectly, yesterday, and at 25 percent less than we paid last year. The Europeans are much more into the craftsmanship; they're okay with a delay if it means better quality. As another example, in many European countries negotiating the price—a given in the United States—is border-line rude and at the very least shows a degree of financial weakness on your part. Buyers there will cut you off even though your competitor's price is higher if they like doing business with them better.

Questions to Consider

1. How does a salesperson close a sale but fail to form a meaningful business relationship? Does this practice lead to repeat sales?
2. Are buyers most concerned with price, quality, delivery, or a combination of these? Explain.
3. How can a salesperson gain an edge in the fashion sales field? What can he or she do to stand out?
4. According to Schwenk, how is doing business overseas different from doing business in the United States? Do you agree? Share your thoughts or personal experiences.

RW EXERCISES

1. List an example of a B2C transaction and a B2B transaction. Compare and contrast the two.
2. Look through a business journal or the business section of a daily newspaper, and clip three examples each of B2C advertisements and B2B advertisements. Note in each whether the seller is a manu-facturer, distributor, or other, and identify the potential buyers.
3. Inspect your wardrobe by looking up each item's label, and note where it was manufactured. Tabulate the results, breaking these down by continent and further by country. Include your comments and opinions.
4. Review the bulleted list of old-fashioned selling fundamentals on pages 63–64, and write an example of how you would apply each fundamental if you were a B2B salesperson.
5. Pair up with another student so one of you acts as the B2B seller and the other acts as the corporate fashion buyer. The seller should have a conversation with the buyer and ascertain from it the buyer's needs and goals, budget, schedule, and any other pertinent data and make an appropriate product recommendation. Note down what the buyer's needs are and the product you feel would suit those needs. Switch roles for a different perspective, and note the new responses.

6. Pair up with another student so one of you acts as the B2B seller and the other acts as the corporate fashion buyer. The buyer should adamantly make an unreasonable request such as an impossible delivery date. The seller should check with the office and politely decline the order, citing the reasons in a clear, professional manner. Summarize the discussion, and note your personal reactions. Switch roles for a different perspective, and note the new responses.

7. Go to an independently owned fashion boutique or store, and talk to the manager. State that you are doing some research for class (show your student ID), and ask where he or she buys merchandise, how he or she decides which lines to carry, and what makes him or her prefer one seller over another. Note their answers, and include your thoughts and comments.

8. If you were a corporate buyer and your job depended on making sound purchasing decisions, which qualities and skills would you expect from the B2B seller from whom you'll be regularly purchasing inventory? Explain how these would affect your long-term relationship with the seller.

9. Visit an independently owned retail store (not necessarily a fashion store), and talk to the manager. State that you are doing some research for class (show your student ID), and ask how many suppliers he or she has, how long he or she has been doing business with each supplier, and who his or her most valuable supplier is and why? Note their answers, and include your thoughts and comments.

10. Explain the value chain and how each business along the chain adds value to a product. What happens when one of the businesses does not deliver value? Give an example.

11. Pair up with another student so one of you acts as the B2B seller and the other acts as the corporate fashion buyer. The seller should pretend to know the buyer for about one month but pretend to be best friends with him or her, regardless. Summarize the discussion, and note your personal reaction to the fake friendship. Switch roles for a different perspective, and note new responses.

12. Pair up with another student so one of you acts as the B2B seller and the other acts as the corporate fashion buyer. The seller should try to get to know the buyer better on a personal level, by asking appropriate, professional questions and exploring topics enjoyable to both. Summarize the discussion, and note your personal reactions. Switch roles for a different perspective, and note the new responses.

END NOTES

1. U.S. Small Business Administration.
   http://app1.sba.gov/faqs/faqIndexAll.cfm?areaid=24.
2. BizStats.com. "Total Number of U.S. Businesses 2000" report.
   www.bizstats.com/businesses.htm.
3. U.S. Department of Labor, Bureau of Labor Statistics, May 2003.
   "National Occupational Employment and Wage Estimates Sales
   and Related Occupations."
   www.bls.gov/oes/2003/may/oes_41Sa.htm.
4. Porter, Michael. *Competitive Advantage Creating and Sustaining
   Superior Performance.* New York: Free Press, 1985.
5. U.S. Bureau of Census. "Statistical Abstract of the United States:
   2001, Table No.722."
   www.census.gov/prod/2002pubs/01statab/business.pdf
6. Testimony before the House Committee on International Relations, U.S. House of Representatives Washington, D.C., October
   21, 2003.

CHAPTER 05

GETTING TO THE SALE

Overview

Locating qualified prospects who are interested in your product and have the ability and authority to make purchasing decisions is a necessary step to closing a sale. In this chapter, we review how salespeople define their prospect markets and identify the various means to reach these prospects. We look at a prospect, a qualified prospect, and an unqualified prospect—or what we call a suspect—and determine how the three are different and in which category your buyer fits. Finally, we explore some of the available resources that can help salespeople locate more prospects and prepare for sales presentations.

Introduction

Before salespeople can sell, they must naturally first locate buyers who need their products. In the real world of fashion sales, potential buyers are called **prospects**, and the act of locating new buyers is called **prospecting**. Salespeople lose 10 to 15 percent of their accounts each year because of changes in product lines, retirement, business failures, market shrinkage, competition, and other developments. If the prospecting element is not included in a salesperson's planning, within a few years his or her roster of **active accounts** will dwindle and a few will become **inactive accounts**. For this reason, it is essential that salespeople be on the lookout for prospects so their account lists don't suffer.

Say Jane Simmons is a salesperson whose territory consists of forty active accounts, and her sales manager expects her to add five to six new accounts this year. Jane doesn't believe that prospecting for new accounts is necessary because she is meeting and exceeding all of the sales projections and goals that management has set for her. She feels secure with her current account base because her volume is increasing. Jane wants to spend more time with these existing accounts to build long-term relationships. While it is good that Jane understands building such relationships is vital to her success, she must nevertheless be realistic and prepare for the future and the unknown. Many times important accounts go to competition because of any number of reasons, including better deals or prices. It is therefore possible that after the first year, due to attrition, Jane ends up with about thirty-four to thirty-six active customers. Because attrition is so gradual, it often sneaks up on many sellers before they even realize it is happening.

For this reason, prospecting for new accounts is an essential part of the successful salesperson's routine during both good and bad times and must be incorporated into the plan for market coverage. Having an organized plan for prospecting allows salespeople to save time and money while securing sales volume from year to year.

Before developing a list of prospects, salespeople should first seek to identify their markets and define customers who will be most likely to buy their products. Salespeople should consider individuals or businesses that stand to benefit from the products they sell and why. They should also be realistic and consider individuals and business that will actually have the ability to pay for their products. Salespeople should investigate whether a need exists for their products or whether they must entice prospects to develop a need. Once salespeople have properly defined the market and potential customer base, they need to figure out the best ways to reach them.

Within the retail environment, salespeople are barely involved with prospecting—as you recall, the fast-paced nature of retail makes building

RW Dictionary

Prospect Potential buyers who aren't already customers.

Prospecting The act of locating and contacting potential buyers with the aim of setting up appointments for sales presentations.

Active Account A buyer who is already a customer and buys on a regular basis.

Inactive Account A former customer who no longer buys products.

FIGURE 5.1

The Many Avenues to Prospecting

A salesperson can obtain a great number of potential customers by instituting a regular prospecting system.

SALESPERSON

1. Ask for referrals from customers, family, friends, and business associates
2. Attend trade shows
3. Network with retail stores and resellers
4. Make cold calls to marketing lists
5. Go through inactive client files

long-term relationships a challenge if not an impossibility, and retail salespeople need to find creative ways to reach out to new customers and get them to return. Therefore, retailers utilize advertising and marketing to locate prospects and attract them to their stores, but rarely do salespeople leave the stores at which they work in search of potential customers. Instead, retail salespeople obtain significant numbers of prospects by asking for referrals from customers, family, friends, and business associates. In B2B selling, prospecting is much more involved, and salespeople must play proactive roles in locating new prospects. By attending trade shows, networking with retail stores and resellers, calling on boutiques, and making sales calls, salespeople can develop new business relationships and obtain new accounts. B2B fashion salespeople must incorporate prospecting into their routine duties to maintain viable client rosters (Figure 5.1) and not wait until attrition dwindles their client lists to begin looking for new buyers.

RW Concept

Salespeople who want to make a sale must take on the persona of a detective—a marketing detective. Like Sherlock Holmes, they must ask the right questions and get the right answers to close the sale.

The Marketing Detective

Many people consider Sherlock Holmes to be the best detective in literature's history. As soon as he reached the crime scene, he would begin to inspect the evidence, speak to people of interest, and ask questions about anything that seemed odd. Often, he conducted research before even arriving at the scene. Holmes used his uncanny ability to ask the right questions and get the right answers to solve, or close, the case.

Salespeople can meet with hundreds of people, but if none of them is interested in their products, then salespeople are just wasting time. Furthermore, it takes a shrewd marketing detective to recognize when a potential customer doesn't have a need for a product or the means and authority to buy it. Learning to recognize unqualified prospects allows salespeople to politely move onto the next prospect and thus save time both for themselves and the prospect.

Wise marketing detectives can adopt Sergeant Joe Friday's approach when gathering information about potential markets and the prospects within them. Joe Friday, from the motion picture and television series *Dragnet*, used the expression "Just the facts, ma'am!" when he questioned witnesses and suspects; he did this to discourage them from giving opinions and instead encourage them to state what they saw. Before setting out to find prospects, marketing detectives must research and get the facts about potential buyers.

Who's Your Customer?

The first step salespeople should take when prospecting is to define the market for their products. The *market* refers to the individuals who or businesses that may have a need for the salesperson's product and are likely to afford it. Polo's Purple Label, for example, is a high-end line that targets affluent businesspeople in mostly metropolitan areas. Therefore, the market for that line includes the select Ralph Lauren stores in New York, Beverly Hills, Palm Beach, and a few other cities where prosperous people live. In contrast, GORE-TEX targets outdoorsy, sports-minded, middle-class people who live in somewhat rural areas since they sell cold-weather products. GORE-TEX, however, doesn't sell directly to end-users. Therefore, its market is made up of resellers and retailers who sell to their target users.

In retail sales, salespeople need product knowledge to define their markets. One of the best and most efficient methods for getting product knowledge is the in-store meeting; in-store meetings engage salespeople with store managers and key suppliers. The meetings also focus on the various products, advertising, promotional events, and the all-important target market. These meetings enable salespeople to better identify potential customers. Another way that salespeople can establish a B2C prospective consumer list is by acquiring information from retail consumers who have shopped in their departments but haven't made purchases. Specific, well-thought-out questions should help salespeople determine if customers are good prospects. If customers are in fact good prospects, salespeople should add their names to prospective customer lists and include necessary product information.

In B2B sales, matters are slightly more complex because salespeople sell to retailers or resellers. Therefore, B2B salespeople have to first define the group of consumers who will purchase the product in question and utilize research and surveys to determine which resellers or retailers cater to the target market. Readers of this text may think of other ways to define their markets, and they are acceptable as long as readers can clearly identify prospects who need and can afford the product in question, the general geographical location of these prospects, and who, in a B2B context, sells to the target market.

Reach Out to Your Prospect

Once salespeople know who their potential customers are, they can go about locating them to make contact. In the retail environment, the prospects are people who enter a store, and salespeople contact them by greeting them with a smile and perhaps a business card. In B2B sales, once salespeople have a clear idea of who makes up their market, they need to physically locate them. Here again the B2B aspect of making contact is more complex and requires additional detective work.

Salespeople must first spend time searching the marketplace to find out where competitive products are sold. For example, if a salesperson represents a designer line of separates for career women and the customer base consists of both boutiques and department stores, the salesperson's plan of action must include researching merchandise in these stores to see where his or her line would best fit. The salesperson must dedicate time to finding stores that cater to this segment of the market. If the salesperson has a specific territory, then researching should be a routine matter. Salespeople have to "shop until they drop," so to speak.

This, however, should not be confused with cold visiting. Cold visiting is when salespeople visit businesses in their territories without making any appointments or doing any research. This method of prospecting is a numbers game; the logic is that the sheer number of visits will generate sales. Cold visiting has fallen out of favor and can even be considered downright offensive in today's sales environment. Unfortunately, there remain some sales managers who insist their salespeople make cold visits that will result in new accounts. In many cases, the focus is on the number of physical sales calls salespeople are making rather than on the quality of these calls. Cold visits can result in sales but are not cost-effective; there are better tools to work with to get results. Salespeople utilize their time if they do their homework and conduct their research before dropping in cold on prospects.

RW Principle

In B2B, it is crucial that salespeople use their marketing detective skills to identify their markets and figure out how to physically locate and reach them.

RW Concept

In recent years, targeted marketing strategies, promotional pieces that are sent to computerized lists, and slick advertising have greatly added to cold calls. Sellers should be familiar with and capitalize on any such efforts to maximize their prospecting routines.

Salespeople can conduct quick research about their prospective customers by merely asking customers where they shop and finding out if customers are satisfied with the selection of merchandise offered. This source of information is invaluable. Some salespeople conduct focus groups to determine if they are satisfying their consumers' needs. These meetings are an excellent platform for learning where consumers shop and give salespeople the opportunity to find prospective customers. Constant monitoring of different media (i.e., newspaper ads, TV commercials, and the Internet) will provide sellers with leads. Newspaper ads are excellent tools for finding out what the stores are featuring and determining if they are prospective customers.

Dialing for Prospects

Using the telephone is one of the most effective ways salespeople can contact potential customers. Yes, we are talking about the proper use of the telephone. Although at times it can be an intense, a frustrating, and a disappointing transaction because of the many calls buyers receive, it is the best and most expeditious way of reaching your target market and qualifying the prospect. As we already mentioned, cold visiting is costly and rarely produces the desired results. Calling prospective customers is a time-saving and cost-effective method.

Many salespeople use the referral method to expand their reach in the marketplace. By speaking with existing accounts, salespeople can reach other people who use the products they are selling and ask these referred people for referrals as well, and so on. Using this technique can help salespeople uncover additional sources of business; to do this effectively, salespeople must get buyers to talk freely. When calling or introducing themselves to a prospect, salespeople should always mention the name of the customer who referred them right away; this will facilitate a smoother, more meaningful sales call.

E-mail can fit into a salesperson's prospecting toolbox—if it's used properly! Salespeople should never use mass e-mails to sell their products. Salespeople should limit their use of e-mail to communicating information about their companies, such as providing prospects with their company Web site addresses. Using e-mail to confirm appointments and providing information requested by buyers are also effective ways that it can come in handy. Salespeople can use it to answer requests for price quotes and delivery information. Properly using e-mail will cut down on the frequency of telephone calls that salespeople need to make to prospects. Some sellers find using e-mail is easier to reach prospects than making repeated telephone calls and leaving messages.

RW Principle

E-mail etiquette: When corresponding via e-mail, it is important to keep the following guidelines in mind:

1. Mind your manners; say "Please" and "Thank you," as appropriate.
2. Be as brief and to-the-point as possible.
3. Avoid abbreviations, Web slang terms, and chat-room symbols (such as LOL for "Laughing Out Loud").
4. Use proper grammar and spell check your message before sending it.
5. Reread your e-mail at least once before sending it.

Direct mail is another important tool that salespeople can use to find new prospects. Many years ago, a local sales representative wrote a monthly newsletter to prospective and active accounts. He included tips about the trade, news about the industry, information on the best way to display merchandise, and the latest fashion trends (he called the section on fashion trends "What's Hot and What's Not"). Furthermore, he never pitched his products in these newsletters. He called the monthly newsletter "Jerry Sherman's Just So Stories." This great prospecting vehicle is discussed further in the case study on page 91.

Salespeople can also send to prospects brochures along with an appropriate letter describing news about their products as an effective means of introducing themselves to their prospects before they make actual calls. It is important that salespeople always include self-addressed stamped response cards with such brochures and remember to mention it in their letters. This method will encourage people who are interested to give feedback and is also a very effective way of salespeople to get their names in front of their prospects.

Be a Show-off!

One of the most productive ways for salespeople to find potential customers is to exhibit in trade shows. Trade shows are ideal environments because it exposes salespeople to new prospects who are in buying mode. The majority of trade-show attendees are buyers who are actually on the lookout for new products and lines to sell. In a way, trade shows are almost like reverse prospecting: Prospective customers seek out resources by shopping at the exhibitors' booths and displays. When they see products in which they are interested, they approach the sellers. Although it is covered in greater detail in chapter 7, keep in mind that sellers must still ask the right questions and get the facts straight to ensure sales.

Exhibitors receive a list of buyers who attend the shows (some trade shows may charge a fee for this service). The list of attendees includes the name of each buyer, his or her e-mail address and telephone number, his or her company, and the company's address. This is a great source of information for finding prospective customers. Many sellers use these lists for direct-mail campaigns that they follow-up on by making telephone calls. A typical response rate from this type of combined campaign is about 3 to 4 percent. Fashion apparel and textile trade shows are held in major cities and local marketing areas during the year. Individually owned retails stores and department stores attend these shows.

RW Concept

The trade shows discussed in this box are held in major cities two to three times a year; cities include New York, Atlanta, Dallas, Chicago, Las Vegas, Los Angles, and San Francisco. Fashion trade shows are also held in smaller cities and are usually sponsored by territory sales representative organizations or by trade show promoters. The following is a list of some of the most important trade shows:

+ **MAGIC**: Owned by Advanstar Communications, MAGIC International is one of the world's largest and most widely recognized organizers of apparel and fashion industry trade shows. The shows encompass every facet of fashion: MAGIC for men's apparel, WWDMAGIC and femme for women's apparel, MAGIC kids for children's apparel, the edge for the progressive market, and International Fashion Fabric Exhibition and I-TexStyle for the textile and sourcing markets. MAGIC, WWDMAGIC, MAGIC kids and the edge, known collectively as the MAGIC Marketplace, are held concurrently twice a year in Las Vegas, Nevada. International Fashion Fabric Exhibition and I-TexStyle are held in New York City. Visit them online at www.magiconline.com.

+ **AmericasMart**: Located at the Atlanta Convention Center in Atlanta, Georgia, AmericasMart continues its tradition of trade shows featuring apparel for women and children and now offers a brand-new showroom floor for apparel, accessories, shoes, childrenswear, intimate apparel, loungewear, and gift-related products. They hold these shows four times per year. Mostly smaller retailers and boutiques in the Southeast area of the United States frequent these shows. Visit them online at www.AmericasMart.com.

+ **Chicago Merchandise Mart**: An important trade show that caters to Midwestern fashion retailers, Chicago Merchandise Mart is organized by Merchandise Mart Properties Inc. in Chicago, Illinois, and offers a convenient, under-one-roof setting in the Chicago Apparel Center, featuring New York–inspired fashion shows and marketing trend reports. The Women's & Children's Market within the show is a to-the-retail trade apparel market specializing in top women's and children's resources for the department or specialty store. Visit them online at www.merchandisemart.com/mmart/.

+ **FAME (Fashion Avenue Market Expo)**: A show for the women's apparel and accessories market, FAME is organized by Business Journals Inc., a communications company that specializes in serving the fashion retail markets. Visit them online at www.fameshows.com

+ **The Intimate Apparel Salon/INTIMA America Collection**: Product groups include lingerie, swimwear, sleepwear, and textiles. Designed to be the largest intimate apparel event in the United States, the show features spectacular runway fashion shows, an exclusive swimwear collection, educational seminars, and international exhibitor pavilions. The show takes place three times a year in New York and is produced by Messe Frankfurt, Inc. Visit them online at www.usa.messefrankfurt.com.

+ **Interstoff**: Managed by Frankfurt Messe GmbH, which has more than eighty trade shows and exhibitions worldwide, making it a major player in the global fashion trade show business. The shows are held in Beijing, Tokyo, Shanghai, Hong Kong, Moscow, Paris, and New York. Visit them online at www.interstoff.de.

Prospecting Resources

In addition to attending trade shows, there are companies whose services include finding and providing information about sales prospects for a fee. Infomat is one such company, and it has been in the fashion industry information and fashion-oriented search engine business since 1996. Infomat helps develop a prospect list for specific sales needs in all categories within the fashion industry in the United States. Its fashion marketing and research expertise targets potential customers to meet sales and marketing objectives for opening new accounts. The information outlet Infomat enables salespeople to find prospective customers, including retail buyers, private label developers, designers, manufacturers, resellers, and exporters. Salespeople have the option to select an already-developed package or request a customized list. Infomat provides lists for direct mailings to fashion industry prospects.[1]

Like Infomat, Dun & Bradstreet provides several information-gathering services. Besides their credit-checking services, Dun & Bradstreet collects, aggregates, and verifies data from thousands of sources daily to provide targeted marketing information. The company's reports cover a vast area of marketing information, from identifying segments and industries to realizing new sales opportunities. These include a summary of key contacts and sales information for a particular company, competition research, and a detailed background and history of any company. Their detailed background and history reports on potential customers are an invaluable marketing tool[2] (Figure 5.2).

Yet another firm that provides this information service is Marketing Pathways.[3] It offers a service that helps salespeople develop profiles of ideal prospects. Marketing Pathways' "Secret Weapon Series" makes it easy for sellers to formulate a crystal-clear picture of the types of individuals they want to reach. It uses a computer-generated questionnaire that is designed to pinpoint the kind of information necessary to identify buyers by personality and behavior.

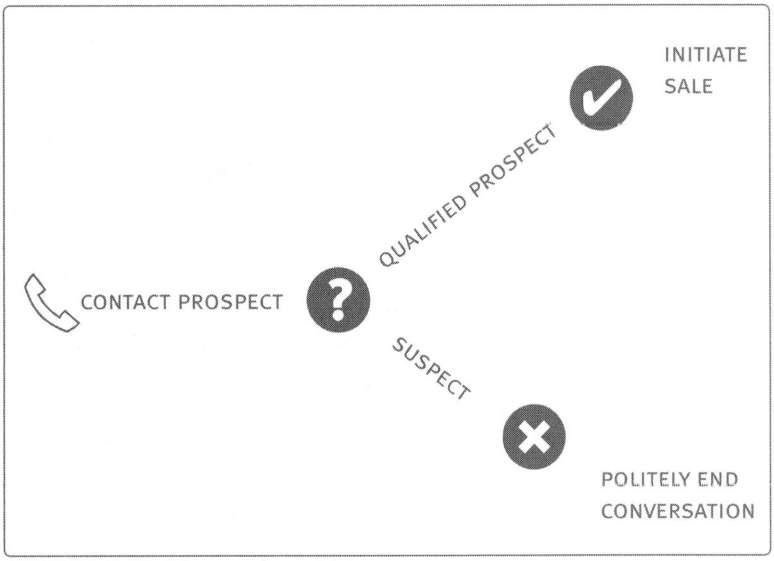

FIGURE 5.2

Using Information to Qualify a Prospect

Answers from a potential customer can help a salesperson determine if they can make a sale or not.

Prospect or Suspect?

Once salespeople make contact with their prospects, they must use their marketing detective skills to **qualify** them. To be a **qualified prospect**, a prospect must meet the following criteria:

+ have a genuine need for the relevant product or service or recognize the possibility of such a need
+ have the financial means to pay for or finance the product of service
+ have the authority to make a purchasing decision

In the real world of B2B, qualifying prospects demands time and research. Remember that although B2B fashion salespeople have relatively few accounts compared with their retail counterparts, these accounts are much more lucrative and require more of their time. Therefore, it is doubly important for salespeople to thoroughly qualify their prospects before investing much time in developing relationships.

Even before calling a prospect, it is a good idea for salespeople to look up prospects in their company files to see if they were former customers. In this case, salepeople should study their files thoroughly beforehand, noting the types of merchandise previously purchased, the frequency and average cost of their orders, and any indication of why they stopped ordering merchandise.

A salesperson can quickly and easily access a prospect's financial means by consulting a credit agency such as Dun & Bradstreet. These firms collect valuable financial information about most businesses and offer it to their clients for an annual fee. Most fashion companies subscribe to such a credit service and make the information available to the sales staff.

If a prospect is financially qualified, the salesperson needs to determine the prospect's need and authority. Salespeople can determine a prospect's need in several ways, but it is preferable to do so discreetly and delicately. Being aggressive or asking outright whether a prospect is interested in buying or ready to buy a product is insulting and reminiscent of the stereotypically pushy salesperson. Being outright gives the impression that the seller isn't willing to take the time to understand the customer's needs in earnest; this eliminates any chance for a meaningful dialogue, which may have developed into a sale.

One acceptable technique that salespeople use is to discuss their products' end users. Doing so allows buyers to determine whether they sell or plan to sell to the same end users, which of course would spark their interest in the salesperson's line. By telling a buyer that his or her dress line targets professional women ages thirty-five to fifty-five and inquiring whether the buyer sells to the same target market or is interested in reaching out to it, a salesperson can immediately determine if their product will fit the buyer's needs. Furthermore, because the question is worded so that it asks about the buyer's end of business, it shows the salesperson cares about the buyer's success and not only about making a sale.

Soon in the conversation, the salesperson should find out if he or she is talking to a buyer with the authority to make purchasing decisions. Most times the salesperson may have to talk with people who do not have this authority, but often it is a necessary step to get a meeting with the decision maker. Remember, the gatekeeper may hold the key to a meeting with the buyer. However, it's best for salespeople to limit conversations with personnel who are not decision makers to show that they value others' time as well as their own. In other words, don't explain product features to the secretary—save these for the buyer and give the secretary only the facts he or she needs to know.

Salespeople should always exercise caution when talking to people who are not decision makers in the companies they represent—the person who's taking messages today may be the buyer tomorrow, so it goes without saying that salespeople must always show respect. Just remember that salespeople can't make sales without having access to the decision makers. An opening question when salespeople are making cold calls is to ask *Who would I speak to about my new collection of career clothing?* This is a valid question that qualifies the prospect's authority in a professional and satisfactory manner.

In the retail environment, it is fairly simple to qualify prospects. It is reasonable for salespeople to assume that if a prospect is in a store, he or she has some need or at least an interest in a product and that he or she has the authority to make a purchasing decision. "Are you ready to purchase something today?" is quite possibly the worst question a salesperson can ask after "May I help you?" It is a negative approach that focuses on a seller's needs to close a sale rather than on the customer's needs. Asking, for example, if the prospect is looking for something for themselves or for a gift, can establish need right away without being too aggressive.

Inquiring whether the customer is buying for a particular event or occasion can also assist in establishing need: if the prospect has a wedding to attend that weekend, then obviously they have a need to buy attire soon. Once the salesperson ascertains a prospect's need, he or she can qualify the prospect's budget by observing what the prospect is wearing—if the prospect is well-dressed, it is reasonable to assume that the prospect can afford the high-end suit he or she is browsing. Do remember that appearances may sometimes be misleading. Try to determine the customer's budget constraints by asking what brands he or she normally wears.

Guilty as Charged

The term *suspect* as used in this text refers to a prospect who doesn't qualify. It is by no means a derogatory term. It simply means that a salesperson suspects that the prospect may be a client but then discovers that the prospect doesn't qualify—the suspect, therefore, is only guilty of not being qualified. If a prospect doesn't meet the qualifying requirements—that is, he or she doesn't have a genuine need for a product or service, doesn't have the financial means to pay, or lacks the authority to make a purchasing decision—then the prospect wasn't a prospect but a suspect.

Without a tried-and-true method of prospecting, salepeople are unable to differentiate between suspects and qualified prospects. Once they determine a customer's status, they can then politely part with suspects and proceed with qualified prospects. Many salespeople don't bother to spend time researching a prospect before initiating a call. They avoid getting essential information, such as finding out the history of a prospect's account and understanding buyer behavior as discussed in chapter 4. Think about the advantage salespeople have when they are able to determine what brands a prospect carries and the price lines.

Good-bye Suspects. Hello Qualified Prospects!

As mentioned earlier, salespeople should qualify prospects as soon as possible and move onto other prospects if they turn out to be suspects. If a suspect has admitted to not having the budget to make a purchase, then there is no reason to waste that person's time. Instead, try and find out when their budget may be updated or revised. If that fails, leave your calling card and wave good-bye. Most salespeople have a very limited amount of time to prospect, so it behooves them to maximize this time and move on from suspects to prospects quickly.

Keep in mind, however, that just as today's assistant may be tomorrow's buyer, so can today's suspect become a qualified prospect tomorrow. When that occurs, salespeople want to make sure that newly qualified prospects think of them first and in a positive manner. In addition to being a nice person, salespeople should part with suspects politely and professionally and leave their contact information or give the them a brochure. It is essential for the salesperson to know who the decision maker is before making the first move. Although we discussed the necessity of reaching the decision maker, many times we have to go through the gatekeeper—the secretary or assistant who monitors the calls and makes appointments for the buyer. This procedure is probably the most delicate one in reaching the decision maker.

Getting the Appointment

Obviously, salespeople must be on their best behavior when trying to reach the decision makers. What do you say and how do you say it to get the gatekeeper to make the appointment or connect you to the buyer? The best approach for salespeople to follow when they are trying to access buyers is for them to be concise and not try to sell their products or services over the telephone. Salespeople should focus the conversation on getting the appointment. They can briefly mention the type of products they sell, but salespeople must avoid trying to give further details.

Say, for example, that a seller is calling to make an appointment with a buyer and an assistant answers the phone. The conversation might go as follows:

Seller: "Hi my name is Mary Bailey, and I represent The Boca Clothing Company. I would like to speak with the buyer Ms. Johnson."

[*Now wait for the assistant to question.*]

Assistant: "What do you want to see Ms. Johnson about?"

Seller: "We are launching a new collection of moderately priced fashions for career women and would like the opportunity to show her what the industry is talking about. The collection will be featured in *W* magazine next month. My research has indicated that your store caters to career women."

[*Again, wait for the reply. If the reply is positive, then you can say something along the lines of the following:*]

Seller: "I will be in your area this week; would she be available Monday or Wednesday? Is the morning or afternoon best?"

When salespeople use the **choice technique**—that is, giving a person a choice of the day and time—they get a better response than they do from just asking for an appointment. Naturally the dialogue will depend on the specific situation. Salespeople should concentrate on getting their appointments, and discussions should be centered on the date and time of the meeting.

If salespeople get a negative reply, for example, that the prospect doesn't carry career clothing, salespeople can ask if the prospect would be interested in entering this market in the future. If the answer is no, then the prospect doesn't qualify.

Making sales appointments saves time and allows salespeople to line up more prospective business by phone during shorter periods of time than by visiting each account cold. It also gives salespeople more prestige and increases the opportunity of contacting the decision makers. Whether salespeople choose to make appointments by phone or in writing, they should keep one important objective in mind: Always have a message, such as an idea that will show the prospect how he or she can benefit from the business. Do not waste the buyer's time with vague and pointless calls or letters. When asking for appointments, salespeople should let buyers know they will be brief and to the point and that their sales presentations will not take more than a short time. Remember that the purpose of advanced calls is to make appointments, not to sell merchandise. Attempting to accomplish both at the same time will make a salesperson's actual visit anticlimactic and weaken his or her presentation.

Chapter Summary

+ Before a salesperson can make a sale, he or she must first locate buyers who have a need for a product. In the real world of fashion sales, a potential buyer is called a prospect, and the action of locating new potential buyers is called prospecting.
+ Because client attrition is inevitable, prospecting for new accounts is an essential part of a successful salesperson's routine and must be incorporated into his or her plan for market coverage.
+ To close a sale, a successful salesperson must take on the persona of a detective—a marketing detective— to recognize when a potential customer does or does not have a need for the product and the means or authority that prospect has to buy it.
+ The first step of prospecting is for salespeople to define the market, that is, the group of individuals or businesses within a specific region who may have a need for their products and are likely to afford it.
+ There are many methods salespeople use to reach their prospects, but attending trade shows and using the telephone effectively are among the most tried-and-true methods.
+ A *suspect* as used in this text refers to a prospect who doesn't qualify. It is by no means a derogatory term. It simply denotes that a salesperson mistakenly thought the suspect was a prospect but discovered that the suspect is not qualified—the only thing a suspect is guilty of is not being qualified.
+ Qualified prospects have a need for a salesperson's product; they can afford and have the authority to buy it.
+ Once a salesperon qualifies a prospect, he or she must not try to sell the product over the phone but rather make an appointment to meet the prospect in person.

+ Salespeople should not linger with suspects because it wastes everyone's time—they should politely move onto the next prospect.
+ When making appointments, salespeople should use the choice technique: *"Would you like to meet on Tuesday or Thursday? Is morning or afternoon better for you?"*

RW CASE STUDY

After Jerry Sherman completed his service in the army as a young man, he went and searched for a job as a salesman. The stumbling block he encountered, as do most newcomers, was that he had no experience. He decided that he would have to make a plan to sell himself to the interviewers.

One of his problems seemed to be that he did not know enough about the companies at which he interviewed—its customers and its end users. He had an interview with a small knitwear company called aileen inc. This time he did some research and had a lady friend, acting as a consumer, call the company to find out the names of some local stores that carried the company's line.

The next step was for Sherman to visit the stores and ask about the product and how it was selling. He found the store personnel very cooperative in giving him the product information he needed. When he went to the interview, he felt quite confident because he believed his research would give him a leg up at the interview—and it did. He was hired for the local New York territory.

Armed with a list of active and inactive accounts and samples in hand, he visited the active accounts first to establish relationships with the buyers. Next, he visited the inactive accounts to find out why they were no longer active. Some of the inactive accounts cited late deliveries, others claimed the company was not cooperative, and still others found other resources—hearing these reasons gave him the "dos and don'ts" of running a territory. He also learned who his competition was and discovered that he had a distinct advantage due to the quality of the product and consumer acceptance of the style and value. Without knowing it, he established a thorough analysis of his product and territory.

He would also drop in at other retail stores. He soon discovered that this cold calling process was a numbers game—a hit-or-miss affair. He knew there must have been a better way of prospecting, so he participated in local trade shows and acquired a list of stores that attended the shows. He asked people in the trade for referrals and looked for new store opening announcements in *WWD* (*Woman's Wear Daily*) and other industry newspapers. These were all prospects.

To make contact with prospects, he sent out a monthly newsletter called "Jerry Sherman's Just So Stories." He sent the newsletter to prospective customers. The letter did not try to sell the products, though it mentioned them. It mostly included tips for the trade and what was happening in the marketplace, including a "What's Hot and What's Not" section. The newsletter was a success—he achieved name recognition. He also included self-addressed stamped postcards with the mailings requesting that recipients contact him. When he received the returned cards, he followed up with telephone calls and made appointments. About half of the people he visited became customers.

To further expand his prospecting, he purchased a list of retail businesses in his territory. The names were combined with the lists from the trade shows and referrals. He decided to make Fridays telephone contact day. Questions were posed to determine during the call if the contact was a qualified prospect. Once he determined this, he would make appointments. After the first year, the territory showed a 45 percent increase in sales volume. Several years later, aileen inc. became a public company with Sherman as vice president of sales and marketing.

Questions to Consider

1. How did it help Sherman to identify his end users and research their buying habits?
2. How did Sherman utilize trade shows and prospect lists to reach potential customers?
3. Why do you think Sherman did not try to sell his product in his letter? What did the tips that he included in his letter accomplish?

RW EXERCISES

1. Explain in your words the meaning of the term *marketing detective*, and give examples of how salespeople can use marketing detective skills to identify their market.
2. Pick one of your favorite shirts or clothing items, and write down its brand name and description. What do you think makes up that line's market and why? How well do you fit into that market? What were the features that made you decide to buy it?
3. Pair up with another student and ask them the questions in exercise 2. Note their answers, and include your opinion.
4. Pick a clothing line, and research it through magazines, articles, manufacturer literature, or any other credible source. Utilizing these sources, price tags, advertisements, styles, and any related factors, identify the market for this line and who the potential end users might be. In your response, describe the clothing line,

its brand name, the sources you used in the analysis, and the results.

5.   Write down your opinion of the pros and cons for contacting prospects via e-mail as opposed to the telephone. Which would work better for making appointments and why? How would you prefer a salesperson to contact you?

6.   Pair up with another student so one of you acts as the salesperson and the other acts as the buyer—it can be in either B2C or B2B. Assume the buyer has signed on the dotted line and is now ready to leave. The seller should ask for references and write them down. Switch roles for a different perspective, and note the new responses.

7.   Look at one of the Web sites discussed in the section "Propsecting Resources" that gather information about prospective customers, and study some of their pages. Note down the information in each site that you thought would be most beneficial to a salesperson and why.

8.   Pick a fashion designer or manufacturer, and assume you are a salesperson working for this manufacturer. Your job is to place a new line in as many retail stores as possible within your district. Identify the line itself, and analyze your market, B2B customer, and end user. Create a letter, mailer, or brochure that you can mail out to the prospects in your area.

9.   Define in your own words what *qualifying a prospect* means and why it is important in sales. Would skipping the qualification process make a salesperson's job easier or harder and why? Give an example.

10. Pair up with another student so one of you acts as the salesperson and the other acts as the prospect in a B2B scenario. The salesperson should qualify the buyer's need, budget, and decision-making authority through casual conversation and subtle questioning. Summarize how the conversation went, and discuss whether the prospect was a qualified prospect or a suspect and why. Be sure to comment on the presence or absence of the buyer's need, budget, and authority. Switch roles for a different perspective, and note the new responses.

11. The next time you go shopping at a store, look at two different items and note whether you are a qualified prospect or a suspect for each of the two items. Examine the presence or absence of the three requirements (need, budget, and decision-making authority) in each case.

12. Pair up with another student so one of you acts as the salesperson and the other acts as the prospect, who turns out to be a suspect. The salesperson should politely hand the suspect a card and invite

the suspect to contact him or her in the future and smoothly end the conversation. Write down how the process went. Switch roles for a different perspective, and note the new responses.

13. Pair up with another student so one of you acts as the salesperson and the other acts as the person answering the phone in a B2B scenario. The salesperson should introduce him or herself and practice talking with the assistant in a polite and professional manner to get the decision maker on the phone. Summarize how the conversation went. Switch roles for a different perspective, and note the new responses.

14. Pair up with another student so one of you acts as the salesperson and the other acts as a prospect who turns out to be qualified. The salesperson should ask for an appointment without trying to sell the product using the choice techniques. Write down your results. Switch roles for a different perspective, and note the new responses.

END NOTES

1. More information on Infomat can be obtained on their Web site at www.infomat.com.
2. More information on Dun & Bradstreet can be obtained on their Web site at www.dnb.com.
3. More information on Marketing Pathways can be obtained on their Web site at www.marketingpathways.com.

CHAPTER 06

SELLING YOURSELF

Objectives

+ Explore further the idea that salespeople sell not only products but also themselves.

+ Understand what is meant by the phrase "dressing for success" and how a salesperson's attire can assist in building relationships with clients.

+ Recognize the importance of getting to know buyers as people and allowing them to get to know you as well.

+ Learn about the professional image construed by a salesperson's commitment to the industry.

+ Review some of the ways a person can become an expert and get more involved in the industry.

Overview

As this text has emphasized, salespeople don't only sell products but also themselves. Therefore, salespeople's appearances and the manner in which they conduct themselves can significantly affect their success in fashion sales. Attire and appearance can impact the way buyers perceive sellers, but salespeople's professional involvement within the industry can have an even wider impact. In this chapter, we explain and explore the various ways a salesperson can present himself or herself as an integral part of the product he or she sells.

Introduction

When salespeople sell products, they show their buyers that they are dependable, ethical, and caring. In short, they show buyers that they are the right person with whom to do business. Salespeople sell themselves as much as they do products. If you wanted to buy a quality leather coat, would you want to buy it from a salesperson at an established fashion boutique or a street vendor who is selling coats out of his car's trunk? Even if both salespeople presented you with the same exact coat at the same exact price, you would most likely purchase it at the boutique because you feel the salesperson there is legitimate. The salesperson at the boutique inspires confidence that the coat will last a long time because it is probably good quality. Shopping at the legitimate business with a creditable salesperson also reassures you that if there were a problem with the product you could return to the boutique and exchange it.

This example shows that while it is important for products to be of merit and thus satisfy a buyer's needs, the salesperson must also be of merit. In essence, sellers must show buyers that they are as good as the products they sell and that by purchasing from them, buyers are getting more value. When salespeople show they have product knowledge, the ability to solve problems, the passion for fashion and style, and the commitment to improve the industry, it solidifies their positions as the top choices for buyers.

A salesperson's appearance, manners, and eloquence can make or break his or her career. The buyer typically sees the seller's face, hair, and clothes and forms a first impression even before the seller has had the chance to say one word. In an industry that's driven by looks and appearance, unkempt hair, a wrinkled shirt, or day-old stubble can give buyers the wrong first impression, which may taint the future of a buyer-seller relationship.

Present Yourself Professionally

About twenty-five years ago, John T. Molloy, the United States' premier scientific image consultant and clothing researcher published his first book entitled *Dress for Success*.[1] The book focused on how men should dress to be successful in the business world. It is interesting to note that he did include only one chapter regarding proper dress for women. One year later, he published *The Woman's Dress for Success Book*,[2] which followed the same thesis as his previous book. Years later, Molloy revised both books and entitled them the *New Dress For Success*[3] and *New Women's Dress For Success*.[4]

Molloy points out that "a woman's success does not depend entirely or even primarily on how she dresses, but dress is an important factor in most women's careers. Research shows that when a woman dresses for success, it does not guarantee success, but if she dresses poorly or inappropriately, it almost ensures failure." Molloy goes on to say, "Most women know men who dress horribly and are very successful. Dressing poorly sometimes does not destroy a man's career the way it does a woman's. If a man is really good at what he does, he is often referred to as 'a diamond in the rough' and can move up in spite of the poor image. This is obviously a double standard and certainly not fair. However, it is the way the real world operates, and you have to deal with it."

Both books concentrated on people being conscious of proper coordination of their attire, how to make an impression, and what colors to wear. There is mention of how to dress for interviews and once a person gets a job. He indicates the importance of power clothes and proper attire for lawyers, doctors, and other professionals. Molloy points out that clothes can make you look more influential, knowledgeable, and pleasant. Molloy's books are great guidelines for many people who are entering the business world.

However, dressing for success in fashion selling is more than just coordination of attire, powerful clothes, colors, and silhouettes. A salesperson's approach should be to understand the ground rules of the dress code of your buyers and their companies. Knowing the dress code and dressing accordingly are the first steps in dressing for success. This is what we call "Empathetic Dressing for Success." Empathetic dressing works in the same way that salespeople utilize empathy to understand the moods and behaviors of their customers and adjust their behavior accordingly. With empathetic dressing, salespeople are aware of their buyers' dress codes and adjust their own accordingly. It is true that when salespeople dress properly, it can promote from buyers positive responses; however, salespeople should be more aware of the culture and dress code policies at their buyers' companies. Salespeople should address several questions before they dress for success. For example, they should find out if their customers' dress codes permit for casual clothing days, whether the dress code is very formal during the week, and just how lax the casual dress code is so they can dress accordingly.

The text is not suggesting that salespeople lose their identities, but it is vital to eliminate aspects of dress that buyers may view negatively. For example, a salesperson who dresses in designer clothing may want to step it back a bit if his or her buyers do not dress in the same manner; in some cases, overdressing can evoke a negative reaction. In fact, a buyer may resent a salesperson who dresses in nothing but designer names, if he or she cannot afford to do the same. To eliminate potential negative reactions from buyers, salespeople should dress in basic yet stylish clothing, usually in colors such as black, navy, brown, or beige. Why add more roadblocks to establishing business relationships with the buyers by wearing attires that may offend them?

Ideally, salespeople should showcase in their attire the products and styles that they sell and proudly wear as often as possible the clothes and accessories that are available at the companies for which they work. If you are selling Ralph Lauren Polo fashions, for example, your wardrobe should reflect that and represent Ralph Lauren's latest trends, styles, and colors. After all, if a product isn't good enough for the seller to wear, then why should a buyer consider it? What happens when a male salesperson sells women's clothing or a female salesperson sells men's or children's clothing? When wearing the products they sell isn't possible, salespeople should at least dress in compatible clothing. For example, a woman who sells traditional menswear should dress in traditional clothing that sends the same fashion message.

Be a Chameleon

In the real world, dressing for success is a commonsense exercise. Salespeople should do their best to fit in to the business environments in which they work. Webster's dictionary defines chameleon as "the ability to change color, change appearance." We are not advocating that salespeople change their persona or be phony copycats of the buyers with whom they work. Rather, we are pointing out that by modifying attire to fit into the business environment, salespeople will steer a buyer's focus away from what the salespeople are wearing and on the benefits of the products they are trying to sell. Clothing should be the background for the seller and never the object of attention. A salesperson's attire should not distract from the sales message.

We recommend that men wear conservative attire—usually a white or blue shirt with a color-keyed striped tie, navy blazer, dark or khaki trousers, and very little aftershave or cologne. It is best for women to wear basic colors, dresses or tops that have moderate necklines, pantsuits, very little jewelry, and not too much makeup or perfume. It is imperative that salespeople find out their prospective customers' dress codes before they visit them. Salespeople may verify this information by asking an operator or assistant at your prospective customer's company. Most of the time, they will be happy to help. In the examples mentioned previously, we've shown how important it is for the salesperson to adapt their dress code to that of their customers. Some companies require more formal clothes—men to wear shirts, ties, and slacks (not denim jeans), and women to wear dresses in acceptable lengths, jackets and skirts, or dress pants with minimal skin showing. On Fridays, most

RW Concept

Sometimes in B2B selling a salesperson cannot ascertain beforehand whether the prospect's company has a formal or casual dress code. In this case, it is always better to dress formally.

companies relax the dress code and allow their employees to wear casual attire. Find out what companies consider casual—don't assume that shorts and T-shirts are acceptable, even on "casual" Fridays. When in doubt, stay on the safe side and always dress appropriately. It is important to dress professionally and look neat at all times.

Appearance and Personal Hygiene

Appearance plays an important part in forming social relationships, especially within the very visual fashion industry. Therefore, salespeople who take care of their appearance and hygiene promote favorable impressions of themselves and have easier times establishing relationships with their clients. Physical appearance forms a basic foundation for any social relationship, especially in today's highly-glamorized world, and particularly within the fashion industry, which revolves around personal appearance. Salespeople who look sloppy violate not only the broad norms that govern basic social interaction but also the values of the fashion industry itself. Salespeople should comprehend that their appearance and personal hygiene impact the sales process and ensure that it is always professional and appealing.

Getting to Know You

Salespeople should allow their customers to get to know them not only as salespeople but also as individuals. How does one person get to know another person? How can the buyer see you as a person first and then as their salesperson? There is no simple answer to this question. Getting to know people takes much work and patience. Honesty, reliability, and knowledge are the standards that will enable salespeople to establish a dialogue with the buyer. Positive experiences will encourage buyers to see salespeople as people—salespeople who earn their buyers' respect, establish themselves as people who will be there when needed. Going beyond the call of duty is one of the best ways for buyers to see sellers as people.

A representative for a well-known line of menswear explains that he always looks to help buyers in areas that do not necessarily relate to selling his product. He recalls a time when one of his buyers was in dire need of an assistant and had difficulty filling the position. Hearing of this problem, the representative set out to find out who in the industry was looking for a job. After a week of making inquiries, he found out that one of his other accounts was downsizing and the assistant to the buyer was looking for work. She was an excellent employee and highly respected in the industry—it took one call to the buyer for her to be hired. Now, who do you think will have a special relationship with the buyer? Most times salespeople are interested in doing only their jobs. They fail to realize

---

RW Principle

Honesty, reliability, and knowledge are the standards that will enable salespeople to sell themselves. Salespeople should establish casual dialogues with buyers and allow buyers to get to know them on a personal level.

that their jobs include helping buyers in areas that sometimes fall out of the scope of their concrete job responsibilities but that nevertheless garner immediate rewards. By finding his buyer a new assistant, the salesperson showed that he cares about his buyer's best interests, even when he doesn't have a personal agenda to fulfill. Going the extra mile gives the buyer the opportunity to know the salesperson not only as a salesperson but also as a person who cares.

Salespeople who focus on more than business alone have the inside track in creating this person-to-person dialogue. How can one achieve this and not be overbearing? In chapter 8, we will discuss relationship development, partnering with the buyer, solving the buyers' business problems, and ethical practices. If the seller wants to form a long-lasting business relationship with the client, it is imperative that he or she recognizes the client as a person with similar needs and desires

Salespeople, in their day-to-day relationships with buyers, must take care not to overstep their bounds. While it's great when salespeople and buyers meet for lunch or dinner, it is also good policy for salespeople not to invade their buyers' privacy and vice versa, of course. Salespeople should avoid getting too involved in their buyers' personal problems; otherwise, they may find themselves part of their buyers' problems. Sellers walk a tight line in trying to let the buyer know them on a personal level, but when the relationship gets too familiar, it is time to step back and not get involved with the buyer any further.

Let's Do Lunch!

One of the best ways for salespeople to sell themselves and improve business relationships is by having one-on-one conversations—and what better way is there to facilitate conversations than by having lunch. It is usually difficult to get to know buyers in office environments. Buyers may be distracted by ringing phones, incoming e-mails, and growing piles of paper in their in-boxes. A lunch meeting during the work week helps put buyers at ease and goes a long way in forging casual business relationships. Some companies may not allow their employees to socialize with their suppliers; however, lunch meetings are an acceptable practice in the fashion industry. The lunch meeting allows time for buyers and sellers to discuss a few matters about the industry, but the main purpose is to allow buyers and sellers to communicate with each other. Sellers should keep business talk to a minimum and forget about getting another order at the lunch meeting. Instead, he or she should keep the meeting as social as possible. The result will be a positive business relationship between the buyer and seller. If a buyer sees that a salesperson is not trying to use the lunch meeting as a means of closing a sale and instead is having an actual conversation, then it will put the buyer at ease and let the buyer view the

RW Concept

The power lunch earns that name because people are more comfortable making decisions in settings where they feel comfortable. Furthermore, going out of the office allows a buyer to concentrate on an order in a relatively stress-free environment where there are no interruptions or distractions.

salesperson as a regular person. It may even encourage the buyer to do business with a clearer head, since he or she is away from the constant distractions of the office.

During lunch, salespeople should take care not to go on about themselves and learn to be good listeners. This is an opportunity to apply their listening skills, which are essential in today's sales environment, where listening is just as important as talking. Salespeople should ask questions and allow their buyers to talk. Doing so may reveal that buyer and seller share similar interests. Nearly everyone has a special interest or a hobby; if a salesperson shares the same interest or hobby as his or her buyers, it helps to strengthen business relationships. Sellers must be patient and realize that they may not discover their buyers' interests at their first lunch meeting. Relationships grow as people experience positive interactions with one another. It is difficult for any salesperson to establish a personal platform with a buyer when the two first meet—but, as salespeople and buyers continue doing business together, they have an opportunity to discuss family, friends, hobbies, and other points of interest.

Promoting Yourself

There is a saying among sales professionals: *Sell yourself first, or you'll sell yourself last.* In other words, if salespeople do not promote themselves— toot their own horns, so to speak—they will be the last ones to close sales. Salespeople who find new and innovative ways to keep their names in the minds of their buyers and deliver what they promise will reap the tremendous benefits of long-term business relationships.

While salespeople should toot their own horns, they must also be careful to avoid letting their egos get out of check. There's a fine line between salespeople subtly reminding their customers of excellent service and boasting about their best service at the expense of their competitors. Nobody appreciates conceit, and salespeople who become overbearing braggarts will end up losing customers regardless of how good they are. To be successful, salespeople should know their products and industry, keep up with the trends, attend fashion shows, and read trade publications such as *Women's Wear Daily* and consumer magazines such as *Vogue* to stay abreast of what's occurring in the industry. The RW Concept on the next page lists some of the important trade and consumer publications with which salespeople should be familiar.

Self-promotion is a continuous process—a successful fashion salesperson never stops doing it. There is probably an infinite number of ways for salespeople to promote themselves, the sole limits of which are their motivation, persistence, and creativity.

RW Concept

Important trade publications are listed below, as follows:

Women's Wear Daily, or ***WWD***, is a definitive voice of the fashion and retail industries. *WWD* is a trusted source for getting industry news; it has a global reach that connects the worlds of fashion, media, finance, and celebrity.

Daily News Record, or ***DNR***, focuses on men's and boy's fashion, accessories, and related businesses. It is a trusted source for its insider's perspective.

Children's Business delivers fashion and market coverage to retailers that carry a wide range of children's products. This monthly magazine provides an annual ranking of the top one hundred retailers of children's clothing and segment-specific, sales-related data for key children's markets.

Footwear News, or ***FN***, is edited for women's, men's, and children's footwear industry. The publication focuses on international, national, and regional news with an emphasis on fashion and marketing. News articles cover retail footwear and accessory fashion trends, merchandising techniques, government issues related to the industry, new technology, imports, and business.

Home Furnishings News, or ***HFN***, is edited specifically for senior retail management in the entire home furnishings market, including home textiles, floor coverings, furniture, housewares, tabletop and gifts, major appliances, and consumer electron-

ics. As such, it covers the broad spectrum of issues relating to home furnishings, including marketing sales, merchandising, fashion direction, financial information, and business analysis.

InFurniture magazine is edited to present fashion trends and business issues that are reshaping the furniture industry. It is edited for senior management in both the retail and manufacturing sectors. *InFurniture* identifies for readers design trends, merchandising tactics, and marketing strategies. It reports the outside influences and examines the ramifications and the underlying meanings of the fundamental shifts taking place in the furniture industry.

Important consumer publications are listed below, as follows:

InStyle invites you to meet celebrities in their homes to see how they express themselves in fashion, beauty, and lifestyle. Indulge yourself with each monthly issue, as you read about what Hollywood's wearing and who's designing it, how to get beautiful things, and much more!

Cosmopolitan is a top young women's magazine famous for its upbeat style, focus on the young career woman, and candid discussion of contemporary male and female relationships. Since its founding in 1886, *Cosmopolitan* has been reporting on modern social trends.

W is elegant, opulent, and colorful. It's the fashion magazine for the deserving

woman. Its lavish presentation has gained *W* the gold medal award for fashion photography three years in a row.

Essence is the preeminent magazine for contemporary African American women, focusing on topics such as fashion, relationships, career, and family. Every issue also addresses cultural, political, and social issues and caters to the African American community.

Elle is a magazine for today's woman. *Elle* brings you fashion, beauty, and accessories for all aspects of living in style.

Glamour gives you the best hair and beauty tips and fashion do's and don'ts.

Vogue is a magazine about fashion shows, news and trends, and more.

Harper's Bazaar is a magazine for the fashion-minded woman.

Esquire is special because it's a magazine for men. Not just a fashion magazine for men, not just a health magazine for men, not just a money magazine for men, but rather all of them. It is, and has been for nearly seventy years, a magazine about the interests, curiosities, and passions of men.

Clear Magazine is the first internationally distributed fashion and design magazine out of the Midwest. It is also the first magazine on the market with a patent-pending clear cover. As a high-end magazine, it focuses on cutting-edge, well-designed products, fashion, and environment styles.

Professional Associations

An effective way for salespeople to sell themselves is to become experts in their fields. Professional associations offer many opportunities to do just that. Every association is governed by a board of directors that is elected by its members. Salespeople should consider running for office or volunteering to help someone who is already in office. Virtually every trade and professional association also has a number of specialized committees, advisory boards, and councils in place whose duties are to explore and develop certain aspects of the industry for the benefit of the associations' members. Salespeople who volunteer to serve on a committee or board that piques their interests will likely find their participation rewarded not only with the satisfaction of being involved in improving the industry, but also with the chance of establishing professional relationships with influential contacts.

The National Retail Federation (NRF) in Washington, D.C., for example, is the world's largest retail trade association, with membership that includes all retail formats and channels of distribution, including department, specialty, discount, catalog, and independent stores.[5] While the organization's main members are retailers, it offers associate memberships to suppliers of products and services to the retail industry, including consultants, manufacturers, schools, and media. A fashion manufacturer's representative could join as an associate member and have access to the NRF's conventions, events, publications, and membership directories.

Arlington, Virginia–based American Apparel & Footwear Association (AAFA) is a U.S. trade association whose mission is to promote and enhance its members' competitiveness, productivity, and profitability in the global market by minimizing regulatory, legal, commercial, political, and trade restraints.[6] Its Government Relations Committee serves as the main eyes and ears for the AAFA on trade, legislative, and regulatory matters at national and international levels. The Social Responsibility Committee identifies and studies global social issues and trends that affect the apparel and footwear industries. The Human Resources Leadership Council develops and implements programs that will assist the membership in all areas of personnel policies, both domestic and global, while the Sales & Marketing Committee helps members sell their products by providing them with information in the form of industry statistics and consumer research. The RW Concept on the next page lists several other trade and professional associations of interest.

Salespeople should make an effort to learn as much as they can about their buyers' businesses and target markets; they should also try to get some press about themselves and their companies. Salespeople should view themselves as brands and make themselves known. They should be active, volunteer to speak at schools and business groups, and write articles and submit them to trade and local papers.

RW Concept

Professional and trade associations are powerful resources where a salesperson can become involved in the industry, learn about market shifts and trends, and meet prospective buyers. The following are just some of the dozens of associations that exist in the United States alone:

+   American Apparel & Footwear Association is the national trade association representing the apparel, footwear, and other sewn product companies and their suppliers. AAFA advocates on behalf of its members to advance the industry's legislative, international trade, and regulatory objectives on issues such as sizing, care labeling, kickbacks, federal prison industries, flammability, product safety, social responsibility, quotas, imports, customs, ergonomics, and government contracts. It communicates information to promote the apparel, footwear, and other sewn product industries worldwide through trade shows, statistics, seminars, and other initiatives.

+   The National Retail Federation is the world's largest retail trade association, with membership that includes all retail formats and channels of distribution, including department, specialty, discount, catalog, Internet, and independent stores; chain restaurants; drugstores; and grocery stores, as well as the industry's key trading partners of retail goods and services. NRF represents an industry with more than 1.4 million U.S. retail establishments, more than 23 million employees, and sales of $4.1 trillion in 2004. As the industry umbrella group, NRF also represents more than one hundred state, national, and international retail associations.

+   The California Fashion Association educates and provides business development assistance to Southern California's apparel and textile industries. It is the forum organized to address issues of concern to fashion manufacturers, contractors, suppliers, educational institutions, and allied associations; all apparel-related businesses benefit. Fashion is the largest manufacturing sector in Los Angeles locally. Nearly 7,300 firms are involved in fashion-related businesses and account for approximately 130,000 jobs in Los Angeles and surrounding counties (employment in the California garment industry surpass New York's head count by 55,000 jobs). CFA is the clearinghouse for information and representation, a collective voice focused on the industry's continued growth, prosperity, and competitive advantage, directed toward the promotion of global recognition for the "Created in California" image. Its purpose is to generate international trade, interact with state and federal agencies, providing valuable assistance with compliance and labor issues, and general interindustry networking. Its mission is to provide a forum for industry networking, provide information about labor law compliance, promote the application of apparel related technology and advanced education, promote the development of international exports, and work toward a positive image for the apparel and textile industry.

+   The Textile Association of Los Angeles is a membership-based group of professionals engaged in textile sales, manufacturing, related products, and services to the apparel industry. The association provides education, networking opportunities, and resource information services locating textiles, related products, and services within the apparel industry. The association provides services through its office, annual directory, and numerous networking events and opportunities to members and the wider fashion (apparel) community. The association also provides scholarships to talented future designers, contributes to charitable causes, and holds community events for inner-city youth. It is a nonprofit mutual benefit association of salespeople who live and work in California, Washington, Oregon, Montana, Idaho, Utah, Nevada, New Mexico, Arizona, Colorado, Wyoming, Texas, Hawaii, and Alaska and engage in the sale of textiles and allied products to garment manufacturers, textile jobbers, and retailers.

Networking

Today, **networking** is an extremely important component of sales. Networking offers salespeople opportunities to meet and forge business relationships with potential buyers, suppliers, peers, and other members of the industry. Networking typically brings together an extended group of businesspeople who share similar interests or who are located in the same specific geographical area. It allows these businesspeople to interact and remain in informal contact for mutual assistance or support.

Within a formal perspective, networking has become a highly organized activity. Recurring networking events such as those organized by the local chamber of commerce and membership groups made up of businesspeople from a wide variety of fields and industries typically fall into this category. Fashion salespeople can benefit from either types of formal networking but may find informal networking more rewarding because they can customize it to fit their markets and buyers. In essence, if salespeople can identify one or two interests that a large percentage of their target markets share, then they need to figure out how to become involved in these interests to create customized networking opportunities. For example, if a seller in Florida notices many of his buyers talk about golf, he takes a few lessons and finds he likes it. Now the seller can ask his existing buyers where they golf, join their club or league, and begin to socialize with them. In addition, the salesperson may meet other potential buyers he never would have met otherwise, and if he does, it will be while playing golf, thus making the development of business relationships happen naturally.

Networking opportunities may exist in unexpected places. For instance, doing something good for the community, such as volunteering or serving on the board of a local nonprofit organization, can open many doors. Buyers and sellers who have a charity or cause in common will not only find satisfaction from participating in such goodwill projects, but also receive recognition by their peers, superiors, and even clients. Another excellent avenue for combining community work with networking is the Rotary Club.

Continuing Education

A word about self-improvement: Never stop learning! Attending seminars and educational programs will give salespeople distinct advantages over their competition. Using the knowledge attained by this never-ending learning situation will become apparent to those they meet. One of the best ways to learn and become involved in the community at the same time is to teach or become a guest speaker. Salespeople should find a school or an organization and spend a few hours each week teaching or speaking about some of the things they learned in the real world. They

RW Concept

The Rotary Club, the world's first service club, was formed on February 23, 1905 by Paul P. Harris, an attorney who wished to recapture in a professional club the same friendly spirit he had felt in the small towns of his youth. The name *Rotary* derives from the early practice of rotating meetings among members' offices. Rotary's popularity spread throughout the United States in the decade that followed; clubs were chartered from San Francisco to New York. By 1921, rotary clubs had been formed on six continents, and the organization adopted the name Rotary International a year later.

As rotary grew, its mission expanded beyond serving the professional and social interests of club members. Rotarians began pooling their resources and contributing their talents to help serve communities in need. The organization's dedication to this ideal is best expressed in its principal motto: "Service Above Self." Rotary also later embraced a code of ethics called The Four-way Test, which has been translated into hundreds of languages.

An endowment fund, set up by Rotarians in 1917 "for doing good in the world," became a nonprofit corporation known as The Rotary Foundation in 1928. Upon the death of Paul Harris in 1947, an outpouring of Rotarian donations made in his honor totaling $2 million launched the foundation's first program—graduate fellowships, now called Ambassadorial Scholarships. Today, contributions to The Rotary Foundation total more than $80 million annually and support a wide range of humanitarian grants and educational programs that enable Rotarians to bring hope and promote international understanding throughout the world. In 1985, Rotary made a historic commitment to immunize all of the world's children against polio. Working in partnership with nongovernmental organizations and national governments through its PolioPlus program, Rotary is the largest private-sector contributor to the global polio eradication campaign. Rotarians have mobilized hundreds of thousands of PolioPlus volunteers and have immunized more than one billion children worldwide. By the 2005 target date for certification of a polio-free world, Rotary will have contributed half a billion dollars to the cause.

As it approached the dawn of the twenty-first century, Rotary worked to meet the changing needs of society, expanding its service effort to address such pressing issues as environmental degradation, illiteracy, world hunger, and children at risk. The organization admitted women for the first time (worldwide) in 1989 and includes more than 145,000 women in its membership today. Following the collapse of the Berlin Wall and the dissolution of the Soviet Union, rotary clubs were formed or reestablished throughout Central and Eastern Europe. Today, 1.2 million Rotarians belong to some 31,000 rotary clubs in 166 countries. The object of rotary is to encourage and foster the ideal of service as a basis of worthy enterprise and, in particular, to encourage and foster the following:

FIRST, the development of acquaintance as an opportunity for service;

SECOND, high ethical standards in business and professions, the recognition of the worthiness of all useful occupations, and the dignifying of each Rotarian's occupation as an opportunity to serve society;

THIRD, the application of the ideal of service in each Rotarian's personal, business, and community life;

FOURTH, the advancement of international understanding, goodwill, and peace through a world fellowship of business and professional people united in the ideal of service.

Source: Rotary Club[7]

should continue sharing some of their knowledge and experiences with people starting their careers or even a lecture series targeted to high school and college students). Most universities, colleges, and community centers offer a wide array of continuing education classes. Effective public speaking and written business correspondence can help salespeople improve their presentation skills, while Tai Chi may offer salespeople stress relief and inner harmony.

Communication

Immediately following the first visual impression that buyers have of salespeople, another impression is formed once salespeople open their mouths. Verbal communication says a lot about a person's character and buyers are attuned to that. Wise salespeople ensure their communication skills are up to par. In many parts of the country, knowing a second language can help salespeople expand their base of prospects, yielding a great number of additional accounts.

The nonprofit company Toastmasters International provides businesspeople with the tools that enable them to become effective communicators and leaders. Toastmasters training helps employees give better sales presentations, hone their management skills, work better with fellow employees effectively, develop and present ideas, offer constructive criticism, and accept criticism more objectively. It is an excellent resource for improving communication skills. The RW Concept below takes a closer look at Toastmasters.

RW Concept

Toastmasters International is a nonprofit organization governed by a board of directors elected by the membership. The first Toastmasters club was established on October 22, 1924, in Santa Ana, California, by Dr. Ralph C. Smedley, who conceived and developed the idea of helping others speak more effectively. More clubs were formed, and Toastmasters International was incorporated under California law on December 19, 1932.

Toastmasters International's administers its business and services through its world headquarters, located in Rancho Santa Margarita, California. It does not employ paid promoters or instructors. It does not have salaried staff except the executive director and world headquarters staff who provide services to the clubs and districts.

At Toastmasters, members learn by speaking to groups and working with others in a supportive environment. A typical Toastmasters club is made up of twenty to thirty people who meet once a week for about an hour. Each meeting gives everyone an opportunity to practice

+ conducting meetings, which usually begin with a short business session that helps members learn basic meeting procedures;
+ giving better sales presentations, working more effectively with potential buyers, developing and presenting ideas, and offering constructive criticism;
+ giving one- to two-minute impromptu speeches on assigned topics;
+ presenting prepared speeches based on projects from the Toastmasters International Communication and Leadership Program manuals (projects cover topics such as speech organization, voice, language, gestures, and persuasion);
+ offering constructive evaluation (every prepared speaker is assigned an evaluator who points out speech strengths and offers suggestions for improvement).

Toastmasters also helps its members build leadership skills by organizing and conducting meetings and motivating others to help them. Club leadership roles and a leadership development program also offer opportunities to learn and practice. Just as Toastmasters members learn to speak simply by speaking, they learn leadership by leading. A company's success depends on communication. Employees face an endless exchange of ideas, messages, and information as they deal with one another and with customers day after day. How well they communicate can determine whether a company quickly grows into an industry leader or joins thousands of other businesses mired in mediocrity.

Source: Toastmasters[8]

Chapter Summary

+ The product is not the only thing a fashion salesperson sells. The fashion salesperson also sells himself or herself.

+ The salesperson's appearance, manners, and eloquence can make or break his or her career.

+ When salespeople are selling themselves, it is vital that they eliminate aspects of the way they dress that buyers may view negatively.

+ Ideally, salespeople should showcase in their attire the products and styles that they sell and proudly wear the clothes and accessories available at the companies for which they work.

+ Salespeople should always aim to fit in with the business environments in which they work.

+ Earning buyers' respect is one way that salespeople can establish themselves as people who are there when they are needed and not just out to make a sale. Going beyond the call of duty is one of the best ways that salespeople can make buyers recognize them as people.

+ Salespeople who focus on more than business alone have the inside track in creating person-to-person dialogue.

+ One of the best ways for salespeople to sell themselves and improve business relationships is through one-on-one conversations. The lunch meeting is an accepted practice in the fashion industry that provides the perfect opportunity for such conversations to take place.

+ During a power lunch, salespeople should avoid talking too much about themselves and instead ask questions and listen to what the buyers have to say. Salespeople should also avoid talking too much about business and instead focus on social conversations.

+ The best way for salespeople to sell themselves is to become experts in their fields. Salespeople should know their products and industry and keep up with the trends.

+ Salespeople should never stop learning. They should attend seminars and educational programs that will give them a distinct advantage over their competition. The knowledge they attain by this never-ending learning situation will become evident to those they meet.

RW CASE STUDY

Karen Walker is a New Zealand–born fashion designer with an international reputation for her original, effortless, and unpretentious style. Karen Walker's womenswear labels are stocked in more than 130 stores throughout the world in cities, including New York, London, Paris, Hong Kong, Los Angeles, and Sydney and in more than twenty cities throughout Japan. She receives editorial coverage, including regular pages in U.S. and British magazines.

How did you get started?

When I was eighteen and in my second year at fashion school here in Auckland, I put [one hundred New Zealand dollars] (about 50 U.S. dollars at the time) into a bank account and with it I bought some fabric, and made a men's shirt. I took the shirt into a little store in Auckland and asked if they'd try to sell it. They rang the next day and said they'd sold it and could they have three more. That in essence is how it's continued over the next seventeen years growing to its current state.

Must you sell yourself first and then your creations?

I think that at the end of the day the most important thing in fashion is the quality of the ideas, but certainly selling yourself is an important part of the equation in order to be able to put them in front of people. However, no amount of pushing yourself out there is going to make a difference if the product's rubbish or wrong for that market.

What information can you share with us regarding working with people?

In terms of working with people, I've always liked to surround myself with like-minded people, whether they are colleagues or clients. In fact, this has been the basis for our entire business; we're a global niche brand, which means that though we only talk to 1 percent of the market, it has the potential to be and is starting to be 1 percent in every major city in the developed world. What that means is that we know our customer intimately and intuitively. We don't need to market research them or tailor our product to different countries or cities because our girl is the same in Hong Kong as she is in New York, in Paris as she is in Sydney. It also means we don't have to explain ourselves. If people get it in the first two minutes they get it; if they don't, we move on. There's no point in trying to explain or convince people of anything. Either they fit with it or not. We call it P.L.U.: *people like us*. This also extends to our team whether they are stylists, hair and makeup, photographers, agents, press agents, or stockists. It's a very important part of our brand's identity and strategy.

Can you relate to any experiences where selling played a prominent role in building your company?

Selling is of course a crucial part of the fashion industry equation. I'm still learning about it though; one thing I have really grown to believe over the years is that you can't force someone to like or relate to your product. If the product's right, they'll get it. If it's wrong, they'll move on. You have to know who you're talking to and work that and not worry about the rest. To this day, selling still plays a crucial role in the business. We've just had a fantastic show at London fashion week in September, and the response has been wonderful, but until we close off sales on November 4 and I see we've hit our target, I won't relax. The fashion business is just that, a business, and without the sales, there's no point. Sure, at this end of the market, the creative side is what drives us, but it's not art, it is business, and one must be responsible for that.

How have your personal dealings with people helped you reach your objectives?

I've always enjoyed the side of the business that's about personal relationships; it goes back to what I was saying about building a team of like-minded people around me. Most people in the fashion business, including myself, got into this game in the first place because of a love of ideas, and a big part of that is also about sharing an excitement for ideas with other like-minded people so [working with] photographers, models, public relations people, designers or manufacturers is a very exciting part of the work and one that is inspiring and energizing. Finding that connection and sparking someone creatively is one of the most exciting parts of this business to me. From those relationships, many different possibilities can emerge. One of my strongest personal relationships is with Heather Mary Jackson, who's worked with us for eight or nine collections now as a stylist. We hit it off the minute we met, were already familiar with one another's work, and five years later, we're still going strong. I also have very close relationships with many of my buyers, many stylists, writers, and editors, as well as the rest of my team, and this helps us to grow as well as gives us satisfaction.

As a designer, you also act as a buyer of piece goods, trim, etc. Can you comment on how you are influenced by the seller's appearance and attire?

If the person you're potentially buying from looks like someone you can relate to on a personal level, it makes you more hopeful of and open to the product they're showing you. But, at the same time, it's sometimes the least likely avenues and people where you find the good stuff, so I'm very open minded about anyone coming to see me with product.

Do the personnel who sell your collections dress and live the same lifestyle as your target market?

Yes, this is vital. It has to all feel true and honest and be the real deal. The men and women who represent our product both at wholesale and retail points are very much representative of the brand.

Can a seller's attire/appearance build a relationship?

In fashion, one's appearance is vital: That's what we're selling.

Do you agree that getting to know the people you are doing business with and allowing them to know you as well is the key to success?

Building relationships is a vital part of any business and is very much a part of the fashion business. In order to succeed, you must know the people you're working with way beyond an exchange of business cards.

Questions to Consider

1. How important is selling yourself to the sales process according to Walker? What is your opinion?
2. What is P.L.U., and how does this approach assist Walker in developing her sales?
3. Do you agree with Walker that the seller's lifestyle and fashion sense are important to the fashion sales process? Why?

RW EXERCISES

1. Have you or a friend of yours ever showed up for a social gathering only to find out you were either over- or underdressed? How did it make you feel? What were people's reactions to your attire? What do you think the effects of wrong clothing will be on a salesperson's success in sales and why?
2. Pair up with another student so one of you acts as the salesperson and the other acts as the buyer's assistant in a B2B situation. Using your interpersonal skills, find out from the buyer's assistant what is the company's dress code, and list what you would wear for a meeting with the buyer and why. Switch roles for a different perspective, and note the new responses.
3. Next time you deal with a salesperson, take notes about his or her attire. Was it appropriate for your business environment? How did his or her appearance make you feel about him or her? How could he or she have improved his or her appearance to inspire more confidence?
4. Think of a time when a salesperson tried to make you see him or her as a person rather than just a salesperson. What did the salesperson say or do, and was it effective?
5. Pair up with another student so one of you acts as the salesperson and the other acts as the buyer at a lunch meeting. Converse with the buyer and try to avoid lengthy work-related discussions; keep it

mostly on a social level. Switch roles for a different perspective, and note the different responses.

6. Why do you think being involved in the community and taking a lead role in the industry helps you sell yourself to a buyer? Give examples of how this might bring about a sale.

7. At your local library or bookstore, find and read an article in one of the leading trade publications listed in this chapter. What is the article's name and its publication date, and which target market do you believe it caters to? How do you think such publications could help the seller better sell himself or herself to a buyer?

END NOTES

1. Molloy, John T. *Dress for Success*. New York: Warner Books, 1976.

2. Molloy, John T. *Woman's Dress for Success*. New York: Warner Books, 1984.

3. Molloy, John T. *New Dress for Success*. New York: Warner Books, 1988.

4. Molloy, John T. *The New Woman's Dress for Success*. New York: Warner Books, 1996.

5. National Retail Federation's Web site, www.nrf.com.

6. American Apparel & Footwear Association's Web site, www.americanapparel.org.

7. Rotary Club's Web site, www.rotary.org/aboutrotary/history/index.html.

8. Toastmasters International's Web site, www.toastmasters.org/about.asp.

CHAPTER 07

THE SALES PRESENTATION

Objectives

+ Understand the importance of maintaining a positive mental attitude before, during, and after a sales presentation.
+ Learn how to proactively plan the sales presentation so that it highlights a product's features and benefits.
+ Explore techniques to effectively show the product and sell it.
+ Comprehend the concept of the sales objection and why encouraging it is part of a good sales presentation.
+ Discover how to anticipate and answer objections correctly.
+ Review the sales close concept and recognize the best time to close without offending the customer.

Overview

This chapter explores the various fundamentals and techniques with which salespeople should be familiar to have successful face-to-face meetings with clients and sell them the right products. A good sales presentation begins with careful planning, research, and a positive attitude; continues with a confident and knowledgeable description of the product; advances with the answering of objections; ends with a client's signature on the dotted line; and leads to a better relationship with the customer.

Introduction

The sales presentation is one of the most exciting parts of selling. This is the time when a qualified prospect turns into a new customer. This is also the time when salespeople get to meet their existing clients face-to-face and improve their business relationships with them. This is when salespeople shine, show how much they care about their clients, and make their sales.

Many salespeople find the sales presentation to be a euphoric moment. It is challenging, thrilling, and fast-paced. It screams "Show time!," "Action!," and "Go!" The first sales presentation with a specific prospect is the culmination of a salesperson's prospecting and research efforts. The next logical step after a salesperson has identified a qualified prospect who has a need and the ability to purchase a product is for the qualified prospect to actually buy the product. If a prospect needs a product that will make life easier and the prospect can afford to purchase it, it only makes sense for him or her to buy it. Unfortunately, things in the real world are not so simple.

Salespeople's mindsets and attitudes, the ways in which they present their products, their product knowledge, the degree of empathy they exhibit, and the way they answer customer objections or questions are just some of the variables that affect qualified prospects' decisions to purchase. Salespeople can control these variables, and typically salespeople will try to resolve qualified prospects' problems with one or more of these variables to convince the qualified prospects to buy.

There are other hidden variables that are out of a salesperson's control. For example, a salesperson could have the most positive mental attitude in the world, but if the prospect's car is repossessed, the prospect's marriage is in serious trouble, or one of the prospect's parents just passed away, then the salesperson will most likely not be able to make a sale under any circumstances. On that day, that is. Although salespeople don't have any control over variables such as these, they must learn to recognize when such variables arise and try again when the prospect is more receptive. The deft salesperson has to be sensitive to the prospect's problems and come back on another day.

Let's begin exploring the intricate workings of the sales presentation and the ways salespeople can gain better control over some of these variables. There are various techniques that salespeople can utilize in their sales presentations to get the orders despite the variables. Positive and enthusiastic attitudes contribute to better sales presentations. This chapter discusses ways for salespeople to overcome disappointments and learn from their mistakes, how showing the product and demonstrating its features is one of the best features of a sales presentation, and the four types of sales presentations (memorized, priority, in-depth, and consultative). It will also cover addressing a buyer's objections; the manners in which salespeople respond to their buyers can lead them to make sales, as well as bring presentations to a close and get the buyers' signatures.

Positive Mental Attitude

Having a positive mental attitude (**PMA**) is essential to a successful sales presentation and can mean the difference between success and failure. Mental attitude refers to the salesperson's inner mindset and the manner in which he or she approaches the client and presentation. Clients want honest and reassuring answers to their questions—they don't want gloom and doom. Being positive is one of the most important characteristics a salesperson must possess. Chapter 9 discusses positive mental attitudes in greater detail.

PMA is contagious. A salesperson's passion and excitement can infuse the client with enthusiasm about the product—after all, the client has a need for a product and will be enthusiastic about it if satisfies his or her needs. Even before meeting his or her client, a salesperson must reset his or her mental attitude. That means putting any negative emotions or problems aside while he or she is selling and assuming a focused, positive attitude. A successful salesperson must not let negative emotions get in the way of the sale. If a customer goes into a department store and meets a salesperson who starts bellyaching about a domestic problem, the customer will probably feel uncomfortable and not want to buy from that salesperson. Salespeople should never share their personal problems with their clients.

The Plus or Minus Factor

To loosely quantify salespeople's mental attitudes, the authors devised the Plus or Minus Factor. In essence, the Plus or Minus Factor measures the degree to which a salesperson exudes a positive or negative attitude. For the sake of simplicity, we chart a salesperson's PMA on a scale of plus 10 to minus 10. Numbers at the top of the chart show enthusiastic, optimistic, fun-to-be-around salespeople, while numbers at the bottom show cranky, cynical grumps. The higher the Plus or Minus Factor, the higher the chances that a sale will take place.

Salespeople with a low Plus or Minus Factor will complain about how terrible business is and how customers aren't buying and demand too much. They will no doubt complain about all the competition, reminisce about better times, and complain about their bosses.

Salespeople with a high Plus or Minus Factor will likely say that business is what you make of it and recognize that opportunities are always there for those who work hard. They believe in the products they sell and genuinely care about their customers. If the day did not go well, the positive salespeople will say, "tomorrow is another day, and it will bring with it another opportunity for success!"

Being positive doesn't mean that a salesperson should be unrealistic. No salesperson will ever succeed while innocently believing that everybody is good and that nothing will go wrong or by ignoring issues that need to be addressed. Everyone has a bad day and sooner or later, even the most enthusiastic and chipper salesperson will have to deal with a rude client or a delayed delivery. If salespeople learn to recognize negative situations that may adversely affect business relationships, they should try to fix them while keeping a positive attitude. In other words, a salesperson should be positive but also realistic.

Internal Rah-Rah

Being a salesperson can sometimes be quite tough, similar to being a football player. Just as a football player drives for a touchdown and gets tackled repeatedly along the way, a salesperson strives for a sale and encounters negative reactions along the way. During a football game, the coach, fans, and cheerleaders motivate the football player who has just been tackled and sacked to get up and keep going. In the sales environment, however, there are no coaches, fans, or cheerleaders. Salespeople must cheer themselves up and keep themselves motivated as a general rule. Psychologically speaking, PMA is an internal coping mechanism that reinforces sellers as they face the daily challenges and disappointments in the marketplace. It is a prime requirement for those that have chosen a career in sales.

During a recent seminar the authors attended, the weather was marred with heavy rainstorms for two days. The discussion on the first morning revolved around the bad weather and how it was affecting business. The negative responses included, "The weather is terrible—rain, rain, and more rain. Who knows when it will clear up?" and "It will ruin business in the retail stores; people will not go shopping in this weather." Positive responses included, "Inclement weather can be conducive to getting consumers out of the house and encouraging them to go shopping." The salesperson with PMA may also react to this situation by saying, "True, we are getting a lot of rain and it may hurt business today, but tomorrow will be another, better day."

Being positive helps salespeople overcome the many disappointments that they confront. The objections voiced by buyers and failed sales can quickly erode the confidence of the most positive salesperson if he or she allows it. To combat negativity, salespeople must treat each disappointment as a learning experience. By analyzing what went wrong, why they didn't get the order, and how they could do better next time, salespeople can make future sales transactions go much smoother. If the salespeople feel they should have paid closer attention to the customers' reactions or did less talking and more listening, for example, then they should make mental or written notes about it and pay closer attention to that element during the next presentation. The sellers must be mentally equipped with a bottomless well of PMA, otherwise their ability to sell will be lost. Clients can pick up on negative statements, which can become the biggest obstacles to making a sale. The positive person generates a good feeling and gives the buyer a level of comfort and confidence. In essence, we are really selling ourselves and our ability to build relationships. The Plus and Minus Factor is the dividing line in deciding the winners and losers.

Show and Sell

Showing a product to a client in a professional manner and using the appropriate presentation technique can be extremely important to the outcome of the sale. In the highly visual field of fashion, clients instinctively prefer to purchase items that they can see, touch, and feel. Therefore, it is important for salespeople to be armed with as many samples—or at the very least visual aids—as possible when preparing sales presentations. It is equally important for salespeople to know how to present the samples and visual aids to their clients.

The four different presentation types are memorized, priority, in-depth, and consultative.[1] Each presentation method is geared toward a different strategy, depending on a product's nature, the buyer's needs and character, and the seller's comfort level.

The following general rules hold true for any type of sales presentation:

+ A good presentation should be simply stated in words the buyer can understand.
+ Salespeople should make both logical and emotional appeals.
+ A confident and friendly atmosphere should be established at the outset.
+ Sales strategies for salespeople who sell to single buyers should be different from sales strategies for salespeople who sell to buying centers, which are groups of individuals who and organizations that have a stake in and influence the final buying decision.
+ Salespeople should bring every presentation to a close by making it easy for the buyer to make a decision.

Let's inspect each of these presentation methods and how to best utilize them.

The Memorized Presentation

One way to organize the presentation is to memorize the key selling points of the merchandise, also known as the memorized or canned presentation. This method is particularly useful to new and inexperienced salespeople who are still developing a personal methodology to selling. It allows them to give buyers the complete story about the merchandise and to make sure they don't miss any key points.

The memorized or script-based presentation has one distinct disadvantage: The script cannot possibly predict and prepare for every conceivable question or objection. Since salespeople who select this type of presentation typically lack comprehensive product knowledge, they are unprepared to deal with objections that are not accounted for on the script. It is not a flexible presentation that allows for deviations from the memorized script; therefore, unusual questions normally mean the end of the presentation. In cases like these, it is always best for salespeople to admit right away that they don't have the answers but promise to return with answers once they do have them.

The memorized presentation should be used only if a product is simple and speaks for itself or if the product is presold through extensive advertising that results in dramatic consumer demand for that item. In the fashion business, not too many products fall into this category. For example, selling products such as basic T-shirts for Hanes may be conducive to this type of presentation. However, sellers need to be ready to discuss the benefits of the new Hanes tagless T-shirts over ones that have the old sewn-in tag. The memorized or canned presentation should provide the answers for as many potential questions as possible.

The Priority Presentation

Within the priority or specific-needs presentation, the salesperson verbally sketches a problem that is either common to many buyers or is of specific interest to a potential client and offers a solution, which is usually suggesting the buyer purchase the particular merchandise that the salesperson is selling. This presentation gives salespeople the chance to shine a spotlight on the problem of interest and concern to the buyer and fix it by the end of the presentation.

For example, if an apparel buyer complains that he is unable to maximize sales on fast-selling merchandise, a salesperson—if the company is large and has the resources to offer it—should encourage the buyer to participate in the Just in Time (JIT) program, which means that merchandise is delivered when it is needed or just in time to satisfy the customers' needs. It also reduces the buyer's costs of carrying extra inventory. In this priority presentation, the salesperson's opening comments should focus on explaining the JIT system and bring resolution to the delivery problem.

Say the XYZ Company has decided that their customer base has changed from the teenage consumer to the young college and career woman. They are looking for resources that market to this consumer within a popular price range. The XYZ executives and buyers have attended trade shows looking for new resources of this type. The priority or special-needs presentation is a natural choice for a salesperson who sells the type of merchandise XYZ Company is looking to buy. The chances of making the sale are likely. The presentation would certainly stress the target market and price range.

The priority-specific needs presentation motivates customers to participate in the selling process and arouses their willingness to act. To close the sale, salespeople must bring together all the aspects of a buyer's problem to show how buying the product will solve the problem.

The priority approach also benefits salespeople because it allows them to address the specific needs of each customer's preconceived values. Customers should be categorized according to how their needs are prioritized.

For example, Customer A may have the following order of priorities:

1. fashion
2. service
3. quality
4. value

Clearly an approach that is driven by a discussion of upcoming trends would be the best in this instance, with some attention given to the company's service record and secondary interest paid to the quality and value of the merchandise in the presentation.

Customer B's priorities, however, may be as follows:

1. value
2. quality
3. service
4. fashion

In this instance, salespeople should emphasize the value of their company's merchandise in relation to its competition and highlight the precautions they've taken to ensure quality control of their merchandise. Fashion and speedy delivery should be downplayed, but not ignored, in this presentation.

The priority presentation is most productive for salespeople who are good extemporaneous speakers and expresses themselves well. Also, by paying attention to the preconceived values of buyers in this presentation, salespeople increase their chances for success. Professional salespeople learn how to avoid getting sidetracked on frivolous small talk and to keep the discussion focused on the merchandise.

The In-Depth Presentation

For major sales transactions, in-depth presentations are often the most productive. The salesperson utilizes surveys, PowerPoint presentations, charts, and other forms of visual aids to impress buyers with the research and development that have gone into the design and manufacturing of a product. Sometimes salespeople even present statistics relating to their market share for that product. This type of presentation can also include demographics, marketing analyses, consumer characteristics studies, and psychographics—this information will give credibility

---

RW Concept

Computerized presentation resources: There are many programs and Web sites that offer practical advice and helpful add-ons that can give your presentation that extra pizzazz. While salespeople may not want to overdo it with the use of sounds and animations, multimedia pieces can help engage buyers and make for a more interesting presentation. The bottom line is that the message must be more prominent than the visual and sound effects.

Microsoft PowerPoint: Using enhanced multimedia capabilities to deliver presentations with more impact improves a salesperson's chances of making a sale. This top slideshow presentation program is a popular choice among businesspeople because it is user-friendly and compatible with most PCs. It is offered as part of the Microsoft Office suite. Visit them online at http://office.microsoft.com.

Pro Presentations: Whether salespeople present ideas with charts, slides, multimedia, or online presentations, it's easy to create effective professional presentations with Harvard Graphics' Pro Presentations. People can simply drag and drop their images and charts between all of the programs included in Pro Presentations. Visit them online at www.harvard-graphics.com.

FindSounds.com: This is a search engine for locating sound files on the Internet. Search by keyword or by category. Salespeople and others delivering slide show presentations may find this site especially useful for locating sounds. Visit them online at www.FindSounds.com.

Entrepreneur: This site offers many articles dealing with creating sales presentations and the effective use of promotional materials. Visit them online at www.entrepreneur.com.

Presentations.com: This magazine site offers articles and ideas to anyone who gives presentations in group situations, including sales professionals. But getting the most from the site requires using the search feature since links to back articles are not obvious. It is best to use Advance Search and adjust the date option. The site also has a Survey of Presentation Methods (in PDF format) that offers an interesting look at the techniques and technologies commonly employed to give presentations. Visit them online at www.presentations.com.

TagTeam.com: This is a service that allows sales and marketing departments to upload selling aids and other promotional materials that anyone can access. It is best for small businesses that cannot afford their own Intranet or Extranet sites. Visit them online at www.tagteam.com.

to the products being sold and also show how they are directly connected to the buyer's target market.

The in-depth method allows for a more polished presentation, which often succeeds in making an excellent impression on clients. However, it is also more time-consuming because it requires that salespeople gather and analyze facts that will help motivate a sales transaction. It is also more expensive to plan and carry out than the other methods, since it often requires high-end equipment, laptop computers, and digital projectors. Therefore, it is usually reserved only for major presentations to larger customers.

The Consultative Presentation

Within the consultative sales presentation framework, the salesperson acts as an adviser and possesses the knowledge and ability to customize the presentation to address and solve the specific problems with which the customer is faced. This type of presentation requires the seller to conduct a great deal of research into the buyer's business, products, and market.

In this method, the salesperson is on the same side of the fence as the buyer, and the presentation deals with providing opportunities for the buyer. The seller takes on a partnership role and shows involvement in finding opportunities and solving problems for the buyer. The salesperson should also have the knowledge and ability to implement these solutions. The consultative presentation is not one that is directed at an immediate order—instead, it aims at building a relationship and taking a serious interest in helping the buyer expand his or her business.

To take on this role successfully, the salesperson must be well versed. The seller is not viewed as someone who wants to make a sale but one who will ride out a problem even if it means not getting the sale at that time. It's the act of giving advice without looking for immediate gains. Sometimes it involves doing a task and not receiving acknowledgment or immediate remuneration. It is the present and future of the selling profession. The business environment is currently in the relationship stage—buyers need partners, not hotshot sellers. This type of selling is not for every customer; customers who are interested only in short-term gains or price concessions are not good candidates since they are interested in what they can get today and care less about tomorrow.

Planning for the Presentation

Planning for your meeting begins well ahead of the actual appointment, with what we call the *pre-approach*. The pre-approach consists of the collection of information vital to the process of the presentation. Information about the needs of the company as well as the buyer (decision maker) provides sellers with a distinct advantage during the presentation because they will be able to ask and answer questions that will establish a better rapport with the clients.

Successful salespeople spend time researching their prospective customers and their companies. Getting to know the buyer's personality and market reputation is also vital to this communication process. Is the buyer a people person or motivated by facts and figures? Is he or she friendly or strictly business? Introverted or extroverted? While all this may seem like issues for a psychologist to analyze, it falls into the category of understanding people to better relate to them. Empathy and research is what makes the communication process work.

The salesperson can obtain such clues to the client's character by asking vendors or business associates within the industry who already know the client. The fashion industry is tightly-knit where everybody knows everybody, so often the salesperson is able to get some feedback. But if the pre-approach yields no good information, salespeople should be doubly attentive during the first five minutes of the presentation so they can pick up any information that will make the presentation more personalized.

Armed with as much facts as possible from the pre-approach, it is time for the presentation. If the salesperson has to wait, he or she should review the presentation plan one last time and act busy. Draft a to-do list, indicating your plans and goals regarding this presentation. Use your laptop or PDA to fine-tune and review your presentation. You will get a lot done this way, and you will feel you have accomplished something positive during your wait. More important, salespeople who are waiting for customers should start brief conversations with receptionists or assistants informing them quickly about their products. Often, receptionists or assistants can provide salespeople with invaluable tips on how to approach a client. Listen to what they say and utilize any information they give you to make the presentation more personalized. Don't over-wait. Salespeople should wait no longer than fifteen to twenty minutes before leaving; a buyer will respect that salespeople have other people to see.

Very often a successful sales presentation depends on how well a salesperson hits it off with a customer. A good first impression is vital, and therefore, appearance and poise should be well-developed sales tools. Salespeople should radiate confidence and address the prospect by name frequently. If this is the first time a salesperson is meeting the buyer face-to-face, he or she should use the first few moments of the appointment to get to know the prospect. Find out as much about him or her as possible, and show an interest in the prospect and the prospect's company. The more salespeople know about clients, the more possible it will be to communicate the benefits of their products.

Salespeople should focus their attention on the buyer's problems and how the merchandise they sell can help solve the problems and boost profits. They should respect the buyer's time and avoid small talk. They should always try to end their presentations with some form of commitment from the buyer (e.g., they will place the order, will review your presentation with their superiors, get back to you shortly, or visit your showroom to see more of your merchandise).

Advance planning helps to ensure that sales presentations will be well directed and orderly and may also increase order volumes, especially as salespeople plan out strategies for getting customers to go from ordering small quantities to ordering more substantial quantities on a recurring basis.

Planning also gives salespeople an advantage over salespeople who do not plan what they will say to their customers. By taking the time to plan ahead, salespeople avoid saying something that will get them off the right track, waste their customers' time, and miss out on opportunities for getting new business.

No Can Mean Yes

One of the main challenges that salespeople face is when a potential client says "No." To a seasoned seller, a "No" response doesn't necessarily mean that the buyer is not willing to buy. Rather, it often means that something about the product—perhaps the manner in which the salesperson presented it—is causing the buyer to hesitate.

Even experienced buyers find it difficult to make decisions sometimes. Anything that seems ambiguous to a buyer may lead that buyer to play it safe and say "No." After all, no one likes to make hasty decisions. Sometimes, buyers want to find out if the seller's information is worthy or to challenge the seller.

The following is a list of what buyers may mean when they say "No" during sales presentations:

+ "I need more information."
+ "You haven't given me a good enough reason as to why I should buy."
+ "You haven't solved my problem(s)."
+ "You haven't shown me the benefit(s)."
+ "Your presentation has not addressed the perceived value I am looking for."

Salespeople must delve into the verbal dynamics involved in sales presentations so they can learn when buyers really mean "No" and when they really mean "yes." How can the salesperson tell if the buyer is hinting that they need more information or are simply not interested? It is very important that salespeople do not get disheartened when they hear the dreaded "No;" instead, they must listen carefully to what follows after it. If the client gives explanations for why they do not want to buy, then it is typically safe to assume that the buyer is giving the seller a chance to address those **objections**. Otherwise, the buyer wouldn't bother explaining his or her decision. For example, suppose the client says the product's delivery time is too late. In essence, he or she is telling the salesperson that if the product were delivered faster, he or she would consider buying the product. The client is giving the seller the opportunity to arrange quicker turnarounds and make the sale.

If clients say boldly that they are not interested in the product or have no need for it, then, in most cases, the "no" probably just means "no." This is a clear indication of a buyer's polite desire to end the sales presentation. Carrying on with more information about the product will usually irritate the client and could possibly even sour the entire buyer-seller relationship. In this scenario, the salesperson should ask if they can meet at a future time when new styles/items will be available. If the response is still "no," then the only thing the salesperson can do is to leave but keep the door open for another day. The salesperson should indicate that he or she appreciated the buyer taking the time to meet and end with a good impression. Keep in mind that you may have to see that buyer again, so a polite good-bye is always in order.

Relationship-based selling has made a strong comeback (it really never left us), but it is returning with different ground rules. First, the buyer and seller should always have the same objectives. Second, their business relationship should be predicated on a long-term timeframe in which both sides trust and respect each other. Third, buyers will always be sure to voice any objections, and sellers must be honest, accurate, and never adversarial. Finally, salespeople should never resort to tricky techniques meant to get buyers to make purchases. Buyers today are more knowledgeable than their predecessors; do not expect them to fall for antiquated pressure techniques. Salespeople should focus on how their clients buy, why they buy, what motivates them, and whether a product satisfies their needs. Sellers should always be prepared to confidently and honestly address objections.

Addressing Objections

The first step in answering objections properly is to refrain from taking them personally or being defensive. Armed with the understanding that objections actually move the sales presentation forward as discussed in the previous section, successful salespeople never let objections bother

---

RW Dictionary

Objection The reason a client offers for not buying a product. Objections are questions or statements that indicate the concerns buyers have about a product or sales presentation. Buyers expect to have their objections addressed and resolved before they consider buying.

them. They accept that objections are an integral part of selling and regard the need to address them as one of the job's many challenges. They strive to turn even the most difficult "no" into a "yes."

Knowing what buyers are looking for and how they go about making their final buying decisions is vital to the outcome of a successful presentation. Salespeople should encourage buyers to voice objections during presentations so they have better ideas of what buyers want and so they can address objections while they have buyers in positions to buy. This opportunity allows salespeople to give answers that can inspire confidence in buyers.

Assume that a salesperson is in the middle of presenting a line of clothing, and the buyer objects about the high prices. The best response is not to fight the buyer's objection, but to craft a smart and honest response. Consider the following possibility and note how it addresses the buyer's objection by adding a positive spin: "Yes, it may seem too high at first, but not if you take into consideration our fashion styles, faster deliver turn-arounds, guaranteed quality, and personal service. Our merchandise has consumer acceptance and is not out of the price range for your target market. In addition, our product includes all the things that you have mentioned are important to your company. Considering all these factors, our prices equal value and that's what your consumer is looking for in today's marketplace. I would like also to give you a list of references from our customers to reassure you as to our reputation and track record." The salesperson here is still trying to get a sale but is not resorting to pressure tactics.

Why Ask Why?

Salespeople can effectively counter many buyer objections by using the "Why?" method. When buyers make objections that need clarification, the best approach can be simply to ask why. Oftentimes, a customer opens up and gives a thorough explanation, which gives the salesperson an inside scoop on his or her thinking process; the salesperson can use the information to tailor the presentation to the client and properly address his or her concerns.

In this situation, objections are used by the seller to encourage the client to open up and talk more freely. This can turn a negative sales situation into a potential "yes." When the buyer details the reasons why he or she does not want to buy, it sets up a dialogue for understanding what is preventing the buyer from buying. In a sense, the objection is the buyer voicing what bothers him or her about the product. Only once the client has voiced his or her doubts and the salesperson fully understands them will the seller be able to address these concerns.

For example, say a salesperson is giving a presentation and stops to ask

---

RW Principle

Objections are an integral part of selling and help move sales presentations forward. Salespeople should welcome objections so they can better understand and address the issues that may potentially prevent a buyer from making a purchase.

the buyer if he or she likes the colors. If the buyer replies "no," the salesperson should immediately ask why. Most likely, the buyer will give a reason that includes the color group he or she prefers. A good salesperson can confirm whether the preferred color group is available; even if the colors are not available, at least the salesperson has discovered what the buyer is looking for and can revise the next sales presentation to include the colors the client prefers.

Your Honor, I Object!

The trained salesperson recognizes certain negative reactions by buyers and learns how to handle these routinely and effectively. Sometimes a buyer's objections are unfounded. They may be rooted in discrimination or arise from a fear of making decisions. Salespeople can overcome these factors by having confidence in themselves and developing harmonious working relationships with their customers.

However, there are some standard objections that can be expected. For example, buyers may say they need more information about the salesperson's company. The salesperson should set forth a strong statement regarding the benefits of the product line he or she sells and how it fulfills the customer's needs. This sort of objection indicates a buyer's interest in a product and is the buyer's way of asking for more details. Buyers may resist making a purchase because they don't want to change suppliers. In such cases, salespeople should try to convince the buyer that the value of the new product warrants change. Anticipating objections and answering them correctly starts the salesperson on the road to a successful presentation. Certain objections are frequently voiced at most presentations. Knowing this, a seller should aim to address these issues before they are mentioned by the buyer and do so with a positive spin. This will counteract a situation where the seller would have had to defend his position on things like pricing. Instead, the seller should first mention the advantages of their company's prices and include them as part of the presentation. The salesperson could mention the anticipated price objection by saying something like "In today's competitive market, we have found that customers are interested in products that provide value, which is the amount of support that we deliver to our customers. Our product provides benefits that are necessary in these competitive days. We offer deliveries that are on time, quality control, and customer service. Most importantly, our products sell, and our resellers make healthy profits as a result." Other common objections that salespeople should be aware of are as follows:

+ price objections—prices are too high or low.
+ product objections—sometimes they object to a product's details, but other times they object to the entire product concept.

+ company objections—the buyer is not comfortable doing business with the company the salesperson represents.
+ personal objections—the buyer objects to making a decision. (The salesperson should be alert to other underlying reasons.)
+ deadline objections—the buyer thinks the delivery dates are too late or too early.

Salespeople should keep their sales presentations flexible enough that they can alter it, so they can properly address any objections a buyer makes. A good idea is to be ready with standard responses to as many common objections as possible so that you are not put on the spot and exude confidence and product knowledge.

Having a positive mental attitude will help the salesperson successfully address unnecessary buyer objections. In all instances, the salesperson should refrain from arguing with the buyer and remain open to objections and other forms of buyer participation. The salesperson shouldn't be so strong-willed as to rule out the buyer's complaint, which very often may provide useful information in altering the product line or the company's marketing direction.

The best salespeople present themselves as helpers and advisers to their customers, rather than as adversaries. Understanding the customer's objections and offering truthful responses can be the best sales tool salespeople have at their disposal.

Closing the Sale

Closing the sale refers to the act of successfully completing a transaction and getting the order. However, the term is a misnomer according to Thomas J. Schwenk, principal owner of Jordon Thomas & Associates. Schwenk says that after you receive the order, it really opens the relationship and is the start of future opportunities.

Schwenk explains the term is misleading because salespeople may believe that their jobs are done once the sale is closed. He points out that after closing the sale, sellers who neglect to follow through and continue to build on existing business relationships will receive far less repeat orders in the future. Closing the sale is a misnomer —you are closing a transaction but in fact opening up a relationship. At the close of every sales transaction, the buyer should exhibit confidence in making the purchase and leave in a positive state of mind.

Many salespeople have difficulty closing, and some are tempted to substitute proper closing methods with shoddy techniques; however, the long-term results will invariably be extremely poor. Salespeople must never use tricks to secure a closing. Any knowledgeable buyer can recognize this form of manipulation, resulting in an abrupt end to what could have been an otherwise successful sales presentation.

The Signal to Close

Most salespeople assume that closing the sale is performed at the end of the sales presentation—once they have delivered the full speech, showed every feature of the product, and presented every benefit. This is simply not true! The best time to close the sale is when the message is understood by the buyer and he or she demonstrates a need for the product. This can happen at any time during the presentation. So, the question is—how do you figure out when the the buyer realizes he or she is going to buy?

The ability to read people is paramount for successful sales transactions, and salespeople can improve this ability by developing strong business relationships. During a sales presentation, a buyer constantly sends out buying signals. For example, a simple nod of approval by the buyer when the salesperson makes a statement or demonstrates a particular design feature may indicate the buyer is interested or has accepted the product's value. A buyer may even come right out and say he or she likes a particular product or one of the product's features. If the buyer interrupts with such praise, a salesperson should take the opportunity to ask for the order right then and there—and do so by stating what the delivery date is and writing up the order. If the buyer is ready, then you've just saved the buyer's time and spared yourself going through the entire presentation. If the buyer is not ready to make the commitment, then the seller should proceed with the presentation.

Just as buyers may nod approvals, they can also send negative signals by shaking their heads or frowning. The salesperson should pay close attention to these signals and question the buyer's reaction in a tactful (not defensive) manner. This, too, can provide the salesperson with an indication of where the presentation is heading. Understanding body language is extremely important and can open the door to closing the sale.

Many salespeople mistakenly wait for buyers to make the first move in closing the sale. While this book strongly discourages using pressure techniques, it does encourage salespeople to be assertive and proactive about closing a sale. Pressure selling is the biggest mistake in the sales transaction. If the buyer feels pressured, he or she will most likely react defensibly, with the seller invariably being the loser.

RW Principle

Asking for the order is not a one-time event. If the buyer is not ready, they will tell you. Try to figure out their objections and answer them, and then ask for the close again later. However, that doesn't mean one can abuse it—asking for the close every other minute will likely ruin the presentation.

Ask for the Signature

Salespeople close sales by asking for the orders. Every successful salesperson develops his or her own style for closing a sale; usually the manner in which a salesperson closes a sale fits his or her personality. However, even with that guideline, the actual method each salesperson uses to close typically varies from sale to sale, depending on the specific client he or she is dealing with, the chemistry between the salesperson and buyer, and the circumstances of the sales presentation. In other words, each closing transaction has its own rules and requires paying attention to the dynamics involved in that specific presentation.

The closing procedure begins when the buyer agrees to take action regarding the salesperson's product. This usually will happen when the salesperson asks for the order. The best approach is to assume that the sale is made. For this to work, you must be instinctively certain that the client has no other qualms or questions. Salespeople should always be prepared to take down orders. They should have a pen and order sheet or their laptops cued up at all times so they can take down pertinent information, such as quantity (i.e., units or dozens) or for fabric yardage, colors, shipping preferences, payment terms, and deadlines. When asking for the order, salespeople should consider giving the buyer a specific choice when taking down orders—for example, a salesperson may ask a buyer whether the buyer prefers to use his or her own order form rather than the salesperson's.

When the paperwork is finished, the sales transaction is complete. Salespeople should remind buyers of the benefits they will receive and thank them for the order.

Once the order has been taken, make sure the customer understands its benefits. Build a series of acceptances, or "yes" answers, and obtain affirmative decisions on minor points like size breakdowns, packing, hangers, shipping directions, and so on. Doing this will eliminate future problems of communication and misunderstandings.

When the order form is completed and signed by the client, the sales transaction is complete. Thank the buyer for placing the order and then stop talking about the product or order unless the client has a question. Once the signature ink is dry, the salesperson should not take up much more of the buyer's time, but instead should gather his or her notes, papers, and visual aids; tell the client when the seller will call next; and bid the client good-bye.

Special-Situation Methods

There are a couple of standard closing methods that salespeople should use only in special situations to expedite the closing of a sale. However, these closings should only be used when absolutely necessary. Misrepresentation is likely to be discovered and will not only ruin the sale but also destroy a profitable business relationship before it even has a chance to start. The two closing methods are as follows:

+ Future event—This method informs the buyer that an event in the near future could affect prices or availability. The following is a good example of what a salesperson would say when dealing with a future event that may truly affect a closing: "With the escalating costs of fuel and energy, prices will increase in the very near future. Buying now guarantees the existing prices upon delivery."

+ Standing room only (SRO)—This method informs the buyer that there is strong demand for a product so a seller may run out of inventory in the near future. The salesperson should use newspaper articles and other forms of documentation to establish credibility. An example of what a salesperson may say in this type of closing situation is as follows: "There are mounting shortages of this type of yarn, and if you don't buy now, I can't promise you'll be able to order it at a later date."

Mastering these basic sales methods and adding your own personal touch will put you on the road to a rewarding career in apparel and textile sales.

Chapter Summary

+ The sales presentation is one of the most exciting parts of selling because salespeople get to meet their clients face-to-face, improve business relationships, and get new sales orders.

+ The pre-approach is the stage where salespeople plan ahead for meetings by collecting information about prospective clients and companies, assessing their needs, and ascertaining who the decision makers are.

+ Maintaining a positive mental attitude (PMA) is essential to success in sales and can make or break any sales presentation. Psychologically speaking, PMA is an internal coping mechanism that reinforces sellers as they face daily challenges and disappointments in the marketplace.

+ In the highly visual fields of fashion and interior design, showing product samples is extremely important to a successful sales presentation.

+ There are four different presentation methods—memorized, priority, in-depth, and consultative. Each presentation method employs a different strategy and is geared toward a specific sales situation.

+ The seasoned seller doesn't balk at a buyer's "No" response. He or she understands it often means that something about the product presented, or the way it has not been presented, is causing the buyer to hesitate; once a salesperson addresses and resolves any buyer concerns, a sale may be possible.

+ Objections are an integral part of selling and help move the sales presentation forward. Salespeople should welcome objections as these allow them to understand and address the issues that prevent the buyer from making a purchase.

+ When an objection is made that needs to be further clarified, the best approach can be simply to ask why. Many times, customers end up letting the salesperson in on their thinking processes.

+ Closing the sale means asking the client to buy and taking the order, thus completing the sales transaction. It is the most delicate part of the presentation. The best time to close the sale is when buyers understand the message and realize they need the product and should buy it. This can happen at any time during the presentation.

RW CASE STUDY

Peter V. Handal provides us with advice and tips through the courtesy of Dale Carnegie Training. He is president and CEO of Dale Carnegie & Associates, one of the largest training companies in the world with two hundred offices in more than sixty-five countries. Handal is also a former CEO of a children's apparel and accessories company marketed under the Just 4 Kids brand. Handal is a widely recognized expert on workplace and executive management issues. He is also a director of the American Association of Exporters and Importers (AAEI) and has held several positions within the AAEI, including chairman from 1985 to 1987. In 1988, Mr. Handal was appointed by the Secretary of Commerce and the United States Trade Representative to the Industry Sector Advisory Committee for Wholesaling and Retailing and was chairman from 1994 to 1996. He continues to serve on the committee.

Many salespeople experience anxiety when making their sales presentations. What methods do you employ to relieve this anxiety?

+ Know as much as you can about your customers: their challenges, their products, and their competition.

+ See the world from the buyer's point of view.

+ Provide value on every sales call.
+ Be an expert, the kind of person [who] clients will call for advice, insights, information, and help, even if it is not directly related to your product.
+ Know what your product does to help current clients, especially specific impact your current clients achieved as a result of doing business with you.
+ Have evidence of return on investment you have achieved for your clients.
+ Don't think of sales "presentations"—this is an interview.
+ Read the book *How to Stop Worrying and Start Living* by Dale Carnegie. It contains thirty techniques on how to deal with stress.

What steps can be used to organize a sales presentation?

+ Plan strategically. This includes research into the company, key decision makers, their market, their challenges, [and so on].
+ Build rapport. In less than two minutes, sell yourself and your company. Don't sell the product yet. Begin the presentation in a creative way that shows you have some understanding of their business.
+ Generate interest. Ask questions to determine key buyer needs and issues so you can sell based on needs, not products. Help buyers see a gap between where they are now and where they could be.
+ Provide solutions. Don't just sell a product. Sell value. Customize your presentation and communicate unique solutions for each buyer. Don't talk about user-related benefits to an executive or financial buyer who may never see or touch the product.
+ Appeal to motives. Reduce procrastination and create a sense of urgency by helping [buyers] see how they will benefit when they have made the change to your solution. Communicate the costs they are facing now in lost money, time, quality, and opportunity. Then, paint a clear picture of their new reality, using your solution.
+ Gain commitment. Make the decision process easy for the buyer.
+ Follow-through. There is very little correlation between customer satisfaction and customer loyalty. To keep customers, we need to constantly anticipate and exceed their expectations. Give added value at every opportunity. Interview your existing clients and determine creative ways to help them be more successful.

Many salespeople are stereotyped as product-pushers. How do you counteract this?

Be a consultant, not a salesperson. Salespeople who act as order takers are quickly being replaced by call centers and Web sites. The salesperson of the future will succeed by adding value to the business relationship, not by just communicating value of the product. We can do two things: solve problems or create opportunities. Help buyers see possibilities they did not imagine: new markets, new territories, [and] new clients. Introduce buyers to other influential people in your network. Be an expert [who] people come to for help.

Can you discuss some ways to answer objections?

Objections are not the same as "nos." They often are requests for more information. Objections are welcomed because without them we might be "out the door."

The first advice I'd give is to make sure we have an attitude that welcomes objections as opportunities to present different perspectives. Then we must be on the client's side in handling it. We must avoid an argument or even the appearance of disagreement in presenting a different viewpoint on whatever the objection is. Handling the person well is more important to handling the objection. As Dale Carnegie says, "Try honestly to see things from the other person's point of view." This will make it easier to be their advocate in overcoming anything that could be a stumbling block to the client[s] getting successful solution[s] to their issues.

During the presentation, when is it a proper time to close a sale?

[Phrases such as] "being closed" is not language that is friendly to buyers. Rather than closing, let's focus on gaining commitments and giving commitments. The proper time to ask for a commitment is when the buyer is ready. We can help them be ready by asking for smaller commitments at every step in the sales process. Salespeople should be asking for commitments throughout the sales process. For example, being introduced to other decision makers, setting the next meeting date, giving us additional information so we can help them, and so on. If the only commitment we ask for is a signed order, it will be more difficult for the buyer. Ask test questions throughout the process to assess the interest level of the buyer. If you get a warm response, ask a slightly more direct question. Look for buying and warning signals, then ask more test questions. Finally, have the confidence to ask directly for a decision. Also, every sales call should contain a commitment from the salesperson to the buyer. This is one way we can add value.

Can you briefly discuss Dale Carnegie's techniques for influencing people?

Mr. Carnegie was always focused upon a *win-win* environment that genuinely showed respect for people. Carnegie felt that without this as a value, you are just trying to manipulate people for your own ends. His thirty different principles for dealing with people start with the focus of building trust and the relationship. He spoke of ways to influence others—with the win-win approach. He talked about how to deal with difficult or negative people in challenging situations with more consistent, positive outcomes for all.

These weren't just *his* principles—they were given to him from some of the most famous and successful people of his day and put into his book *How to Win Friends and Influence People*—a must read for any salesperson.

Questions to Consider

1. What does Handal mean when he says a salesperson should aim to "be a consultant, not a salesperson"?
2. Do you agree with Handal that there is very little correlation between customer satisfaction and customer loyalty? Why?
3. How can a salesperson sell value in addition to the product? Give an example.
4. How can a salesperson know when to close the sale according to Handal?

RW EXERCISES

1. Think of a time you displayed PMA during a negative circumstance. Describe what occurred and note the effects your positive attitude had on the situation.
2. Pair up with another student so one of you acts as the salesperson and the other acts as the buyer, either in a retail or B2B setting. First, the seller should display a negative attitude during the sales presentation. Second, the seller should display a positive, enthusiastic approach. Write down how each approach affected the process and outcome of the presentation. Switch roles for a different perspective, and note the new responses.
3. Why is showing the product essential to a successful sales presentation? Give personal examples.
4. Create a fictitious line of clothing, with your name as the designer brand. Briefly analyze the target market and price range. Formulate the guidelines, scripts, and visual aids for each of the four presentation methods as they would apply to your product.
5. Pair up with another student so one of you acts as the salesperson and the other acts the buyer, either in a retail or B2B setting. Act out several short sales presentations where the buyer gives different

buying signals. The seller should interpret these signals and ask for the order in an appropriate manner. Take notes on how each scenario went. Switch roles for a different perspective, and note the new responses.

END NOTES

1.   Sherman, Jerry and Eric Hertz. *Woman Power in Textile & Apparel Sales.* New York: Fairchild Publications, 1979.

CHAPTER 08

Objectives

- ✦ See how forming personal relationships and business partnerships with buyers is the backbone to selling.
- ✦ Understand why a salesperson's job really starts once the sale is completed.
- ✦ Learn how to properly follow-up on a sales order, and review ways to deal with dissatisfied customers.
- ✦ Recognize the vital need to confront potential or existing issues quickly and honestly, and find out how to best inform clients about problems.
- ✦ Acknowledge a salesperson's role as a problem solver, and comprehend how that role strengthens the buyer-seller relationship.
- ✦ Explore the various methods that salespeople use to keep themselves visible to their customers.
- ✦ Realize the importance of business ethics in sales and how violations can negatively affect a salesperson's long-term performance.

FOLLOW-THROUGH AND RELATIONSHIP DEVELOPMENT

Overview

Some sellers believe that once they make their first sales, they are done. This chapter shows why the relationship between a seller and buyer begins once that sale is done. This chapter reviews the steps that salespeople need to take to follow-up with their clients. We also discuss how a salesperson can capitalize on interactions with clients to further improve the business relationship. Finally, we stress the importance of adhering to business ethics and how ethical violations can damage not only a relationship with one client but also with other clients.

Introduction

Theodore Levitt is the former chairman of the marketing area at the Harvard Business School and former editor of *Harvard Business Review*. He says, "The relationship between seller [and] buyer seldom ends when a sale is made. The relationship intensifies after the sale is made."[1] He adds, "The sale starts a courtship to the point where a business marriage begins, and the quality of this marriage determines whether there will be continued or an expanded business relationship, or troubles and divorce; how well the marriage is depends on how well the relationship is managed by the seller."

Once completing a sale and getting a buyer's signature on the order form, the seller should immediately put through the order to production and plan his or her follow-up strategy. To make a sale, a salesperson needs to establish a business relationship with the client based on trust; but once the client places an order, the salesperson must show that he or she continues to earn that trust. To maintain a positive relationship that will yield future sales, salespeople should routinely check up on orders, resolve any issues that come up, and keep buyers informed of their orders' progress. If a seller fails to take these steps, the chances of making future sales are seriously curtailed.

Ethics and honesty are integral to a relationship's development after a sale. If sellers are not honest with their buyers about problems as soon as they arise, then buyers will feel betrayed and probably refuse to do business with them again. Sellers who confront problems and keep their buyers informed, no matter how bad the news, will most likely become known throughout the industry for their ethical principles and will enjoy an enhanced client base that grows through word of mouth.

While it is important for salespeople to attract new clients, it is equally important for them to retain their existing clients. Active accounts purchase about 40 percent more than new accounts. Furthermore, it costs many times more to sell to prospective customers than it does to sell to existing customers. Salespeople must take one sale and shape it into a business relationship that yields multiple repeat sales.

"I do! I do!"

If Levitt's marriage metaphor is expanded on, then a sale can be likened to a wedding ceremony: The act of signing the order form symbolizes the vows. In essence, a buyer asks the seller whether a product will be delivered as promised, and by accepting the order, the seller answers, "I do." In turn, the seller asks the buyer whether a product will be paid for, and by signing the order form, the buyer answers, "I do."

Just as a pair of newlyweds works hard to begin their life together on the right track, a buyer and seller work hard to create a healthy and mutually beneficial business relationship. In a business relationship, the buyer and seller skip the honeymoon phase and dive directly into the marriage phase; the buyer prepares for a new product or line while the seller places the order so that the production department can start manufacturing it.

The events that follow often determine whether the "marriage" will be short-lived and end once the product is delivered or whether it lasts for years of repeat business. If a salesperson simply places an order with production, moves onto the next prospect, and never calls on the buyer again, the business relationship ends when the sale is made. Such salespeople reason that production does not concern them and whether their clients are happy depends on the way the production and delivery departments handle matters; while this theory is understandable, the circumstances in the real world dictate otherwise. In this case, chances are the buyer will also never call on the seller, and the business "marriage" would dissolve following the completion of the initial sale.

However, salespeople who remain involved in the fulfillment of the order can use this phase as a pretext for calling on the client to not only keep clients up-to-date on their orders' statuses and make sure they are happy but also to develop their relationships. As we discussed in chapters 3 and 4, developing the business relationship with the client is the backbone to selling success and is vital not only in generating repeat orders but also in creating new business through referrals.

The Right Side of the Fence

The buyer-seller relationship has evolved over time. Years ago, buyers and seller sat on opposite sides of the fence, but today buyers and sellers work together for common goals. Sellers recognize that they need buyers to stay in business, so they have someone to whom they can sell their merchandise; therefore, sellers need to take an active role in helping buyers succeed. In addition, when sellers team up with buyers to identify a new product line that better suits the buyers' needs, sellers improve their own bottom lines. To maintain good relationships, the seller must be willing to give and receive.

Sellers must understand what their buyers want before they even start relationships with them. Buyers want their sellers to be team members and have a high degree of ethics and integrity. They want to feel comfortable and trust that sellers will actually do what they promise. A relationship cannot progress unless the seller is able to be a problem solver, provide the buyer with excellent customer service, and satisfy the buyer's perceived value. The seller can ensure a lasting relationship by making sure each and every transaction goes as smoothly as possible. Sometimes the best times for sellers to get buyers to trust them is when problems come up because buyers get to see for themselves if and how sellers solve problems. Professional salespeople must always be proactive to solve problems buyers may have with their products, such as late deliveries and merchandise that is different from what buyers expect.

Your Job Starts When the Sale Ends

In many ways, a salesperson's job begins in earnest once the buyer signs the order. This chapter stresses the importance of caring for customers after sales are closed because it is the best way to keep customers happy and coming back for additional orders. True, getting the client's signature on the dotted line is important; but a signature is virtually meaningless if the salesperson does not stay on top of the order, if the product is not delivered correctly, or if the customer is not happy with the delivery. Dissatisfied buyers not only refuse to do business with sellers, but also spread the word to other buyers and cost sellers business with new prospects. It is essential for the seller to be committed to a long-range view and work beyond the single sale and toward a successful business relationship with the buyer.

There are several basic, yet important, steps sellers should take when closing a sale: Follow-up with production departments on an order's progress, tackle delivery problems head-on, keep clients abreast of progress and be truthful about problems, find out how clients like or dislike the products they buy, and ask for another order. Sellers add to these steps or customize them; as long as doing so assists sellers in maintaining positive relationships with their buyers, it is acceptable.

Follow-Up Internally

Technically speaking, it is not a salesperson's job to produce an actual product. However, a salesperson's job certainly includes keeping track of the department responsible for this part of the process. It behooves the salesperson to stay on top of the production department, without micromanaging them, of course (the salesperson should have good relationships with all parties with whom he or she works to ensure positive communication). For example, a salesperson wants to address problems that come up with color as soon as possible—not wait until the product is ready for delivery to check if everything is okay, or worse, remain quiet as if a client won't notice and complain.

Although buyers may check directly with the customer service depart-

---

ment on their delivery statuses, they also count on their sales representatives to monitor their orders for them. After all, sellers are the ones who promise buyers that products will be delivered according to agreed-upon specifications by certain deadlines. Buyers have enough to worry about—issues with a company's production department shouldn't be one of them.

Successful salespeople, therefore, develop systems to keep track of orders as they progress through the production line and aim to discover and rectify potential problems before these turn into disasters. Some use computerized programs to keep track of orders, while others use a desk calendar or a pack of index cards. All are valid methods as long as they alert salespeople to important dates by which key phases of the production should be completed. Obviously, there is no need for a salesperson to follow-up on every part of the production sequence—but he or she should focus on the three or four major points along the line and determine the expected production time for each.

At times, it helps to work things out backward. For example, say an order for a new product line is to be delivered in one month, but the salesperson knows that shipping to the buyer takes four days, the packaging takes three days, and the assembly takes one week. The salesperson cannot just assume that all raw materials should be there and ready for assembly at least two weeks before the delivery date. If they aren't, then it is likely the product will not be delivered on time unless a drastic action is taken to remedy the situation. It is crucial, therefore, for salespeople to keep track of important production dates using whatever system is best for them and touch base with managers of the appropriate departments or sections to find out if things are going according to schedule.

Keep the Client Up-to-Date

Regardless of whether production of an order is on, ahead, or behind schedule, it is good business practice for salespeople to keep in touch with their buyers regarding progress around the most critical production dates. In effect, such practices achieve more than one objective since salespeople not only let their clients know the stage of production at which an order is but they also give salespeople the opportunity to show buyers they really care. It can be extremely beneficial for salespeople to follow this technique, particularly in the beginning stages of a relationship with a new client, where every action the salesperson takes or does not take can set the tone for the rest of the relationship.

Most important, perhaps, is the fact that each time a salesperson calls a client with progress reports, the client hears the salesperson's name and voice one more time. The more times a salesperson speaks with a client, the more likely that salesperson reinforces the idea that the client should go to him or her for future orders. It goes without saying that salespeople should contact their clients only when they have meaningful information to provide and not every half hour. It is vital that salespeople not abuse their "rights of access" to their clients. For example, clients might appreciate and even expect daily updates on urgent rush orders, but grow annoyed with daily updates on routine orders.

Tell the Truth

Salespeople must never lie to their clients. Salespeople who keep their clients informed of their orders, even when the information is bad news, gain their clients' respect and trust. If salespeople lie or keep quiet about something potentially wrong with an order, such as knowing that the deadline will be missed or the color is off, nine times out of ten the client will eventually find out about it and never buy from those salespeople again. Also, it is infinitely easier to tell the truth in all cases than it is to fabricate lies and then attempt to recall which lie was offered to which client. Telling the truth also makes good business sense. Salespeople have much to remember without having to worry about telling and keeping up a lie. When production- or delivery-related problems come up, salespeople should first consult with the appropriate people in their companies to try to find alternative solutions. Only when they discover that there is no resolution must the salesperson face up to the problem and inform the client as soon as possible.

Consult with the Client as to Consequences

Some buyers are not bothered in the least bit regarding delays while others who are under time constraints may be very upset. Salespeople must remain calm at all costs if their news of delays (or other problems) should cause clients to become highly agitated; salespeople should try to avoid taking sides. Instead, salespeople should remind their clients that they are calling to inform buyers about problems because they care. In this role, you are essentially walking a tight rope and you should speak with caution.

If a salesperson's company is clearly at fault for a delay in production, the salesperson should offer an apology or clear it with a manager to offer a discount on the order. As long as a salesperson has not promised delivery on an unrealistic due date, an order cancellation at this stage is not the salesperson's fault. It may behoove the salesperson to detail how he or she is going to fix the problem, as doing so will encourage that client to work with the honest salesperson again in the future.

Follow-Up After Delivery and Ask for Another Order

Soon after the product has been delivered to a client in good order, the seller should call to see if the client is satisfied. If the client seems unhappy, the salesperson should try to find out why over the phone or even make an appointment to see the client as soon as possible. It is better to confront problems early on while there is still a chance to rectify matters. If buyers are indeed satisfied, then salespeople can safely scratch the order off their pending lists and file away the paperwork. But they also get to remind clients of the good service they have provided, ask clients if they need to place orders for anything else, and set up appointments to discuss future orders.

Dealing with Dissatisfied Customers

Your buyer may become dissatisfied, with or without a reason, at any point after the close. Your job as a salesperson, and as a people's person, is to identify the problems, find out the reason behind the dissatisfaction, and come up with solutions. One of the best ways to accomplish this is to ask the customer why he or she is dissatisfied and listen carefully to what they have to say without interrupting. Don't assume you know why they are unhappy or jump to conclusions after they utter the first sentence.

Salespeople need to privately and objectively ascertain whether the client is upset about a mistake with the order or about a mistake the client made that he or she is now trying to resolve. Making this determination is possible by not only having a conversation with the dissatisfied customer but also by consulting with the production or delivery managers. If you have a delivery sheet signed by one of the buyer's employees on June 15 and the buyer is blaming you for delivering in July, whisk out a copy of the dated delivery sheet and show it to the buyer. If, in fact, a delivery was late, then clearly the client has a sound basis for being upset. Depending on the company's policy, the salesperson may need to refer this to a manager to resolve such an issue. Or, the company may give the salesperson some license to offer a concession and take care of the upset client on the spot. In the latter case, it is up to the salesperson to ascertain what happened and decide on a remedy.

Issues may arise due to all sorts of organizational errors. If the quality of the product or item does not match the sample, then it is probably something the salesperson should bring up with the production supervisor. If the client is being called by accounting to get an invoice paid, but the client had already mailed it in weeks before, then the head of finance is who the salesperson wants to see. When talking to the production supervisor or the head of finance, the salesperson should keep in mind they do not know the buyer. Therefore, the salesperson needs to give them as much information about the client so they can make an intelligent decision about handling such issues. For example, if the client orders $1 million in stock each year, giving the client a 10 percent discount to compensate for a late delivery will be negligible compared to the loss of the account altogether.

Building a Common Ground

This book stresses the importance of salespeople and buyers sharing a common ground, and this chapter discusses how to go about getting there. Salespeople need to find things that are of interest to both their clients and them. Once sellers can identify one or more **points of interest** with their buyers, they can build a relationship that stands the test of time. All salespeople need to do is listen to and observe their clients.

When salespeople use routine business phone calls as opportunities to chat about things other than business, they may find that buyers share the same views or preferences on one or more topics. It is also vital that sellers observe their buyers and their buyers' offices and clothes for clues. For example, upon entering the buyer's office, the salesperson scans pictures, awards, and other memorabilia hanging on the wall or resting on the desk for this common interest. Suppose the seller notes a picture of the buyer playing golf, and the seller plays golf as well—right there is a point of interest. Make sure you talk about these points of interest at an appropriate time when the buyer is receptive to such conversation—talking about golf when the client is late for another meeting is hardly the way to create a relationship. Avoid discussing religion or politics at all costs since these are loaded subjects that can backfire.

By letting buyers know the sellers share their interests and by talking about these topics further, sellers can begin to build relationships with the clients that are based on more than just business transactions. One caveat is that this can't be faked. If a seller pretends to like what the buyer likes, it will end in disaster because eventually the buyer will somehow find out. If a buyer invites a salesperson to play a round of golf and that salesperson hates golf, he or she should politely refuse and suggest a round of tennis or some other activity they both may enjoy instead. As discussed extensively in chapter 7, salespeople should tow a delicate line when it comes to relationships and how personal they become—it is true that things need to get a bit more personal for business relationships to develop, but salespeople don't want to become entangled in personal problems such as divorce or legal issues. Although many sellers will tell you that the social environment plays the most important part in achieving their sales goals, it can be dangerous to mix the two if the seller is not cautious. Actually, the seller must be cautious in deciding where the relationship is going. Keeping the relationship on a business level means there is less of a chance for the relationship to diminish due to personal issues. We all know that social relationships may often spur personal problems. These in turn can erode the objective perspective that both the seller and buyer must maintain.

This is not to say that the seller cannot ever go to lunch with the buyer or invite the buyer to a barbecue. The occasional social interaction can be quite helpful in cementing a strong business relationship. It is when the business relationship becomes too personal that we often find trouble brewing. While it is mostly true that empathy can trigger the start of a relationship, it cannot be the only basis for a long lasting buyer/seller relationship. Performance, satisfying the buyer's needs, and solving problems are still the deciding factors as to whether a relationship will last.

Relationships are built on trust and personal experiences, but are tested by performance. For salespeople to develop a stronger business relationship with the customer, they must deliver what they promise within deadlines and in a professional manner. If a salesperson fails to provide a customer with the product, service, and follow-up, he or she will not be able to achieve a long-lasting relationship, no matter how much in common he or she has with the buyer. Let's say that Paul Arnold is a sales representative for a major textile company. Paul is a graduate of an Ivy League college, knows all the right social manners, and has a great personality. When Paul starts his presentation, he impresses buyers with the eloquence in which he communicates his message. He shows charisma and makes an instant positive impression, but he lacks an ability to make judgments and fulfill his promises. As a result, he promises to fulfill orders he cannot possibly deliver and loses his clients to the competition as a result. Even with the gift of public speaking, unless salespeople are able to deliver on their promises, they will never be able to develop solid business relationships with their buyers. Salespeople must keep focused on their customers' objectives and make it their paramount priority to meet these objectives.

What's Your Problem?

In chapter 3, need is defined as a problem that customers wish to solve or something they feel they should have. In other words, a buyer's problems and needs are closely related. When people think of the word "problem," they mostly imagine a negative connotation. However, the successful salesperson views problems differently from most people. For a salesperson, every problem presents an opportunity that may

RW Concept

To the successful salesperson, problems are often welcome: Every problem presents an opportunity that if he or she can offer a solution for will result in a sale and a satisfied customer.

result in a sale and a satisfied customer, if the salesperson can manage to find a resolution. Salespeople who are good problem solvers make successful sales; the attitude of a problem solver is probably one of the most important characteristics of a successful salesperson. After all, sometimes a client may have a need for a product because it is the solution to a problem he or she has. Salespeople need to listen and ask the right questions to identify a client's problem and be able to recommend the right product.

Recall the RW Concept in Chapter 3 that denotes that need is "a problem the customer wishes to solve or something the customer feels they should have." In other words, the buyer's problems and needs are closely related. Traditionally, problems have had a negative connotation. For most of us, life is full of problems, and others' problems are the last thing we want to hear. That is not the case in selling—the seller should be genuinely curious to hear the buyer's problems. The key to being a problem solver and a successful seller is first and foremost learning to appreciate problems as opportunities and then keeping an open-mind attitude so that one can find a solution.

A buyer's problem may be as simple as "I want to add women's large-size sportswear to our stores" or as complex as "I'm trying to reach out to Hispanic women in their 30s." It behooves the seller to fully comprehend the nature of the buyer's problem and to help them solve it if their merchandise relates to these needs. In the first example, the buyer may want to satisfy the demand for larger-sized clothing and strengthen the women's department since they are getting many requests for this category, or in the second example, the area demographics are changing and they have noticed an increase in the Hispanic population. The salesperson hearing this would realize that the buyer is having a problem satisfying his or her own customers' needs and that the void in these categories is at the heart of this issue. As long as the seller solves the buyer's problems in this manner, the buyer will never even dream of talking to the competition.

In Case You Forgot

Ideally, salespeople keep in touch with their buyers and their office staff on a routine basis and should do so either in person or over the phone; however, at times, it is wise for salespeople to send greeting cards. These written communications, especially birthday or anniversary cards, can show that a salesperson cares enough about a client and help cement a business relationship. However, simply sending the *Thank Yous* and *Reminders* is meaningless unless it is followed up by personal face-to-face contact. Some salespeople spend a disproportionate amount of time corresponding when they should be spending it in direct contact with their customers. Many salespeople use written material as a substitute for doing their job—getting out there and meeting with the client in person is the true measure of being proactive. Salespeople should always maintain a delicate balance of sending correspondence to their clients and visiting them.

The practice of sending thank-you cards or reminders is a method used primarily in retail sales, as discussed in chapter 3. Salespeople who work on commission are the ones who mostly rely on sending thank-you cards. Most salaried personnel are not as concerned with this important aspect of doing consumer business. Reminders are always a vital element in the day-to-day business relationship.

In the real world of B2B selling, thank-you cards and other reminders are used occasionally, but it is more customary to verbally give thanks after an order is processed. Courtesy dictates that saying thank you and sending reminders are valid and integral parts of the relationship-building process. Still, in this modern age of computerized communication, written thanks and reminders always stand out.

Business Ethics

Salespeople can be smart, professional, show empathy, and know their products inside out, but if they do not possess a sense of business ethics, they are destined to fail. Business ethics provides sellers and buyers with the guidelines that protect and preserve the business relationship. As this text continues to stress throughout, trust is one of the basic ingredients of the business relationship.

Lying, deceiving, misrepresenting, and not telling the whole truth are all manifestations of ethical problems. When salespeople lack ethics, they are eventually exposed as frauds and the buyer-seller relationship is destroyed. Would you trust someone who lied to you in the past? Salespeople must always be ethical to successfully develop and maintain business relationships. They must ensure that their customers get what they were promised and find resolutions to any problems that arise. They must also avoid making promises they know they cannot fulfill.

Chapter Summary

+ A sale can be likened to a wedding ceremony, where the signing of an order form represents the marriage vows.
+ The buyer-seller relationship begins in earnest once a sale is made and processed, and the degree to which a seller is involved in the

post-sale follow-up can determine the business relationship's overall success.

+ Sellers recognize that they need to take active roles in helping buyers succeed because when buyers fail in business, sellers have no customers to whom to sell merchandise.

+ There are several basic steps the seller should take following the closing of a sale: Follow-up with production departments on an order's progress, tackle delivery problems head-on, keep clients abreast of progress and be truthful about problems, find out how clients like or dislike the products they buy, and ask for more orders.

+ When buyers are unsatisfied, salespeople must determine the cause of the dissatisfaction and resolve any problems to the best of their abilities so that the relationship can continue.

+ One of the things that can help maintain ongoing relationships is to find a common denominator or point of interest—things that are of interest to both the seller and buyer.

+ Every problem presents an opportunity for salespeople to offer solutions that may result in a sale and satisfied customer.

+ Birthday or anniversary cards and occasional written reminders can show how much salespeople care about their clients and can help cement positive business relationships.

+ Ethics plays a major role in a relationship's development after a sale is completed. Buyers inevitably discover unethical practices so it behooves salespeople to be honest and keep buyers informed of an order's progress, even when the news is not good.

RW CASE STUDY

Oscar Feldenkreis is the president and chief operating officer for Perry Ellis International. While reflecting on his twenty-plus years of experience in working with such major buyers as Kmart and Macy's, Oscar comments on the importance of building and strengthening relationships in the field of fashion sales.

What role has the concept of developing business relationships played in the success of Perry Ellis International?

I have always treated everyone with respect—from the secretary or receptionist to the assistant buyers and buyers and merchandise managers. When I went to call on stores, I would bring bagels and coffee to develop the feeling that they and I are on the same playing field. That's how I developed a great relationship with them. The assistant buyers became buyers, and buyers became divisional merchandise managers. As time progressed, the people I had met at the entry-level ranks became important decision makers and gave me the opportunity to grow with them because they trusted me. They trusted me because I wasn't an individual who looked to get an order right off the bat. Personally, I feel it's important in salesmanship to first understand what makes a person tick—when is their birthday? [When are] their children's birthdays and graduations? What are their favorite sports? I always try to invite their spouses to dinner, and in so doing, they [can] see me as real person.

I am not so interested in the order as much as I'm interested in building a relationship and trust. My forte is to build a foundation with people based on trust, and they will develop a level of confidence [that] will help build the business. I always try to look for a niche or an avenue to develop that relationship so that if I wanted to call them on Monday or Tuesday, I [have] a reason to call. You have to understand that not everyone whom I did business with wanted to develop such a relationship—some insisted on a strictly business relationship, and I always honored that stand. They were not open to a relationship as I described. It all comes down to understanding people—selling is really more psychological then some think. You have to know where they are coming from. I would spend time with the accounts to learn how they think, understand their business philosophy, and what they expect from vendors. It is crucial to understand their operation systems, being on the scene when they needed me, and learning the customers' end of the business is crucial.

In 1982, we started calling on Kmart. I would go overseas with the Kmart buyers in order to cater to their needs. When the buyers would place their orders, I would be right there with them, and then I would make sure they received the samples and merchandise they ordered from my resources overseas. As the business developed, I always treated other accounts such as Macy's, May's, and other major retailers in the same manner. I managed my relationship in the same format. As a result, in 2002, we received from one of my accounts the largest order in our company's history—for 1 million units. In 2003, we decided to go public; we were growing in leaps and bounds. My father always taught me that you cannot depend on one customer; you have to diversify. We were one of the very few that were able to sell to all channels of distribution—while we were selling Wal-Mart and Kmart, I was able to also sell Macy's and other traditional department stores, and at that time, no one was able to sell to these two different types of retailers.

How do you deal with delivery problems?

In today's day and age, delivery and execution is probably the single most important aspect of the relationship. Of course you need a good product as the basis of any relationship, but if you cannot deliver the product on time, what's the point? I strongly believe you must fulfill your commitments—I like to sleep at night and not worry about making the commitments. I am very proactive regarding making certain promised deliveries are indeed delivered on time. I was educated on the manufacturing end, and I understand where and how a product can be produced, the time factor in purchasing the raw materials, and manufacturing it into a product ready for delivery. I know the pitfalls and the pros and cons in the productive cycle. It's important to know where to produce the product using your knowledge and utilizing the proper resources. We deal with factories all over the world, so for example, if the order calls for a garment that required a bias cut [that] involves more manufacturing know-how, I would go to a country where they know how to produce this complex garment. Cost also enters into the equation, and I educated myself about where I can get a better product that is cost effective and will be delivered on schedule.

If something goes wrong with the order—the merchandise is not as ordered or not delivered on time—how do you go about discussing it with the customer?

Firstly, I always keep the customers abreast of what's happening with the product or order during the manufacturing cycles. And if there is a problem, I would definitely be proactive in getting involved—for example, suppose we determine the fabric has flaws, which is the biggest problem when it comes to quality assurance. We must notify the customer of this before it is delivered and offer a replacement delivery. We must give the customer an accurate delivery date. Because most of our products are produced overseas, we must know the delivery schedule for shipments from various countries overseas and the time it takes to deliver this merchandise to the [United States] by boat or air. If something goes wrong, we don't wait for the customer to inform us if we are able to see the problem first.

How do ethics play into the business relationship?

"Ethics equals performance." If you have consistently performed in the past, exhibited an ethical record, and proven that your dealings are honest and that you have not taken advantage of the customer, then you have nothing to worry about. But there is an expression called "bait and switch," where the seller shows the buyer Item X and actually produces something else that may appear similar but is not the same. We do not participate in anything of that nature. A while back, one of our customers wanted to buy silk shirts at a specific weight for the price. When I found out that we couldn't deliver the product at this price, I went back to the buyer and told them I could not take the order and that if they wanted that weight, it would be more expensive. Many companies will try [to] get away with it—we don't. What they see is what they get. It's better to be honest upfront and tell the buyer the truth because being dishonest will eventually catch up with the seller. It's a fact of life—tell it like it is!

What do you do with an unethical buyer? How do you deal with such people?

I do not deal with unethical people—customers or suppliers! I recently had a situation with someone we have been dealing with for twenty years where he began to take advantage of our relationship through unethical actions. So I cancelled an $8-million-dollar account. Firstly, getting out of this type of relationship shows power—in life, you have to stand for something. Secondly, if the water becomes muddy in dealing with someone—you have to make the decision whether to get out of it, otherwise the mud rubs off on you. We have an expression in the industry: "The first markdown is the best markdown." If someone goes against a pre-arranged agreement, you have to get out of this relationship because eventually the unethical behavior of not adhering to the original agreed situation will eventually lead to disaster. Once they break the rules, then it will be only a matter of time until the relationship will be broken, too.

How do you remind your accounts that you want their business?

I believe in visiting the accounts as often as possible in order to know how they are doing, [to] learn what makes that corporation tick, to see if there are any new happenings, and to generally be part of their business. It's a matter of studying the nature of their business and be there as much as you can. Some companies don't want their salespeople to travel in order to keep the expenses down, while some salespeople who pay their own expenses tend to cut down on visitations with the rise of gasoline prices and travel expenses. I am a proponent of having our salespeople travel to the customers as often as possible because it is important for the customers to know that we want to go to them rather than them always coming to us at a market week or at a trade show. Today, it's more important than ever to understand the trends in demographics. For example, look at the explosive growth of the Hispanic population within the U.S. population. This Hispanic growth is greatly influenced by Mexicans entering this country, not just South Americans. It is important for salespeople to understand this growth and how it will affect your specific customer. The more knowledgeable we are about this demographic trend and others, like the increased growth in the African American and Asian communities, the more likely it is to find it necessary to address changes in styles, colors, and sizes in order to satisfy these emerging consumer forces. As long as we are cognizant of these population changes, we will an advantage over a lot of our competitors. It is vital to know who is shopping in the different retail stores in the different locations and the consumer profiles for these stores. Salespeople have to put the pieces of the jigsaw consumer puzzle together to get a better picture of their customer's customer.

We talk about the relationship with customers as a partnership—is it really a partnership?

At the end of the day, the partnership between a seller and customer has a value, but the value is limited as to the true loyalty the partnership is all about. One must realize that the seller is only as good as the product and only as good as the day and year of your performance. Each year you have to start from zero. Today, only performance counts—many customers have a very short memory of what you did yesterday. It is imperative to understand that many retailers have gone out of business. Many manufacturers have only half the market [that] they had in the past. The retail climate is very competitive. In the past, we had more of a market, and today's dwindling market puts another twist on relationships. As I said earlier, "relationships are based on performance," and today it is more apparent than it was in the past. We have to understand the dynamics of today's marketplace and put relationships in the proper perceptive: In essence, we must understand the buyers' profile[s], understand their strategies, and get to know their business[es] better than they do! Knowing today's environment and conditions will give a company a competitive advantage.

Questions to Consider

1. How important is the staff in the buyer's office? Should a salesperson treat a secretary or a buyer's assistant the same as they would the buyer?
2. How can business relationships be augmented by learning about the buyer's family or personal tastes?
3. What are some of the ways to deal with delivery problems so that a business relationship does not suffer? Can you think of any others?
4. How important is ethics to business relationships according to Feldenkreis? Do you agree? Share your thoughts or personal experiences.

RW EXERCISES

1. Think of two times when you bought something from a salesperson. What were the terms? What did you and the seller agree to do as part of the sales contract? Did the salesperson deliver what he or she was supposed to? Did the salesperson's performance lead you to buy from him or her again?

2. Pair up with another student so one of you acts as the salesperson and the other acts as the buyer, either in retail or B2B, and assume you just closed a sale. First, the seller should not follow-up at all on the order and wait for the buyer to call him or her. Second, the seller should reenact the scene, this time calling the buyer with the order's progress. Write down how each approach affected the business relationship and the outcome of each approach. Switch roles for a different perspective, and note the new responses.

3. Imagine a situation where a seller has closed a sale and got the order. Go through each step and outline what the seller should do within this scenario to accomplish a smooth follow-up. Explain what, in your opinion, is the importance of each step.

4. Pair up with another student so one of you acts as the salesperson and the other acts as the buyer, either in retail or B2B, and assume you just closed a sale. The seller should go through each step of the follow-up sequence. Write down how each step affected the business relationship and whether it resulted in a second sale and why. Switch roles for a different perspective, and note the new responses.

5. Recall a time when you were not satisfied as a fashion customer, and analyze the problem. Was the product defective, or did you take issue with the salesperson? How did you react to the problem as a customer, and how did the salesperson deal with it?

6. Pair up with another student so one of you acts as the salesperson and the other acts the buyer, either in retail or B2B, and assume something went wrong with the order. The seller should listen carefully, identify the exact problem, and take steps to rectify it if possible. Write down how the seller's approach affected the business relationship and the outcome. Switch roles for a different perspective, and note the new responses.

7. Give two examples of how a seller can find a point of interest with a buyer, and note how you think this point of interest would affect the buyer-seller business relationship.

8. Think of two examples of a problem within the fashion industry that present an opportunity. Note the solutions a seller can offer to turn the opportunity into a sale.

9. Have you ever received correspondence from a fashion retailer or boutique? What was it about? How did it make you feel as their cus-

tomer? Did it lead to an eventual sale? Include your thoughts and comments.

10. Pair up with another student so one of you acts as the salesperson and the other acts as the buyer, either in retail or B2B. Through conversation, listening, and observation, the seller should identify a point of interest with the buyer and proceed to utilize it to cement the relationship. Write down how the seller's approach affected the relationship. Switch roles for a different perspective, and note the new responses.

11. Think of a time when a person lied to you. Detail the circumstances, what happened, and how it affected your relationship with the person. What do you think buyers would feel if a seller lied to them?

12. Pair up with another student so one of you acts as the salesperson and the other acts as the buyer, either in retail or B2B. Assume the seller got the order and is following up on it, but is omitting significant information from the conversation in hopes that the buyer won't find out about it. Write down how the seller's unethical behavior affects the buyer and the business relationship. Switch roles for a different perspective, and note the new responses.

END NOTES

1. Levitt, Theodore. "After the Sale Is Over." *Harvard Business Review*, 1983.

2. Harvard Business School Web site. Faculty & Research page. http://dor.hbs.edu/fi_redirect.jhtml?facInfo=bio&facEmId=tlevitt&loc=extn.

CHAPTER 09

MANAGING A SALES FORCE

Objectives

+ Understand the responsibilities, duties, and functions of sales managers.

+ Review the sales experience and managerial knowledge required from sales managers.

+ Examine the role sales managers play in recruiting salespeople and building cohesive and qualified sales teams.

+ Comprehend the vital need for planning in managing a sales force.

+ Explore problems managers are likely to encounter on the job and workable solutions to these issues.

+ See the reasons why implementing motivational programs can significantly improve overall productivity and morale.

Overview

Similar to the inability of drivers to manage traffic at an intersection where the stoplights aren't working and there are no police present, a sales force can't manage itself. A leader with the necessary knowledge, experience, authority, and motivation to set territories, establish goals, direct, and arbitrate conflicts keeps a sales force from becoming confused. The long-term success of any fashion company is dependent on a sales manager who is not only knowledgeable about properly managing and motivating a sales force, but also who earnestly applies his or her knowledge at every turn.

Introduction

Average sales forces are headed by national sales managers, territorial regional managers, or both, depending on their size. Owners of smaller companies typically act as sales managers. Sales managers are extremely important in the fashion industry because they are ultimately responsible for the performance of the sales staff and for the growth and success of the companies they represent.

Morale, productivity, and retention are all organizational factors that are crucial to balanced operations in and the sustained growth of a business. Whether these factors are present or not can be directly traced to the management style of a sales manager. Sales managers who know their duties and responsibilities and take effective steps to implement them are worth their weight in signed sales orders. The actions of sales managers directly impact the success rates of salespeople who report to them, but they also carry significant ripple effects that can make or break the very foundations of an entire company.

What are the responsibilities and duties of a sales manager that makes it such an important position? How does a sales manager go about accomplishing these duties and tasks? How does he or she manage a sales force? This chapter answers these questions and reviews the patterns of organizational behavior associated with the job.

The Sales Manager's To-Do List

The responsibilities, functions, and duties—or what we refer to as RFDs—of sales managers are many, but one of the primary ones involves recognizing problems and making decisions on how to best deal with them. For more than fifty years, Peter F. Drucker has been one of the leading experts on management and the responsibilities associated with it in the business arena; he has been called the father of modern management. Drucker is an author, a consultant, and a teacher, and his twenty-nine books have been published in many languages.[1] In his books, he discusses why the managers who succeed must possess the ability to not only manage their subordinates but also manage themselves. Leadership is based on performance, not personality. In his discussion about the quality of leadership, Drucker states that leaders must demand high standards of themselves and others and create an environment of trust to be successful. They must also set goals for their subordinates and be able to accurately define problems, find answers, and make decisions that test their decision-making skills against the final outcomes. Drucker points out that knowing what their responsibilities are

People Building A sales manager's chief RFD, it is the act of finding and developing salespeople so they can be more productive and confident about achieving their goals.

In the 1970s, before the concept of equal opportunity entered the fashion selling business lexicon, the ideas of traveling and saleswomen who worked outside of the office were very rare. In an effort to develop their sales forces, manager's coined the expression "manpower development." Fortunately, today our industry has a better representation of women in sales, and "manpower development" evolved into "people building."

"When I was involved in sales management, I was once asked by a reporter from *Women's Wear Daily* during an interview to describe 'What business I was in?' I replied, 'the people-building business.' I went on to say that the manager's main job is working with people and having the ability to help them reach greater goals than they ever imagined. That's what management is all about—working with your own people and treating them with respect and getting them to go one step up the ladder to reach their goals. Just to give orders, goals, training is not enough—we must work with our people and help them

CONTINUED ON NEXT PAGE

and being able to successfully carry them out are primary prerequisites for being successful managers; this text will examine each one.

People Building

A manager's chief RFD is **people building**. Managers are charged with finding good people who they can develop to be more productive and more confident in achieving their goals by preparing them to recognize changes in the marketplace and deal with those changes. They must inspire salespeople to feel confident about themselves. Salespeople who know how to overcome obstacles and changes that may affect their results are more productive.

Monitoring overall sales by objectively reviewing salespeople's performances by region to determine if sales goals will be achieved requires administrative skills. Sales managers must act as coaches and motivators, keeping up morale and adjusting sales activities of sellers who are falling behind. Recruitment and retention fall under this function, which we discuss later in the chapter.

Productivity Facilitation

Another RFD is monitoring and improving the productivity of salespeople as well as their entire sales forces by conducting empowerment meetings, boosting morale, establishing sales projections, and utilizing managerial and corrective tools to help individual salespeople meet sales goals. Managers must be conscious at all times about their salespeople's behavior and performances and deal with any negative aspects as they occur. Procrastination is the road to failure—when things go wrong, proper analysis and action are the only ways to find the solution. In Chapter 11, we discuss this RFD in more detail.

Operational Communication

A third RFD is relaying and explaining the policies and structures of the companies for which the sales managers work to their salespeople and sales forces and providing the resources to allow salespeople to operate at their full capacities and enable them to accomplish their goals. The ability to communicate information that results in successful outcomes is an important part of successful management. Managers need to be able to tell their subordinates how they can work more efficiently without causing resentment. All in all, Drucker believes people must work smarter, not harder. One of the most important responsibilities of managers is self-management and the ability to focus on problems and find solutions.

The role of a sales manager is indeed a complex one. Sales managers not only deal with making decisions, motivating others, and having gen-

CONTINUED

become champions, be there when they need us, and, what's most important, give them the confidence that they can do it! Give them the tools to reach their goals and continually strive to help them achieve greater heights and successes. Encourage them not to be afraid of making mistakes, and let them know it can be a very positive learning experience—encourage them to make decisions."

—Jerry Sherman

eral control of their sales forces, but also have to be intimately involved in the internal structures of the companies for which they work. They must take a leading role in providing sales staffs with information and support about company goings-on throughout the different departments. For example, treating production and on-time delivery as top priorities ensures a smooth operation of the sales force. Without accurate production and shipping information, the sales force will lose creditability with their buyers and lose future business.

Training

Still another RFD is training the sales staff by routinely organizing training seminars and programs to keep the sales force informed of new products and provide a venue for practice and improvement in general and specific sales methods. There are many types of training programs aimed at different objectives. Training programs must be customized for the specific purpose they serve and keep marketing objectives as a top priority. For example, if an established fashion manufacturer was launching a new division with a completely new sales force, then training programs and objectives would focus on targeting specific markets and include extensive sessions on product knowledge, selling strategies, and identifying target markets. There would also be a strong emphasis in salespeople's abilities to open new accounts. The sales force's goals could concentrate on getting new customers rather than on getting specific dollar amounts. Managers would have to judge salespeople's performances on the number of new customers they obtain rather than the total amounts of money they generated in sales. This idea is discussed in further detail in Chapter 10.

In addition, sales managers must also take effective steps to address instances of nonperformance, even if it means letting go nonperformers. Dr. Lawrence J. Peter, who with Raymond D. Hull wrote the *The Peter Principle*, argues that "in a hierarchy every employee tends to rise to a level of incompetence" and that, "in time, every post tends to be occupied by an employee who is incompetent to carry out its duties." It therefore stands to reason, according to Dr. Peter and Mr. Hill, "that work is accomplished by those employees who have not reached their level of incompetence." Although many people in sales disagree with his hypothesis, it does prove true in many companies. Some companies that face financial troubles can attribute it to a management team that fails to properly audit their personnel's performance. One of the questions that sales managers must ask themselves when dealing with a seller who is not performing is "Do we have the wrong person selling?" When a company loses market share, it can often be attributed to the wrong people selling, and if the problem of having the wrong people selling is not resolved, then the wrong people are also managing. In other words, a company is saddled with salespeople and possibly sales managers who are ineffective at their current positions. It is therefore crucial for sales managers to be alert about their sellers' performances and be ready to take appropriate steps when it dips below expectations, as covered in further detail in chapter II.

Filling a Sales Manager's Shoes

Some of the best sales managers are people who excelled as sellers first and, because they possess the characteristics and skills necessary for managing others, climbed up the ranks. Their experience in selling gives them a substantial advantage in performing their duties. If a salesperson can effectively and profitably manage his or her own sales territory, then there is a good chance that he or she can develop into a successful sales manager who has responsibility over an entire sales force.

If a salesperson has developed all of the techniques necessary for running a successful territory—time budgeting, account building, prospecting, and maintaining a profitable account list—then they are in a good position to guide other, less experienced salespeople in managing their own territories. The transition from selling to sales management is, in fact, not a difficult one for most people. The characteristics of a good salesperson—attention to details, following through on prospects and sales calls, being assertive yet truthful in dealings with customers and corporate management—are also essential to the success of sales managers.

Keep in mind that just because salespeople are able to do the right things as salespeople, this does not mean they automatically make good sales managers. Managing yourself is completely different from managing others. Peter's Principle states that salespeople will perform incompetently if they are not suited to the structure that management requires. In many cases, the best sellers become candidates for management positions because of their selling expertise. But, leadership as Drucker states, "is performance, not personality." When promoting candidates to management positions, corporate management must take into account whether salespeople can make the transition from running things mostly on their own to working in a more structured environment and in closer proximity with upper management, bearing with office politics, and handling the pressures that a management position brings. Developing sales projections, setting up goals, auditing performances, and dealing with salespeople's and buyers' personal problems can be a taxing proposition.

Perhaps the greatest problem sales managers may face is not being able to motivate others and, especially, themselves. The ability to self-motivate is a major asset for any manager to have and one that not everybody is capable of having. The big question is "Who motivates the motivator?" Sales managers must effectively push themselves and their sales forces toward growth and success, at times with little to no guidance from superiors. By association, sales managers must be resilient and able to handle disappointments and not let negativity affect their management of others.

As we discussed earlier, salespeople do not just write down orders. They must act as well-disciplined business managers whose chief objectives are to earn profits for themselves, the companies for which they work, and their customers. This is why they often find themselves as top candidates for promotion to sales management positions.

Sales managers must manage the people who make up apparel or textile companies and motivate them to achieve sales and profit goals. They must harness the abilities of other people to accomplish the corporate objectives of the firms for which they work and must learn to work through other people to accomplish the sales goals for the companies they represent.

RW Dictionary

80-20 Rule States that about 20 percent of the sales force sells about 80 percent of the company's business. These percentages will vary somewhat from company to company.

Recruiting

When it comes to a comparison between sales personnel and productivity, there's a guideline known as the **80-20 rule**. It states that about 20 percent of the sales force sells about 80 percent of a company's business. In other words, a small percentage of the sales force brings in a major part of the business. Why should a small percentage of the sales force contribute to so much of the total sales? Couldn't a manager hire only people who fit the profile of the top producers? Managers have gained a bad reputation for hiring the wrong salespeople. It seems strange that sales managers who are so involved with decision-making on a daily basis would fall short in the personnel selection process.

+ **We hire in favor of our own image**. If the applicant finds a common denominator with a manager, this can sometimes become the main reason for getting hired. The hiring manager may feel that the applicant speaks the same language as he or she, that they share the same background or education. People who are like each other like each other.
+ **Do we have the right candidate for the job?** Many times in the anxiety to fill a position, hiring managers tend to forget that candidates must be the right fit for a job's qualifications. If the territory is

made up of small accounts with limited growth potential and the candidate is overqualified, then it will probably make for a short-lived relationship since the applicant won't feel challenged. Conversely, if a candidate is new and inexperienced, a hiring manager can do more harm than good by giving that candidate a mature territory—that person will likely feel overwhelmed. No matter how good a candidate seems, they must fit in with a job's requirements for both skills *and* experience.

+ **How we go about checking references.** Many times the reason that there are increases in new hires who don't work out is that managers don't do a thorough job of checking references. Companies are not allowed to bad-mouth an ex-employee regarding references—especially in writing. That's a given—the best way to check the references is to talk with buyers who have worked with the applicant. Remember we said *talk*, not write. Managers must be willing to go that extra step before they hire someone.

+ **Before finalizing the hiring process, managers should conduct a final wrap-up interview.** We recommend that a final interview be arranged before hiring. You may see the person in a different light. Also, it is always good to have another executive or one of your trusted salespeople sit in at the final interview to get a different perspective. This is a perfect opportunity to see if the candidate knows the job requirements. We have found many surprises as a result of final interviews.

Without competent salespeople, a fashion company is doomed to fail. The sales manager is typically the executive who makes the final hiring decisions concerning new sales positions. In that capacity, the sales manager must be knowledgeable in conducting effective hiring interviews, evaluating prospective salespeople's characteristics, selecting the best candidates, and negotiating employment terms.

A fundamental part of effectively hiring good salespeople is defining the sales position scope and requirements: the amount of previous experience necessary, the size of the territory in question, and the types of clients with whom the new hire will work. Once these are clearly defined, interviews will be more meaningful because they will enable managers to better relate candidates to job requirements. Most sales managers use profiles of their most successful salespeople to determine the characteristics, approaches, and work values they prefer in potential hires. The interview should determine if candidates fit the established profiled.

In general, it is a good idea to keep the interviews as relaxed as possible. An informal approach is the best way to determine if a candidate is right for a company's sales force, and the most effective determining factor is how a candidate answers questions during the interview. Is the candidate selling him or herself? Did the candidate research the company? Is the candidate giving responses in a way that highlights his or her skills and experience? It is common sense for candidates who go on interviews to find out as much as possible about the companies at which they are interviewing, as well as the policies, positions in the market place, competition, and the people to whom they market.

Usually, the end of the interview is the most crucial part—the candidate is normally more relaxed, and hiring managers can use the opportunity to see the real person by asking a few more questions. For example, the interviewer may find that some of the questions during the interview weren't addressed. At the very least, the following questions should be covered before saying good-bye:

+ Why do you want to join our company?
+ Where do you see yourself in three to five years?
+ What do you dislike most about buyers?
+ What do you like best about buyers?
+ Who is your role model? Why?

Managing People's Problems

As salespeople rise through the ranks of the apparel and textile sales field, they find that their success often depends on how well they get along with other people. Especially important is the ability to cope with people's problems—the range of interpersonal conflicts arising from the competitive nature of the business. The most common problems that sales managers face include the following:

+ internal competition from salespeople on their own staff
+ resentment and jealousy from other employees regarding their success
+ insecurities of people who feel threatened or injured by the success of another person in their department
+ inability to relate to their superiors
+ being left out of the loop because they don't play into office politics

In some cases, it is best for sales managers to overlook other people's problems and find a means of cooperating with the troublesome people, in spite of the obstacles these people present to sales managers' success. Calling attention to a problem often exacerbates conflict and causes a hostile person to become an even more disruptive influence. However, in other cases, such as in sexual harassment, sales managers must devise effective plans and take firm action to resolve them.

As a people-oriented profession, fashion sales management places great demands on its staff to get along with others. Solving business problems is not enough to guarantee a successful career in this field. Sales managers must be good at understanding other people and able to work harmoniously with others to attain a company's common goals. The following case studies demonstrate some of the problems you are likely to encounter in your progress through the ranks of the apparel-textile sales field, along with some suggestions for handling them.

End "Run-Around-the-Boss"

Joan is a sales manager with a well-known textile company. While her superior, the vice president, is away on business, she is instructed to report directly to the president of the company. Joan seizes the opportunity to cement her relationship with top management. In the absence of the vice president, she attempts to interact with the company president on a business and social level. She and her husband invite the president and his wife to dinner and play tennis with them on the weekend. In the office, Joan directs all of her sales reports to the president himself.

Once he returns, the vice president doesn't take long to notice Joan's new approach. He discovers that he is being bypassed in the reporting process and that Joan—one of his key executives—is no longer responsive to his instructions. Consequently, the vice president accuses Joan of insubordination and asks the president for her dismissal. The president, who finally feels abused by Joan's aggressiveness, consents, and Joan loses her job. Joan's strategy in going around her superior ultimately backfired, leaving her without a job. Her mistake, though serious, is a common one, and in a sense she was lured into it by the periodic absence of her superior and the need to report directly to the company president while the vice president was away.

To avoid the "run-around-the-boss" problem, it is important to maintain an appropriate attitude of respect for and attentiveness to the immediate superior. When sales executives need to interact with top management, they should speak highly of their immediate supervisors and exhibit respect for them.

The "Kid Glove" Problem

Shortly after accepting a sales position with a small textile company, Joe finds that management is giving him special attention and consideration. As a rookie on the sales staff, he is not subjected to the hard criticism frequently directed to his veteran counterparts. Joe is called aside privately by the manager and encouraged, in a gentle manner, to improve upon his shortcomings.

Joe's account list consists of many small but secure customers, none of which presents a difficult challenge. When a big prospect is assigned, the sales manager gives it to one of the veterans on the force. Likewise, when a tough problem arises with one of Joe's accounts, someone other than Joe is always asked to clear it up. While Joe's position looks comfortable from the outside, it will grow increasingly difficult for him to function effectively with this company and to earn the respect of his peers and managers. He is being "shielded" from the difficult decisions and tough problems of the sales business, thus losing valuable experience. By assuming only small, safe accounts, he is being denied the experience of working with major customers, earning profits that such large accounts provide for companies and salespeople, and advancing through merit.

Joe must make it clear to his superiors that he does not want or expect special consideration. It is important for Joe not to allow the fellow salesman to take on a superior, condescending attitude. Through hard work and insistence on his right to do his job, Joe must earn everyone's respect and demand that he be regarded at all times as a full-fledged member of the sales team.

Dealing with Bias

John has spent five years as a salesperson for a men's sportswear company and has been promoted to sales manager in charge of a twelve-person sales staff. John is also the youngest person on the sales staff. Prior to his promotion, he was the number-one salesperson in the company for three consecutive years. John attained the highest percentage increase in sales, opened more new accounts, and had the best track record for retaining existing customers than any of the other sales staff during this period. He was highly praised many times for his territory management, people, and administrative skills. Although he is prepared for some resistance from his former peers and deftly manages to earn their respect in most areas, one salesperson presents a more difficult situation.

Bill, a salesman with the company for more than twenty years, openly resents John's promotion. Bill's performance in the past was excellent, but there was a decline in his sales volume during the previous year. Bill has blamed his recent poor performance on the product. Bill is also a self-avowed opinionated person and frequently makes disparaging comments about younger people in sales and management. Bill has never indicated that he was interested in a management position, and upper management never considered him for this position based on his weakness in administrative duties and his attitude. Up to now, John, who is twenty years younger than Bill, has managed to avoid Bill's comments by staying out of earshot. But now, as his superior, he is forced to hear Bill's negative comments at sales meetings and group lunches about the company's policies and its people.

After a while, John can no longer put up with Bill's attitude and suddenly calls him into his office to announce that he has been terminated. By firing Bill suddenly and without warning, John gains the resentment of other salespeople. They now view him as a highly emotional person who overreacts to situations. They fear that he could one day react to them the same way if he doesn't agree with his views. As a result of his actions, many members of the sales staff have become increasingly hostile and uncooperative toward him. Some have been heard to say, "I'll just do my job and nothing else."

John's error was in not attempting to earn Bill's respect for his sales and management expertise. Managers do not have the luxury to internalize feelings when negative remarks are made. Nor can they let the personality of an individual interfere with the decisions they make. It is difficult but important to understand that this is business and that it is not personal. John passed up many occasions to demonstrate his ability in helping Bill solve particular problems with his accounts. By turning against him, rather than working with him to earn his respect, John lost an experienced salesperson and seriously damaged his rapport with the rest of the staff.

Suppose John had sit down with Bill away from the office and had a real open conversation with him to clear the air. What if John had asked Bill to tell him off the record what was bothering him? What if John had honestly discussed Bill's attitude and remarks and explained to him that it was not appropriate behavior and, therefore, not welcomed in the company? If true, John could also tell Bill that some of the younger salespeople made remarks about Bill's age and that he reprimanded them as well because he does not tolerate that type of attitude. What if John came right out and said he was willing to let bygones be bygones?

John could have used this conflict to discuss Bill's feelings about the company's direction and Bill's sales performance. What if John offered suggestions and a strategy for Bill to improve his performance and ensured Bill that he would be supportive. Bill may have seen John in a different light, as someone who cared. Bill may have realized that it did not pay to be judgmental and prejudicial and possibly may have tried to get rid of the negatives that held him back. In any event, if John had tried to work with Bill one-on-one, Bill could have become a more productive member of the team.

When working with dissident or problematic staff members, sales managers should try to win their confidence by being supportive and trying to help them reach their goals. Frequent counseling sessions with dissident staff members may result in better relationships or help to establish common goals that transcend the initial conflicts. Exploiting conflict may result only in damaging a manager's or a dissident salesperson's career. Sales managers who deal effectively with other people and overcome obstacles emerge as leaders.

Go Team and Rah-Rah!

Chapter 7 discusses how tough it can be to be a salesperson sometimes. We likened a salesperson who is striving to make a sale to a football player who is trying to score a touchdown. Just as offensive players refuse to give in to defensive plays, so must salespeople strive to make their sales, regardless of negative responses along the way.

During a football game, the coach, fans, and cheerleaders motivate players who have just been tackled to get up and keep going. In the sales environment, there are no fans or cheerleaders. Therefore, it is extremely important for sales managers to be supportive of their salespeople and coach and cheer them along the way to the sale. How does a manager do that? One way is implementing motivational programs. These programs aim to help salespeople reach their sales goals by setting up incentives beyond standard commission. The main motivating force for many salespeople is recognition, and the major motivating force for the individual is to feel that they belong in the team.

What about contest awards and bonuses? Money is important, but personal recognition is often a more significant motivating force. Monetary award programs are important but are not long-lasting—they motivate immediate action but tend to distract the salesperson from thinking about long-term growth. Having a contest to see who opens the most new accounts can motivate the sales force, and increased sales may be a successful way of motivating the sales force, but only because of management's expertise in managing the activities of salespeople during this contest. In the wrong hands, however, these contests can be more hype than substance. Experience has proven that this blitz for opening new accounts may bring in the numbers—but what type of new customers is the company getting?

This book stresses that success in sales is all about building long-term business relationships. Most times, because of the anxiety to receive an award and the pressure to achieve some individual sales, salespeople open new accounts indiscriminately—many of these customers cannot benefit from the products they buy, so they won't be back for repeat orders, while other customers do not have the financial means to increase their business. Numbers alone will not lead to growth—rather, quality customers who we can benefit from the products they buy con-

RW Concept

In sales, sales managers should provide salespeople with the advice and moral support they need to cope with rejection.

tribute to the health and growth of a business. If managers want to have contests, they would be wise to base them on overall performances and consistent results. The winners will be salespeople who increase their volumes and maintain levels of growth over a period of time, not just for a season or a few weeks as many of these contests are conducted. Setting up contests with parameters based on semiannual or, better still, annual performance will give a better idea of who the top performers are—these are sellers who should receive rewards and recognition because they have helped the company grow over a reasonable period of time. Motivation programs and other sales and marketing activities must be based on long-range objectives. The quick-fix award programs are just that— quick.

Planning for Results

Sound decision-making requires sound planning. Sound planning incorporates all of the factors and actions that will ultimately bring about the intended results: achieving the sales goals for the department, training the sales force on a new line, and hiring two new salespeople. Sound planning allows sales managers to make accomplishments at the companies they represent. Managers know that poor planning equals poor results, and they must carefully look at all the options and their ramifications before carrying out any plans. Planning requires them to visualize the steps that lead to a particular plan's success or failure. A great amount of time, research, and energy must be involved in planning for desired results.

Unfortunately, many managers do little or no planning to maximize the results of their sales forces. Such managers just follow the action and, when the action stops, so does the progress toward achieving the sales goals. Instead of leading their salespeople toward results in an organized fashion, they throw caution to the wind and address problems when they arise. While this may seem like a good strategy to some, its basic flaw is that by the time problems arise, it is often too late to compensate for lost productivity. Therefore, proactive managers who plan ahead are able to stay on top of the progress of sales goals, instead of sitting at their desks with their fingers crossed, hoping for results that may not come.

By properly planning, managers are forced to evaluate their time and as a result become more productive. The old adage of, "Plan your work, then work your plan" is still the preferred method of management for successful sales managers. The sales manager must keep the following points in mind when planning out strategies:

+ Planning ahead is the key to reaching the goal.
+ Planning requires an individual to do some careful and methodical thinking.
+ Planning requires time and patience.
+ The consequences that a plan may have if it doesn't work need to be determined.
+ The time it will take to fulfill each part of a plan needs to be determined.
+ Figure out who is involved in the plan and what their RFDs are in the scheme of the plan.
+ Formulate the individual tasks for which each team member is accountable and have a method to evaluate his or her performance.
+ Monitor the plan to stay up-to-date on overall progress.
+ Have an exit plan that lets you modify or terminate the plan if it is not successful in the time allotted to avoid excessive costs.

It is important that managers have exit strategies built into every plan to avoid damage to the company and its resources. Planning cannot be based on emotions or instincts. If managers embark on a program because it's a great idea and they think it will work, then they need to keep in mind that failure may cost them their jobs. Planning is everything if everything necessary for success is included in the plan.

Successful managers who plan properly are also wise to demand proper planning from the salespeople who work for them. Since all salespeople have an array of sales goals, it is important for them to sit down and work out how they will accomplish these goals and figure out the steps required to reach their sales goals.

Getting to Know Your Salespeople

RW Dictionary

SWOT Acronym that stands for strengths, weaknesses, opportunities, and threats; it is a marketing term that denotes an analysis of these areas and is essential for strategic planning in any business.

Before starting to manage a sales force, it is imperative for managers to conduct an audit—a human audit of salespeople. They must get to know the SWOT—strengths, weakness, opportunities, and threats—of each salesperson, just as they would evaluate a business entity. In Marketing 101, SWOT is defined as an analysis that is essential for strategic planning in any business. The purpose of the SWOT analysis is to alert a company of its leverage by defining its strengths and opportunities and its problems by analyzing its weakness and threats. SWOT helps companies define changes in buying behaviors, new competitors, and other market conditions that impact a company's bottom line. The success of this analysis and strategic planning can come about only through truthful analysis and objective thinking.

Taking this one step further, why not set up a brainstorming session within your company for the salespeople and have them do a SWOT analysis on themselves? Think about the advantages of knowing what your salespeople are all about. The manager's job is to understand each person on his or her sales force; think about the impact this would have if the manager understood what that person perceives as his or her strengths, weaknesses, opportunities, and threats. The positive side of this exercise is that by the salesperson providing this analysis, the manager can take steps to improve areas needed for the salesperson to succeed and also benefit the sales manager's position in the company.

Knowing the SWOTs of their salespeople will also give managers direct insight into the opportunities for which certain salespeople are looking. Some salespeople may desire promotions, and managers can use SWOT to determine if these salespeople qualify as candidates for future management positions.

Managers can thus use SWOT to help certain salespeople reach their goals and to determine who is having trouble so managers can help to improve their productivity. What better way of increasing productivity than by working with those with strengths and helping improve on their strengths, giving them more job satisfaction, increasing their sales, and retaining outstanding sellers. It also helps sales managers determine if there are problems within a salesperson's territory, whether it regards competition, objections to the product, or areas of planning.

Chapter Summary

+ Average sales forces are headed by national sales managers, territorial regional managers, or both, depending on the size. Sales managers are ultimately responsible for their salespeople's performances and the growth and success of the companies for which they work.

+ One of the primary RFDs—responsibilities, functions, and duties—of sales managers involves recognizing problems and making decisions on how to best deal with them. They also include people building, productivity facilitation, operational communication, and training.

+ People building refers to the act of developing people to be more productive and confident in their abilities to achieve their goals.

+ Productivity facilitation refers to the monitoring and improvement of the productivity of all salespeople and the entire sales force.

+ Operational communication refers to the relaying and explaining of company policies and proper structures as well as providing the necessary resources for salespeople to operate effectively.

+ Training programs are designed to teach sales methodologies, give instructions on company procedures, and provide information about new products.

+ Some of the best sales managers are people who excelled as sellers and also possess the characteristics and skills necessary for managing others.

+ The "80-20 rule" states that about 20 percent of the sales force sells about 80 percent of a company's business. These percentages will vary somewhat from company to company.

+ Managers who hire in favor of their own images are anxious to fill positions, don't check references thoroughly, and fail to conduct a final wrap-up interviews before hiring is finalized tend to hire ineffective people.

+ The most common sources of people problems that sales managers face are internal competition from salespeople in their staffs, resentment and jealousy from other employees regarding their success, insecurities of other people who feel threatened or injured by the success of another person in their departments, an inability to relate to their own superiors, and being left out of the loop because they don't play into office politics.

+ In the rough-and-tumble sales environment, it is extremely important for sales managers to be supportive of their salespeople and coach and cheer them along the way by instituting motivational programs.

+ Sound planning and decision-making skills are crucial to success in sales and sales management.

+ A manager's job is to understand each person on his or her sales force; assess their strengths, weaknesses, opportunities, and threats; and work steadily on improving them.

RW CASE STUDY

Jerry Sherman, M.B.A., D.B.A., was vice president of sales and marketing for several multimillion-dollar fashion apparel corporations. In this capacity, he was also responsible for the sales staff and implementing sales training programs. Sherman has lectured at sales and marketing seminars internationally and is a recognized expert in fashion sales and marketing. He has held adjunct teaching positions at the Fashion Institute of Technology in New York City; Lynn University in Boca Raton, Florida; Miami International University of Art & Design in Miami, Florida; and most recently at Johnson & Wales University, College of Business in North Miami, Florida. He is the author of numerous trade articles and is coauthor of *Woman Power in Textiles & Apparel Sales* and this book, *The Real World Guide to Fashion Selling and Management.* Jerry Sherman and his coauthor Sar Perlman are partners in Sherman & Perlman, Integrated Marketing.

Can you describe the role of a sales manager?

The sales manager's role is to provide leadership. This requires the ability to inspire, orchestrate, and facilitate the success of the salespeople. The sales manager must have the energy and enthusiasm to develop salespeople and deliver results. Hiring and assigning the right people for a specific territory is a critical role a sales manager must play. A true leader understands the needs of the salespeople and is able to satisfy these needs by practicing a bottom-up management style.

What are the responsibilities, functions, and duties of a sales manager?

The sales manager is basically responsible for the success of the sales force that he or she leads. Increasing sales with consistency and continuing with overall growth by adding new customers and customer relationship management (CRM) is a major responsibility of the sales manager. Hiring and retaining the right salespeople, training, establishing sales goals, and measuring the performance of the sales team are paramount for successful sales management. Accurate sales forecasting and sales support are important to the success of this position. The sales manager must be able to put together a sales strategy that is realistic and have the ability and talent to move the business ahead. He or she must generate an energetic environment. The sales manager must act as a teacher, trainer, and coach and be able to communicate the objectives of the company to the sales staff. The sales manager's responsibility is not limited only to hiring but also for firing those who have not performed. In addition to these responsibilities, many companies assign major accounts to the sales manager.

What type of experience and managerial knowledge is required from a sales manager?

A proven record of success in dealing with people is a must. Coaching, mentoring, and communication skills are essential. The sales manager must possess a background that demonstrates the energy and enthusiasm that achieves results. He or she must have charisma, vitality, and a positive attitude. They must be able to communicate excitement to their sales staff. Experience in the sales field is essential. The ability to organize paperwork is another requirement. The sales manager should posses the highest level of integrity in order to lead.

What type of problems are sales managers confronted with? What can they do to solve these problems?

One of the main problems that a sales manager is faced with is how to motivate the sales force and what to do when members are not reaching the agreed-upon goals. What to do with underachievers is essential in managing a sales force. When a member of the sales force is not performing, it is the responsibility of the sales manager to do all that is possible to find out what the problem is and try to solve it. A meeting should be held when the problem first occurs to determine if it is a personal problem or a sales problem. If it is a personal problem, the manager should try to find an area of support to help this individual overcome the problem. If it is a sales problem, such as not performing due to a lack of a proper work ethic, poor planning, or [lack of motivation], then the sales manager must work with the person to determine if there is a remedy. At times proper coaching and additional training can solve the problem. It is vital to give the salesperson a time frame in which to improve and to discuss the outcome if the results are not as expected. If after proper notification and coaching we find the performance is still below expectation, then [terminating] the person is the only option. It is also important for the other members of the sales team to see that when someone is not performing they are given every opportunity to succeed. Keeping a nonproductive person on staff defeats the success of the company's objectives. They are taking up room from another person who can be beneficial to the company's efforts. The turnover rate of the sales force is another problem that sales managers are confronted with. Not only is it costly but also if the rate of separating salespeople is too high, the company runs the risk of not attracting new sales talent. Management must be alert to bad morale problems and should deal with them before they become a major problem. Face-to-face meetings should be held to determine the exact problem. After the problem is brought to the surface, the sales manager can decide whether it can be resolved. Many times a problem is self-imposed. Sometimes it could be due to jealousy after seeing the success of someone in the peer group who [receives] promotions. Frequent one-on-one sales meetings and constant communication with sales staff members can prevent most bad morale problems.

How do sales managers go about hiring the right people?

Finding salespeople who fit into the culture of the company and match the culture of your customers is critical in the hiring process. Selling includes three Cs—challenges, competition, and customers. I look for people who like a challenge and are self-motivated, who also like to win but understand the need for a working relationship with others. Although it has been said that many successful salespeople don't like structure, I look for those who will accept structure when they understand that it is necessary for the job function. The track record of performance is important because the past activities will usually predict the future. What activities did they participate in college? Were they involved in people-to-people activities? If they are experienced sellers, I want to see what they have achieved and why they are in the job market. Mostly, we look for people who have a high degree of ethics. This is hard to determine in the interview process but checking the background of the applicants can indicate this important trait for selling professionals. As we say when we see them in action, "truth will out."

Questions to Consider

1. Do you believe in bottom-up management? Why?
2. What would you say is the most important responsibility of the sales manager? Why?
3. Do you feel that it is essential for a sales manager to be an outstanding salesperson to manage the sales force? Explain your reasons.
4. What do you believe is the best way to motivate salespeople?
5. If you were a sales manager interviewing someone for your sales staff, what characteristics would you want the interviewee to have? What qualities should he/she have to fit into the culture of the company? Explain.

RW EXERCISES

1. Why do you think one of the primary RFDs of a sales manager involves recognizing problems and making decisions on how to best deal with them? Give an example of how this might manifest itself in the real world.
2. Pair up with another student so one of you acts as the salesperson and the other acts as the manager, either in retail or B2B. Set up a scenario that requires the manager to practice each of the primary RFDs discussed in this chapter. Write down how each RFD affects the seller-manager relationship and what you think its effect would be on productivity. Switch roles for a different perspective, and note the new responses.
3. Assume you are a sales manager in a company and you need to hire another salesperson. Write down the scenario details (e.g., what type of company it is, what product lines it specializes in, and so on), and define the position. Be sure to include the position's scope and requirements, amount of previous experience necessary, the size of the territory, and the type of clients with whom the person will work.

4. Pair up with another student so one of you acts as the sales manager and the other acts as the interviewee, based on the scenario you created in exercise 3. Act out the interview process with the position's definition and interviewing principles covered. Write down how the interview went, and state whether you would hire the interviewee and why. Switch roles for a different perspective, and note the new responses.

5. Do you think the ability to solve people problems is vital for success in sales management? Why? Give an example.

6. Pair up with another student so one of you acts as the sales manager and the other acts as the salesperson who has a people problem. Attempt to address the problem with the salesperson, keeping in mind the principles discussed in the chapter. Write down how the conversation went, and state whether it was successful and why. Switch roles for a different perspective, and note the new responses.

7. Give an example of a time that you planned a project in detail. Did you achieve the intended result? How did the plan play into your success or failure?

8. Create a scenario where you are a salesperson, either in a retail or B2B environment. You have just agreed on your sales goals with your manager. List the goals, and create a fictitious plan of how you intend to go about achieving them.

9. Do a SWOT analysis on yourself as a student. Where are your strengths? What are your weaknesses? Can you see any opportunities to improve your studies? What could threaten your success, and how can you overcome these threats? Turn your analysis in to the instructor.

END NOTES

1. Some of his more popular books include *Managing for Results*, New York: Harper & Row Publishing, Inc. (1964); *The Practice of Management*, New York: Harper & Row Publishing Inc. (1954); "Peter Drucker on the Profession of Management," *Harvard Business Review* (1998); and *The Essential Drucker*, New York: HarperCollins Publishers (2001).

CHAPTER 10

TRAINING AND TOOLS

Overview

Sales training is a vital part of fashion sales management. It allows the salesperson to practice sales methods in a stress-free environment where errors can be observed and corrected without costing the company lost revenue. But sales training includes much more than methodology; it must also relay information on existing and new products, technological updates, and practices in writing and verbal communication. This chapter reviews the purpose of sales training in the fashion industry, the aspects of sales training that should be covered, and traditional and contemporary training methods.

Introduction

Some executives are purported to forbid the use of the word *training* in relation to their sales forces. They look for expressions such as "motivational sessions," "learning seminars," and other buzzwords in its stead. The late Stanley Marcus, former president and chief executive officer and chairman emeritus of Neiman Marcus said during a sales seminar for retailers many years ago at the Dallas Merchandise Mart that "the word *training* is for animals and not to be used for people." He was adamant that use of the word was demeaning.[1]

While that connotation of the word may be true, it does not change the fact that sales training is necessary. Marcus is right in his statement to the degree that training should never be carried out in the same manner that a person would train a dog—that is, in a dictatorial fashion that does not consult with the trainee's understanding. If a manager simply tells a salesperson to do something in a certain way without ensuring the salesperson understands the reasoning behind it, the salesperson will make a mistake in that area sooner or later. Sales is not a rigid procedure where salespeople can carry out the same set of instructions in all cases. Sales requires a fluid and dynamic interaction with people, and the salesperson must understand what he or she is doing because that is what ultimately drives the development of the business relationship with the buyer.

Throughout the fashion industry's history, we find that the word training remains a viable description for educating and improving the skills of people. Soldiers in the military receive training, emergency personnel receive training on disaster responses, and nurses receive training on hospital procedures. Industry spends a great deal of money on "assertiveness training," which is a method of training individuals to act in a bold, self-confident manner. Webster's dictionary defines training: "to instruct so as to make proficient or qualified." This definition, which is the one we are interested in for the purposes of this chapter, provides insight into what constitutes training and why it is necessary. In most cases, further instruction and continued education can provide tremendous benefits for salespeople in gaining more self-confidence and improving their performance.

The bottom line is that no matter how you interpret the word, the need to improve people's skills will never change; only the methods change. In the years to come, training efforts will likely increase and become more sophisticated to gain an edge in an increasingly competitive marketplace. Call it what you will, successful companies are constantly increasing their budgets for "people development." The success or failure of any training program depends on the methods used and not the words.

In this chapter, we describe some of the different methods currently used by fashion companies and the benefits and disadvantages of each. It is interesting to note that the training process is beginning to shift from being product-oriented to being more people-oriented.

Is Sales Training Necessary?

Show us a successful sales force, and we will show you an ongoing sales training program focusing on product knowledge, people skills, selling skills, mathematical skills, individual management skills, and communication skills. Sales training must encompass all facets of the business of sales to provide the salesperson with a well-rounded foundation upon which to build his or her style of selling.

One of the latest trends—one which is frightening indeed—is management's tendency to shy away from teaching selling methodology in their training programs. Many managers make the mistake of thinking that their products will sell themselves. They reason that educated buyers will recognize their products' benefits and buy them regardless of a salesperson's actions.

However, as we've learned in chapter 7, buyers can have objections to buying, regardless of how well informed they are. They also need a salesperson's assistance when making decisions. If a company does not offer courteous, knowledgeable sales assistance to help buyers overcome their objections, then buyers will most likely take their business to a company that does.

We know that professional buyers will make decisions based on benefits that they can recognize. Personal selling enables sellers to communicate the benefits of their products and consummate sales. B2B selling relies on the relationship between a buyer and seller as much as it does on the product being sold. Besides cultivating that relationship, the seller has the role of presenting a product's benefits to the buyer and answering any questions or objections. A salesperson must be trained and receive routine refreshers on the selling methods that have been found to be most workable within the company.

The phrase "practice makes perfect" applies to sales methodology as well. Salespeople who receive quality training will improve their performance. In today's business world, it is naive to think that a salesperson does not need training on how to best sell and present the specific lines or fashion items that a company offers. At the very least, sales methodology training should include several presentation models, the answers to the most common buyer objections, ways to recognize buying or nonbuying signals, and what actions should be taken to close a sale.

There is nothing wrong with salespeople learning how to develop

RW Principle

Salespeople cannot apply training mechanically. Instead, it is important to remember that training should be viewed as a way of adding to or improving on the various selling methods and that the final judgment on which method should be applied or how it should be applied rests with the salesperson during the actual sales presentation.

methods in which to close sales and gain relationships. We are not talking about using trick methods or gimmicks—these selling "techniques" are dinosaurs that belong to the distant past and will never work in today's market. What we are talking about is raising the salesperson's awareness of the mechanics of the sale, the personal selling methods, the presentation approaches, and the ways to negotiate a sale. Sales managers who formulate a training program that focuses on a solid foundation of selling methodology allow salespeople to practice their sales presentations and offers to them ways to answer common objections.

Aspects of Sales Training

While selling methodology is important, sales training cannot be limited to that and must also cover product knowledge, relationship development, communication techniques, organizational strategies, and technology updates. Today's buyers are more sophisticated than ever. They have access to a complex network of research resources, they understand what they need and when they need it, and they arrive to the sales meeting armed with an incredible amount of information, not to mention offers from the seller's competition. What this means to the fashion manufacturer or retailer is not that the salesperson is now irrelevant. On the contrary, it heightens the salesperson's relevance—if buyers can be counted on to study the company's price lists or brochures, chances are they will also ask questions or demand that issues important to them be addressed. Chances are buyers will also be educated enough to tell whether the people with whom they are dealing knows as much as they do. Training that offers product knowledge is therefore extremely vital to a salesperson's success.

However, sellers must be equally skilled in the area of people knowledge. The first part of people knowledge is relationship development. The salesperson should understand the need for building a business relationship with the buyer and the methods to develop and grow this relationship. We cannot underestimate the role of today's seller as an ambassador for the company he or she represents. The seller who is aware of the dynamics of the selling situation, understands what motivates the buyer, and recognizes the importance of reliability and honesty in a business relationship will not only enjoy success as an individual salesperson, but also will create tremendous goodwill for the company within the industry. Training in the human factor will pay dividends in understanding the variables in the buyer-seller relationship.

The other part of people knowledge is general communication skills. Salespeople constantly interact with others: buyers, the buyers' office staff, and the managers and staff in their own company. If you can't express yourself, then how are you going to get your message across? Communication training is vital and must include listening skills. Today's salesperson has to have a command of the language and be able to speak and write articulately and effectively. Companies should pay adequate attention to the speaking and writing skills of their salespeople. Many sales can be made and some that seem to be lost can be saved by the proper use of language and written communication. Attention should also be given to sending e-mails and postcards thanking the buyer or to making quick telephone calls to keep in touch with buyers.

Training programs that include speaking and writing skills are more in demand today because many sellers are not properly trained in these two essential areas. Companies that are getting the edge over their competition are incorporating communication training into their training programs. To improve public speaking skills, training should include extemporaneous speaking. An example of this may be a meeting where the participants are given a subject to speak to the group about for three minutes. This is followed by a peer group evaluation and critique session. Many people have difficulty speaking in public or under pressure, and practice under simulated conditions can often help ease the fear and anxiety associated with public speaking. "Use it or lose it" certainly applies to public communication, and the more a person speaks or writes, the better that person becomes. Companies that hold speaking and writing training meetings tend to gain an advantage over their competitors. Fashion companies such as Original Penguin have their salespeople do a written and an oral presentation of their new lines at their sales training meetings.

One of the major recent additions to sales training has been instruction in the use of electronic media. From wrestling with palm pilots to negotiating access to the company's network while on the road, salespeople constantly deal with technology to close sales. Training sellers in the effective use of technology is not an easy task because it requires constant updates due to the many rapid advances in the ever-changing field.

To be successful in today's market, salespeople should be able to not only manage their time effectively but also operate their own virtual office while away on sales calls. Due to the increasing necessity of using the Internet, cell phones, laptop computers, and Web-based video conference calls, salespeople must be proficient with the various software programs and devices that are involved. They must also be able to acquire information from the company databases to be more efficient in dealing with their buyers regarding delivery dates and order status. Training should also encompass the use of computers for sales presentations and proposals. The type of training in the past, which in many cases depend-

RW Concept

By definition, salespeople must have excellent communication skills. The skills of presentation, articulation, and persuasion are invaluable to the salesperson and form the foundation of all sales methodology. Without a solid command of the language, these skills cannot be effective.

ed on hype, will not work today—training today must be directed to make salespeople more knowledgeable than they were in the past.

Type of Training for Salespeople

Now that we've established the importance of training, let's examine some of the different training methods used today by sales managers in the fashion industry to enhance their sales forces' product knowledge, sales methodology, and presentation and communication skills. Training programs can be divided into in-house and out-of-house programs.

There are probably as many different methods associated with training as there are sales managers. However, whether it involves a personalized or a team approach, sales training must improve selling skills, people skills, and product knowledge and institute behavioral changes where it is needed. If the training program accomplishes that, then it has justified its existence. The individual's total involvement in the process usually spells success.

Training Out-of-House

Out-of-house seminars or other structured training programs can take place in the same city where the company is located or in a different area. The main point is that the out-of-house program is organized and run by an outside firm that specializes in delivering such sales training sessions. Typically, such programs have better access to big-name experienced guest speakers and are run by knowledgeable training consultants.

Many companies have their salespeople attend company-paid seminars or have their sales personnel attend programs dedicated to improving their performance. Many companies also encourage their sales personnel to attend other noncompany-sponsored programs and will reimburse their employees for attending. Some companies provide business scholarships in local colleges for their sales personnel. Successful sellers are those who are proactive in the learning phase of sales. The true professional never stops learning and finding out what's happening in the business environment.

We would be remiss if we didn't mention the importance of written sales training literature, manuals, and motivational videotapes by sales experts (see RW Concept on the next page). Salespeople can read or listen to these at their leisure, and the material can often provide them with invaluable training tips and offer new approaches to common issues. Proper training programs result in sellers who develop their own sales personalities. They have confidence in what they are selling and approach every situation with a very positive attitude.

RW Concept

While the difference between in-house and out-of-house may at first seem to be the location where the training is delivered, this is not the case. In-house training can, and often does, take place at a venue away from the company's facilities, while out-of-house can take place on-site. The difference is who delivers the training—company employees deliver in-house training and outside consultants deliver out-of-house training.

Training In-House

In-house training programs are conducted by sales managers for their staff, which is why it is called in-house, since it is not an outside consultant who is coming in to do the training. Meetings are held at company offices, hotels, conference rooms, and other favorable learning environments. These meetings are the perfect platform for getting to know salespeople and evaluating their performance with the objective of increasing their productivity.

Ideally, in-house training sessions should have outside experts as guest speakers, and in fact, in-house training can be more effective because it deals with present conditions and problems within the company while at the same time presenting the opportunity for access to guest speakers' advice and expertise. The only downside to the in-house meetings is that when those who are running the meeting are not well-versed—although they may believe that they are—the results of the meeting may be flat or even negative.

Many participants at in-house training meetings learn a great deal not only from their managers but also from their peers. These meetings should be conducted in a manner that makes salespeople feel they are free to voice their opinions and generally participate in the events. This can turn an ordinary meeting into one that is very effective. In-house programs may feature any one or a combination of the training components that follow.

PERSONALIZED ASSESSMENTS

A broad training program that provides general information on product specifications, presentation methods, and policies is not cost effective in today's competitive marketplace unless it also includes an individual assessment of each salesperson's strengths and weaknesses. In-house training sessions can be successful if they are customized to the needs of the individual. Many training programs avoid the human factor.

In Chapter 2, we indicated the characteristics of successful salespeople and how these have a direct impact on their performance. A training program ideally assesses the degree to which each of these characteristics is present in each participant. It is important to review the performance of participants to determine their areas of strengths and weaknesses regarding their individual characteristics. How do salespeople handle rejection? How do they relate to a situation in which the buyer wants a delivery date that is unreasonable? Do they take the order or tell the truth and take the chance of losing an order? How do they handle a conflict between the companies they represent and their buyers? Are they emotionally secure? Can they keep their cool under adverse circumstances?

By assessing these traits, we are able to pinpoint the specific problems each seller may face in achieving his or her goals. In developing the personalized training program, the emphasis should be geared not only toward direct specific remedies for characteristics that are lacking, but also toward definite practice to improve and strengthen characteristics that are highly developed. The objective is to seek improvement in all areas that, in turn, will increase productivity.

Suppose that Mary and John are two salespeople who participate in a company's training program. They each have different strengths and weaknesses. Mary thinks of herself as highly empathetic, but she is not a strong closer and has trouble facing rejection. Mary tells the sales manager about a buyer with whom she has a great business relationship. During her most recent sales call, the buyer told Mary, "I am not doing the amount of sales I should be doing; therefore, I am not buying anything at the present time, and I am sure you understand my circumstance." Upon hearing this, Mary accepted this situation instead of offering the buyer product opportunities that will help increase sales. The manager recognizes that Mary confuses the concept of empathy with sympathy; empathy requires primarily that the salesperson understand a buyer's situation, whereas sympathy demands that the salesperson become emotionally involved in a buyer's predicament. Mary became emotionally involved with the buyer's problem and thus was unable to see the opportunities that the problem presented. A training program that doesn't address Mary's weakness would be worthless.

Management has the responsibility of showing Mary that her strength in gaining relationships is a powerful asset and the key to closing sales. Her ability to establish relationships puts her in a perfect position to increase her productivity. Channeling this strength in the proper direction will lead to an increase in her business. However, by just complimenting Mary on her ability to build relationships, her manager won't be able to show her how to improve her closing abilities. The sales manager must indicate methods of recognizing when and how to ask for an order—after all, her relationship building has given her the opportunity of having one foot in the door. Why not put the other foot in? Mary has to be conscious that in every presentation there are opportunities for a sale whether it is at the current moment or at a future time. She must communicate a strong desire to make a selling transaction because of the business relationship she has established. She also needs to capitalize on her strengths. Because buyers like her, it is probable that she will gain their trust, which will then produce sales. It is also a good approach to have Mary explain to the other salespeople her method of gaining this trust. This platform will give her recognition, and it may also raise her understanding of just how powerful this ability is in the selling arena.

Unlike Mary, John is a great closer. He has reached his goals most seasons, but as of late, his sales have dropped off. John is quite knowledge-able about the product he sells and gives great presentations, but the sales manager notes that at times John tends to exaggerate information, product benefits, and delivery dates just to get his orders; he has even been reprimanded for doing so. John is a hard worker but is so intent on succeeding that at times he loses sight of how important honesty is. Obviously, John does not need to practice closing sales, but instead should focus on the importance of honesty and self-discipline. To be effective, a sales training program that addresses John's weakness directly makes sense and will show him how to overcome his problem.

Personalized sales training sessions must also look at the positives and build on them. Although Mary's weakness is closing deals due to her sympathetic approach, she has several strengths that should be recognized and strengthened as part of her training program. She has the ability to get along with people, she is well liked by her clients, and she can build relationships. The ideal program should not only indicate her weaknesses, but also reinforce her strengths. Likewise for John.

PAIRING UP

Another in-house training component teams up two salespeople to go on a specific number of sales calls together. The idea is to put together a team where one salesperson's weakness is the other salesperson's strength and aims at having the two learn from each other.

If Mary and John were to pair up on sales calls after having had training on their weaknesses, Mary could learn much about the closing process from John, and John could learn the importance of integrity and relationship building from Mary. In many cases, this can be a more productive method of training because the participants are involved in a peer process, and there is no boss to monitor their every move. With proper management guidance, this interchange can be an extremely dynamic training method. Pairing the weaknesses and strengths of both parties should be discussed with the two salespeople before they engage in this exercise—they must be willing to participate. It must be explained to the team that is being paired up that they must observe each other so each can draw his or her own observations and conclusions. After the team finishes the exercise, management should step in and discuss the observations with them.

A skilled manager will also be cognizant of the fact that working on improving the strengths of sellers will yield better performances from them. Having a good closer is not the answer for long-term growth, but knowing how to close and still keep a long-term relationship with a buyer will increase the productivity of the seller.

CLASSROOM-TYPE SESSIONS

Some sales meetings take place in classroom settings and are usually held on a seasonal basis or before a new line or collection is being introduced. The sales managers or sales trainers act as teachers and distribute outlines and meeting agendas that describe the sessions' objectives. Reading the written assignments is part of this exercise and usually some type of testing is given to determine if the information has been understood. The sellers are then graded as they would be in a regular classroom setting.

The agenda may consist of company policies, product knowledge, marketing, production, financial information, and sales methodology, including proper methods to close sales. Emphasis may be centered on company policies—the do's and don'ts in contacting a customer. A great deal of time is spent on product knowledge—that is, the raw materials and equipment used in the manufacturing process. Design concepts are discussed in great length along with the proper ways to give a sales presentation. Marketing research is often incorporated into this setting, offering sellers updated information regarding demographics and how it affects their territories and customers. Research and development programs are also introduced.

This venue is a great place for guest speakers, designers, and marketing and production executives. Computerized or interactive tutorials and fashion update videos fit well into this type of program. A successful classroom program should require group projects where sellers can rotate through different roles. Managers act as mentors or teachers and are not necessarily looked at as bosses. This type of training environment benefits both sellers and management because of the close communication it promotes. This type of venue is used only for a company that has a captive sales force; in-house meetings are the preferred venue for independent sales representatives.

ROLE-PLAYING OFF SCRIPT

The best way to learn something is to become intimately involved in the learning process. How do we intimately involve salespeople in this process? Training should incorporate real-world experiences and environments to be as effective as possible. A well-designed training program incorporates role-playing, in which sellers participate in real-life situations, facing issues that they will be confronted with during their day-to-day jobs as sellers. One way to institute a role-playing situation is for the participants to be given a story without instructing them on how to handle the situation. They have to react to the situation while playing a role.

Videotaping the participants during such a session and playing it back to them can prove quite effective; however, it is more beneficial to allow the participants to do their own evaluations. Doing this enables the participants to see themselves in action and evaluate how they react to given situations. By voicing their critique of their own performances in front of group leaders or members of the audience, they have a chance of learning for themselves without the pressure of being subjected to a group critique. Conducting a role-playing session and having the audience critique it before participants have a chance to comment on their own performances bypasses the learning process of sellers seeing what they did right or wrong. The group's participation should be invited only after participants have critiqued themselves. The audience also benefits by observing what has transpired.

A word about role-playing—just as it is imperative that the participants understand and observe the results, it is vital that the roles be based on actual events with real-world conclusions.

ROLE-PLAYING BY SCRIPT

Some companies conduct video role-playing training sessions using a script. The participants act as buyers, sellers, or any other characters and perform their tasks as written in the scripts. The participants are merely actors and actresses and are not involved in the actions of the character they are playing. The script is written with the objective of encouraging audience participation. The scripted subject matter could be a better way to present the product or how to handle a current problem.

After the role-playing exercise, the group offers comments, as moderated by the group leader. This type of role-playing scenario reduces the pressure on the individuals who participate because they are just acting a part. The audience is more attentive because they will be asked for their comments, which will be noted by management.

A scripted role-play can be developed in-house, wherein the strengths and weaknesses are played out by the salesperson who has a specific weakness. This can serve as a demonstration to that salesperson of the weakness and how the sale is lost because of it. In this case, neither the person playing the buyer's role nor the person playing the seller's should be told what the other person's role is.

For an example, lets say the seller in this script has a great relationship with the buyer, but the seller has not been able to close the sale due to a lack of assertiveness and being too sympathetic (as was Mary's case in the example on page 182). The script reads that the seller has called on the buyer several times but has not received any business. The salesperson has researched the buyer's company and knows that his or her product is as good as or superior to the competition with whom the buyer is currently doing business. Instead of having the salesperson play the seller's role, it is more beneficial to have him or her play the role of the buyer, which is where this salesperson needs improvement. In this scenario and in the scripted role, the salesperson is instructed to tell the seller that he or she is not in a position to buy. The seller's role will be that of a seller who has a great relationship with the buyer but is reluctant to ask for the sale for fear of ruining the relationship. The buyer will be told to just say something along the lines of, "My sales have been off; I am not ready to buy anything right now. See you next time. I don't have an **open-to-buy**." The seller following the script will not ask for the order but instead will talk about things that they are both interested in to keep the relationship going.

Once the salespeople finish their role-play exercise, they should change the script, and this time have the seller properly answer the buyer's objections and make the sale. It should become evident to the salesperson who has trouble closing sales after playing the buyer's role in both instances that he or she has to be more focused on making the sale, and that if he or she does not answer objections and ask for the sale, someone else—namely the competition—will.

Important Tools Used by Salespeople

Any item that a salesperson may hand or present to a potential buyer is considered a selling tool. Let's start with the business card, which is typically the first thing the salesperson gives to a buyer. Buyers receive so many business cards that most are thrown away or misplaced. How will your business card stand out and get the attention of the buyer? What makes your card unique?

A business card should be simple—short and to-the-point copy delivers a better message. The use of heavier paper stock is very important—glossy or special matte stocks also stand out to buyers. Say it in color—remember that fashion is a very visual industry, and the look of your business card and other materials reflects your creativity. Full-color cards are preferred, but if cost is prohibitive, try using two elegant colors that together give the impression you want to convey. Some sellers have their pictures on their cards, which helps buyers put a face with the name on the card. How about unique card dimensions—use a vertical card or a custom-shaped card rather that the ordinary, boring horizontal card.

Have your company prepare brochures with the product style numbers, prices, and delivery dates each season and include interesting copy on each style and gist of the line. A professional-looking piece with this information can be used during your presentation and help you close more sales. Such a brochure should be in color and be printed on good paper stock. Handing a poorly designed or badly printed promotional piece will reflect negatively on you and your product. If the piece is not attractive, don't show it.

As covered in chapter 7, visuals are vital to any presentation. For major clients, develop a PowerPoint presentation customized for that customer. Get a professional to design your visual aids so they look attractive and powerful.

Devise a monthly newsletter that includes your picture, and provide tips to the trade (refer to the case study on chapter 7). Report on industry happenings that are important to your buyers. If you can't do the writing, then hire someone to do the writing using your input (many budding news reporters and college students will gladly moonlight and ghostwrite the newsletter for a fee). Get yourself known. Promote yourself and your company—get your name out there!

Chapter Summary

+ Sales will never be a rigid industry where salespeople can carry out procedures in a mechanical fashion.
+ Sales training is necessary to building a professional and effective sales force.
+ Sales training must encompass all facets of the business of sales to provide the salesperson with a well-rounded foundation upon which to build his or her style of selling.
+ "Practice makes perfect": Salespeople who receive quality training often will improve their performance.
+ Training programs can be divided into in-house programs run by sales managers or out-of-house programs run by outside consultants who specialize in organizing such programs.
+ The in-house program can contain any one or a combination of the following components: personalized assessments, pairing up, classroom-type sessions, and role-playing sessions.
+ The personalized training component includes an individual assessment of each salesperson's strengths and weaknesses and provides the means to address these individually.
+ The pairing up component teams up two salespeople with complementary skills to go on a specific number of sales calls together so they can learn from each other's strengths and properly address their own weaknesses.
+ The classroom component is usually held on a seasonal basis or before a new line or collection is being introduced; the sales manager and sales trainer act as teachers.

+ The role-playing component invites sellers to participate in real-world sales situations that are acted out under simulated and controlled conditions and are then critiqued by the role-players, the group, and the group leaders.

+ Handouts and business collateral, such as business cards or brochures, that a salesperson can give to potential buyers are selling tools and should look professional to enhance the sale presentation.

RW CASE STUDY

Peter V. Handal, who was profiled in chapter 7, provides us with answers to more questions. Turn to page 131 to read more about him.

Could you discuss the importance of sales training?

Sales training is more important today than ever before. We are in a world of fast change, increasing competition, and more educated consumers. This means salespeople are going to be asked constantly to do more, to do it better and faster, and to do it with fewer/less resources. Training salespeople to be more effective, productive, and professional is probably the most efficient alternative there is to this challenge. Salespeople cannot be satisfied staying at their current skill levels anymore than professional athletes or musicians can be.

How does sales training help the salesperson on the job?

Selling is both an art and a skill. Both can be learned, developed, and polished by coaching, not just learning new ideas, but also by practicing what works best with a skilled and experienced coach—someone who can make them better than they were. Motivation and knowledge are important, but it is skill that will win the sales on a consistent basis. Skill only comes from practice and good coaching.

What type of sales training methods do you conduct—role-playing, lectures, and so on?

Yes, these and more. Role-playing is important as long as it is coached for best practices and not just used to reinforce current ways of doing things. Lectures give people new ideas but not new skills. What works best is the "looping" approach that starts with a small improvement idea being practiced [or] coached until people can do it adequately. Then send them out into the real selling world for a week to practice it. Come back a week later and fine-tune the skill, add another step to it, and repeat the process. The "loops" get bigger each time with more being added each week until the salesperson has this process [down] as [his or her] new habit.

What type of sales-related topics are covered in your training program?

Selling can be broken down into phases, steps, or processes—whatever one would like to call them. Being a master of each step or part of the selling process should be the goal of every salesperson. Selling by accident is just as bad as not selling at all sometimes. If I don't know how I made a good sale, it will be hard for me to repeat it. This can be demoralizing to a salesperson. The different areas of the selling process that we focus upon in Dale Carnegie Training are

1. building rapport and gaining favorable attention,
2. creating interest,
3. providing solutions,
4. creating and understanding buying motivation,
5. gaining commitment.

We also include skill development in overcoming objections, pre-approach, and self-management areas as well as in follow-up and post-selling best practices.

Do you tailor the training program to address the individual salesperson's weak points? If so, how?

Whether conducted in an open program or an in-company group, all training must be customized to meet the needs of individual people. We must first find out where a person's ability in a certain area is right now before we try to make changes. We do this before, during, and after the training process.

Many training programs yield short-term results. How does your program differ?

Short-term results can come from just getting a few good ideas. It is important to remember two key concepts in sales training. Habit is stronger than knowledge, and people don't do what they know. They do what they have always done. Sales training is about behavior change, and this comes from good coaching with follow-up, feedback, accountability, measurability, recognition, and reward. Our trainers are thoroughly screened, recruited, hired, and trained from only those with successful backgrounds and professional reputations. We pride ourselves on our extensive trainer development process. That is why we consistently get good results for our clients, and they consistently come back to us.

How can you measure results of your training programs?

Three ways: [First,] we measure all of our training with an assessment form that gives us the participant reaction to our training methodology. We don't even bother to track "satisfaction" anymore. We measure how we "exceeded expectations" of our clients. [Second,] we have customized survey tools and assessments to measure the different needs and levels of selling abilities before and after our training. [Third,] the true ROI of any sales training lies in the increase in amounts of sales as measured over time in dollars. This can be set up in advance to factor in time and other potential factors that could impact selling abilities.

Would you like to add any other comments? It would be appreciated.

To fully understand the selling process today, we need to factor in what today's buying process looks like. Buyers first are preoccupied then are disinterested in what you are selling. Next, they are doubtful that you can do what you claim, and then they want to procrastinate even after they have seen good reasons to buy. Finally, they are fearful to change what they are doing right now. You may notice that these five steps of the buying process match evenly against the five steps of the selling process referred to above in question 4.

Questions to Consider

1. In your opinion, what is the difference between knowledge and skill? How can training help improve each of these factors?
2. What is the concept of "looping" according to Handal? How can it help the salesperson improve his or her skills?
3. Do you agree with Handal that "people don't do what they know. They do what they have always done"? Why?
4. What is your understanding of Handal's statement that "Selling by accident is just as bad as not selling at all sometimes"? Do you think it's correct or not? Why?

RW EXERCISES

1. Do you think sales training is necessary? Why? What are the benefits and disadvantages of sales training?
2. Recall an instance when you dealt with a salesperson who was not professional or helpful. Do you think training would have helped him or her? If so, how? If not, why?
3. List the aspects of the business of sales you think should be included in a training program, and detail why you feel each is important.

4. Can you think of any topic that does not belong and could be omitted from sales training, such as work safety? Where would each of these topics fit better, in your opinion?

5. Which program do you think works better: in-house or out-of-house? Why?

6. Which of the previously mentioned components do you think should be included in an in-house training program? What are the benefits that you see for each?

7. Pretend you are the sales manager at a fictitious fashion manufacturer or retailer. Prepare and conduct a sales training program in class where the other students act as the salespeople. Select the type of program and components you wish to include and plan how to carry these out. Remember to briefly tell the class about the type of business and merchandise your company offers and the target market and price range before starting your presentation so they can participate and get involved. Use visual aids, handouts, and any other tools you feel will contribute to the success of the program. Hand in an outline to the professor at the end of the presentation.

8. What is the importance of professional-looking business collateral? How do you think these could impact the success of a sales call?

9. Visit the high-end fashion department at a retail store or a private fashion boutique, and review the business collateral that salespeople use there. Analyze colors, sizes, and looks, and comment on how these affected your desire to buy from that salesperson.

END NOTES

1. Marcus, Stanley. *The Viewpoints of Stanley Marcus: A Ten Year Perceptive.* Denton: University of North Texas Press, 1995.

CHAPTER 11

MEASURING PRODUCTIVITY

Overview

To properly manage a sales force, the sales manager must be knowledgeable in measuring productivity and taking the right steps to
steadily increase the number and volume of sales. It is important for
the manager to set the proper sales goals, recognize which sellers are
lagging behind and which ones are doing well, and implement the
appropriate training and organizational actions to improve the productivity of the department. Without a tangible, realistic system of setting goals and measuring performance, a sales manager will be unable
to guide the sales force—and ultimately the company itself—toward
success.

Introduction

A business that is not expanding will become stagnant and eventually wither away because of routine customer loss. A company relies on its salespeople to drive sales forward and generate enough new and repeat business to keep the company ahead. But how much is enough? Should the salesperson with the smaller territory be expected to produce the same volume of sales as salespeople with larger territories? What about the amount of new business as opposed to repeat business—should salespeople be allowed to fall behind on their new business as long as they keep their overall volume high?

Sales managers face these questions and other similar issues on a daily basis and have to make critical decisions based on their assessments of the situations and their understanding of the dynamics of sales organizations. Productivity can and must be measured on an individual and a group level. The sales manager should formulate guidelines and statistics by which to evaluate not only the performance of each salesperson, but also the overall success of the department as a whole. In this chapter, we will discuss the different ways performance is measured.

Drops in productivity can be traced to a host of reasons. Individual sellers are affected by personal problems, such as a weakness in one or several aspects of the sales process, a dramatic change in the way the salesperson approaches clients and delivers sales presentations, or a problem in the seller's personal life that is distracting him or her from work. But obstacles to productivity may be present on a company-wide level, producing a performance issue across the department. An example of that could be the installation of a new but malfunctioning computerized order system.

Regardless of the reason, it behooves sales managers to get to the bottom of declines in productivity and address the situation as quickly as possible to restore normal sale volumes. In this capacity, sales managers must draw on their knowledge in sales methodology to spot and reinforce weaknesses; they must also employ their people skills to initiate meaningful dialogues with salespeople that encourage them to share their personal problems. The task of measuring productivity can be daunting and stressful at times, but managers who shirk their responsibilities in this area will do their company and sales force a great disservice. Let's begin by taking a look at what a realistic sales goal is and how to set such a goal in a manner that invites participation and commitment from the seller.

Setting Goals

Creating sales projections and realistic sales goals that are agreed on by both managers and salespeople is the first step to mastering productivity. Sales management must constantly monitor all sales activity, including increasing sales volume, opening new accounts, and retaining present ones. This necessitates implementing methods to improve productivity. These methods and how best to achieve them will be one of the main areas we will discuss in this chapter. Arranging and facilitating agreement between management and salespeople is extremely vital in fulfilling a company's overall sales projections.

Goal setting can be a delicate affair, and having the individual salesperson accept and commit to this goal or sales projection is vital to its success. In this chapter, we discuss how management arrives at sales projections and what methods they use to communicate these numbers to their selling team. How does a company arrive at a sales projection and set up a realistic goal? Developing the criteria for sales projections is one of the most involved areas for both the company and the salesperson. It is vital that this projection be reasonable and attainable. The projection must be reasonable because it must reflect an honest dollar amount to be attained; if this amount is unrealistic, it can be demoralizing for the salesperson, which can do more harm than good.

Sales projections and goals must be distributed with each launch of a new line or the beginning of each season. The entire sales force should be given their goals and quotas regardless of their ranking in the company because productivity knows no exceptions. The top sellers today could easily lose their positions tomorrow if management neglects to be involved with their performance. Monitoring the activities of salespeople in an unbiased manner is a must for the sales department to run well—otherwise, it would not be long before people accuse management of favoritism. Guidelines must be established and updated with the times, but within that framework, the salesperson must always be involved in the setting and attaining of sales goals.

It is important to understand that there are high-sales producers and there are others who are struggling to achieve their goals. The evaluation process and the weight of the final numbers must include parameters that are fair to all segments of the sales force. It is also worth mentioning again that a small percentage of the sales force brings in the major part of the business. As discussed in chapter 9, this situation is referred to as the "80-20 rule," which traditionally has been a guideline to measuring the productivity of the sales force. The rule states that about 20 percent of the sales force sells about 80 percent of a company's business. These percentages will vary somewhat—they could be 25–75 or 30–70, but the rule

RW Dictionary

Sales Goal A quantitative target for a sales-related statistic that the salesperson can achieve within a season, year, or other specified time frame.

RW Principle

Unrealistic goals not only are potentially demoralizing but also distracting to a salesperson, forcing him or her to focus time and effort on achieving something unattainable often at the expense of other important goals.

RW Dictionary

still stands. The top 20 percent producers may be in this category due to their territory assignment—for example, larger cities versus smaller towns—or because they are assigned to high-volume accounts. Then, there are "super salespeople" who will excel due to their selling skills and exceptional talents and will perform regardless of the territorial or account assignment. The sales managers' objective is to measure the performance of all sales personnel, regardless of their sales volume or standing so that every salesperson has a realistic goal he or she can meet.

In establishing the final goal, the manager must take into account the type of territory, account assignment, previous and current volumes, and trends in the specific marketplace and territory. The territory's **buying power index (BPI)** is often a significant factor in setting the sales goals. It is used to forecast demand, and its market can be a region, state, or county.

BPI includes population, income, and spending data. This information is published each year by *Sales and Marketing Management* magazine. The data is available in research libraries on CD-ROM and for purchase. The raw data for this information is collected from the U.S. Bureau of Census, Bureau of Labor Statistics, and National Center for Educational Statistics. Each county in the United States has a BPI percentile assigned to it, which indicates its buying power. The BPI is calculated by first comparing, in a percentage format, the local population, income, and retail sales to the comparable U.S. totals, which serve as the 100 percent figure. For example, if XYZ county retail sales, population, and income make up 1 percent of these measurements in United States, then it could be said that XYZ county has a BPI of 1 percent.

While marketing personnel use BPI to compare market potential and measure demand and purchases in a specific market for a state, county, or zip code, sales executives can use it as a tool in establishing sales projections and goals and measure productivity. If XYZ county's BPI is 1 percent and the total yearly sales for the company is $10 million, then the BPI for that county will be $100,000 in sales for the year. This can be figured into the sales projection and goal for the salesperson, which translates to that county, which should produce $100,000 in total sales for the year. As we mentioned, this is not an ironclad rule—other factors, such as an increase or decrease in population buying power, must be considered for goal setting and performance evaluation. However, most fashion territories are set up geographically and incorporate more than one county. Management would then compute the individual counties' BPIs and other measurements that make up the total territory as the salesperson's sales goal.

It is also important to incorporate the company's sales history of the county, that is, the dollar amount shipped and addition or loss of customers, into this equation. For example, if a salesperson's volume for last year in XYZ county is 3 percent of the company's sales, this would super cede the BPI percentage of 1 percent. So, if the projected sales are $10 million, we can project $300,000 as the goal for XYZ county, as opposed to $100,000 if we were to factor BPI alone.

Some fashion companies do not use BPI at all. Some use sales history for each territory as the benchmark for setting upcoming goals. Others set goals to fit the company's sales projections, so if the company aims to increase sales by 10 percent, then every salesperson is expected to increase performance by 10 percent as well. Still others may use a combination of the two factors or formulate a completely different method to set goals. The BPI method, or any other method, for establishing sales goals must be carefully and periodically analyzed for the information it offers and its effectiveness.

Adjusting to Change

Nothing ever stays the same and that includes the business of sales. Changes in territory, trends, and market conditions must be considered in developing sales objectives. Market conditions that should be taken into account include increases or decreases in unemployment, population shifts, demographics, and consumer spending at a retail level. The sales manager must ask several questions before finalizing the sales goals to ensure that it is realistic in the context of current and past statistics and market shifts. Here are a few of the things that must be considered.

+ Are we losing or gaining customers in this territory? What is the percentage of increase or decrease?
+ Is there above-average attrition in the territory? If so, why?
+ What is the national attrition rate, and how does it compare with the individual salesperson's performance?
+ Is the salesperson neglecting his or her customer base?
+ Are sales increasing or decreasing? Why?
+ Is the area in an economic rise or decline?
+ Is competition spending more time and money to build this territory?
+ Are there any other changes in the territory?
+ Is the salesperson calling on the wrong prospective customers (Figure 11.1)?

Ideally, the sales manager's study of the most recent season should yield an analysis of the salesperson's performance along one or more of the performance categories detailed on page 199 in Table 11.1.

External Factors

Market conditions can and do have impact on sales performance. These external factors cannot be controlled by the salesperson and must therefore be taken into account when evaluating the salesperson's performance.

SALESPERSON

1. **Unemployment:** An increase in unemployment often leads to a slowdown in purchasing.
2. **Population:** A population increase or decrease translates to more or less end users. This affects the buying decisions of retailers and wholesalers.
3. **Demographics:** A major change in the age, ethnicity, or income makeup of the population similarly affects the buying decisions of end users, retailers, and wholesalers.
4. **Consumer spending at a retail level:** The overall condition of the economy and the consumer's confidence in the economy affect the end user's buying decisions.

RW Concept

The sales manager must remember that the purpose of the evaluation is to improve the salesperson's performance or recommend termination if no improvement is shown. If an evaluation is not benchmarked against real tangible productivity issues and goals, then it has no merit and becomes simply a useless administrative exercise.

The sales manager should remember that if negative changes are not a salesperson's fault, then the sales goals must be adjusted to a reasonable number so as not to demoralize the seller. Having attainable goals can be a motivating force in itself when the salesperson reaches these goals.

If the territory or account listing has an established sales history, then the past sales volume, the number of active accounts, new accounts, and attrition should be factored into the sales goal. After proper analysis of this history, the sales manager has to include this information into the final sales projection and into the company's planned projection for future growth. For example, if the territory or account list has been increasing at a rate of 10 percent per year and the company estimates an increase of 15 percent, it is reasonable to project this 15 percent increase in this salesperson's territory. However, if the trend is downward in the territory due to external reasons—such as changes in demographics, additional competition, or a rise in unemployment in the territory, then management must pay attention to these negative items and reduce projection for the goal to be obtainable.

Evaluating Performance

Setting or creating sales goals is not in itself enough to reach them—it is imperative that methods be developed for evaluating the successful achievement of these goals. There are several steps managers can take to evaluate performance. Companies differ in their approaches to sales management; however, the final objective of the performance evaluation

TABLE 11.1
Performance Categories

Performance Category	Explanation	Recommended Goal Adjustment
The salesperson did well.	The salesperson reached his or her goal last season, and no other changes took place in the market.	There is no need to adjust for change.
The marketplace improved.	There was a substantial improvement to the territory's economy, employment rate, or demographics, so the salesperson should be able to substantially outperform last season's sales.	The goal should be raised accordingly.
The company's product lines did well.	The lines sold exceptionally well across the board last season.	The sales goal should be raised.
The product lines did poorly.	Most salespeople had trouble selling the new lines, and buyers kept complaining about styles or functionality.	If product lines remain same, then goals should be lowered accordingly.
The marketplace deteriorated.	A major client moved to another territory, or the economy in the territory has suddenly plunged.	Goals should be lowered accordingly.
The salesperson did poorly.	The salesperson failed to reach his or her goal because of inadequate performance.	Goals should not be lowered; instead, they should remain the same, and the sales manager should embark on corrective actions with the salesperson (see page 206).

should be universally focused on providing a means to systematically improve sales for the company.

It is also vital to use criteria that will accurately measure a salesperson's performance. There are different ways to measure productivity. The weight of performance depends on the individual sales manager's assessment of his or her sales force. Some managers feel that quantitative performance is more important than qualitative performance. Both

RW Concept

Sales is a people-oriented field and is therefore dependent on a certain degree of human and circumstantial unpredictability. Results in sales may not always immediately be evident in numbers and take months to materialize. A manager cannot expect instant results every time and should take into account a salesperson's diligent efforts and progress toward improvement.

measurements are important, but it must be pointed out that in selling new products qualitative measurements rank high on the scoreboard because of the extra effort and time factor in getting results. Combined quantitative and qualitative performance is the standard way to measure productivity.

The following are some of the quantitative factors that managers use to measure results:

+ measuring sales volume
+ number of calls that resulted in appointments
+ number of presentations the salesperson has made
+ number of presentations that resulted in orders
+ total ratio of presentations to orders closed
+ the amounts of the orders
+ number of new accounts sold
+ last year's sales compared with this year's

The following are some of the qualitative factors:

+ appearance
+ product knowledge
+ communication and presentation skills
+ attitude
+ assertiveness
+ perseverance
+ commitment
+ company loyalty
+ awareness of their competition

Let's look at a general outline for a simple evaluation process.

When Do We Begin Evaluating Performance?

We've set the goals before the season or year gets underway. Now the season is in full swing. How can the sales manager monitor which salespeople are on target to reach their goals and which may need assistance to improve their performance? Some sales managers prefer to review performance soon after the season begins, while others wait until the season's end to draw up an official review. We side with the former—waiting only loses sales and revenues for the company, and an informal assessment of performance about four weeks into the season can help salespeople to get over their weak starts and improve their overall figures for the season.

Getting the Information

Since goals are set in numerical quantities, such as the number of orders, volume of orders in dollars, number of new accounts, and so on, it should be fairly easy for the organized manager to determine if salespeople have in fact reached these numbers. Most companies recap a salesperson's weekly activities by developing a computerized report. All orders are sent to the home office by the salesperson daily and are tallied the end of each week. Companies may vary the type of weekly report, but most gather the following information:

+ dollar amount of weekly sales
+ percentage of weekly sales to goals
+ number of accounts sold versus active accounts
+ category of accounts sold—active, new, inactive
+ styles and colors sold—for production purposes

Management must analyze the data and take steps to inform the salesperson whether there are any problems. For example, Dora has a sales goal of $100,000 with an active account roster of fifty accounts. Hypothetically, if the selling season is ten weeks, she should maintain a minimum of $10,000 in sales each week. The first week her total sales were $3,000, and she sold three accounts. The results of the sales manager's weekly report will indicate a red flag, and management can spot a potential problem early on. It is better to take steps at the beginning of the selling season when the downward trend may be stopped than to wait for several weeks into the season to discover that Dora may not reach the projection. This type of management control not only helps the salesperson but also is essential for the success of any company to know what's happening when it is happening.

The Evaluation Process

The sales manager now has a written list of the specific sales goals set with Dora, as well as a verified report with Dora's figures for each of these goals. In the same manner that we utilized a system to determine if a goal should be adjusted higher or lower based on internal and external factors we can adopt some guidelines to determine if a salesperson achieved the goals set for him or her, and if not, why. Many sales managers develop their own methods and categories for performance evaluation, giving weight to the factors that they deem most important. Table 11.2 is a sample breakdown of what these categories may look like.

The manager should review the salesperson's performance in an objective and fair manner. The evaluation must be easy to understand and precise in specifying what the salesperson did right and wrong. If the

	TABLE 11.2 Performance Evaluation	
Performance	**Evaluation**	**Recommended Action**
Outstanding	The salesperson reached all or most goals, despite deteriorating market conditions or unpopular product lines.	Consider special award for the salesperson's outstanding performance.
Good	The salesperson reached all or most goals based on his or her own efforts, in a relatively unchanged market.	Commend and reward the salesperson's performance.
Satisfactory	The salesperson reached most of the main goals. or The salesperson failed to reach some major goals because of market conditions outside of his or her control.	Commend the salesperson for goals reached, and work to correct goals that suffered.
Below par	The salesperson got close to most of the goals. or There is a substantial improvement to the territory or the popularity of company's lines that caused an increase in sales and meeting of goals, not the salesperson's efforts.	Take corrective actions (see pages 202–206).
Poor	The salesperson failed to reach most of his or her goals because of inadequate performance.	Take corrective actions (see pages 202–206).

sales manager fails to define the evaluation standards and how it is done, then it is likely that the salespeople will soon feel the evaluation is carried out with caprice and bias—the resulting damage to productivity can be tremendous. It is ideal for the evaluation to be given to the salesperson in writing as well as verbally.

Productivity Facilitation

One of the most important duties performed by sales managers is to function as productivity facilitators. It is all too easy to just give salespeople their goals, sit back, and evaluate them at the end of the season. However, over the long run, this lazy practice will harm sales. The successful sales manager must be proactive.

Improving a sales force's productivity is vital to the success of any business. This can be done by conducting empowerment meetings, boosting morale, and providing the team with additional sales tools as discussed in Chapter 10. But, let us assume the salespeople have these tools and know how to use them. Now what needs to happen to improve their productivity? Sales managers must establish the sales projections as discussed earlier in the chapter and utilize the various managerial and corrective tools at their disposal to help individual salespeople meet their sales goals.

Salesperson's Agreement

In *The Practice of Management*,[2] Peter Drucker defines *management by objectives* (MBO) as the act of getting employees involved in reaching their goals and objectives and having a voice along with management in final decision making. A time frame is established to evaluate performance and results. A successful MBO program encourages feedback by both management and employees. Management by objectives incorporates the SMART method for determining the soundness of the objectives.

+ Specific
+ Measurable
+ Achievable
+ Realistic
+ Time related

The actual action of setting goals is often overlooked as a performance facilitator. The first and most important management tool of the sales manager is the salesperson's determination. It is a proven fact that when people are involved and feel as if they are part of a project, their performance increases. When people are pushed against the corner, they fight and may even resist sound, constructive ideas simply because these are thrown at them without their input. However, give people some input on a project, let their voices be heard, let them participate in the process, and they will truly become part of the project and work hard for its success.

This is why evaluations must be based on agreed-on sales objectives. This principle should apply to setting up sales objectives and the evaluation of performance by the individual after they are agreed upon. Managers who sit down with salespeople to discuss goals before sales are finalized—whether they are to increase volume or open up new accounts—will usually be satisfied with the outcome. A typical scenario may play out as follows:

Sales Manager:	In keeping with our policy of first discussing your sales goal, I would like you to let me know what your sales projection is for this season. Please consider that we have increased our advertising and public relations budgets. We have also increased our production facilities. You were asked to submit your sales projection after seeing this new line. Could you tell me what your projection is for this season?
Salesperson:	Last year for this season, my sales were $35,000. I feel with the loss of one of my leading accounts, Ilene & Company, which is now purchasing from overseas sources, it will be quite a stretch to reach this figure. I am projecting $31,500 in sales for this season.
Sales Manager:	We feel your goal this season should be $36,000. We realize that Ilene & Company contributed 10 percent of your volume ($3,500) for the season last year. However, the average order for your territory was $1,500. If you could open three additional new accounts and maintain that average per order, this would give you a $1,000 increase over last year's sales. Do you feel that this is a reasonable goal?
Salesperson:	Yes, I now think this is quite reasonable due to the increase in the company's marketing and production efforts. I will put more time into prospecting and drumming up more business. I will try my best to achieve this goal and maybe exceed it.

We previously discussed how we should go about developing the sales objective—what we did not discuss is that it works best when both parties are involved in the objective and the method of evaluating the results. For instance, assume a salesperson has agreed with his or her sales manager that he or she can increase sales by 15 percent because this is an attainable goal. The account base is very strong in his or her territory due to the dynamic growth in the population and because several large companies are moving their headquarters there. So, the usual attrition of about 10 percent will not occur in the territory this season.

The salesperson has made a commitment and unless something unforeseen occurs, he or she will work hard to achieve these goals. If the salesperson doesn't increase the customer base by 15 percent, only he or she will be to blame because it was the salesperson who agreed on the objectives. In fact, if the salesperson doesn't make the agreed-on numbers, management can work with him or her to improve this aspect of the sales objective. Maybe, instead of making six sales calls a day, the salesperson can make seven calls per day.

Shadowing

Shadowing can be an extremely helpful tool for sales managers because it provides them with direct insight into what salespeople are actually doing in the field. Before starting this exercise, it is imperative that sales managers discuss their roles and relieve salespeople of any anxiety or nervousness that can occur when supervisors observe them closely. Managers must assure salespeople that shadowing is not a negative experience but rather a learning one.

When "shadowing" a salesperson, a manager is following that person for the day, listening to the manner in which the salesperson makes phone appointments and evaluating his or her telephone etiquette, making commentary on certain events, and attending all sales presentations. While with the salesperson, the sales manager should resist getting involved in the sales presentation itself. The manager must remain a spectator and observer of the sales presentation, making notes of what the salesperson is doing well and where he or she is lacking. Shadowing offers the manager a chance to see how the seller reacts to real-life situations, something that no simulation or training exercise can ever offer.

Based on the day's analysis, the manager can then create an accurate assessment of the salesperson's strengths and weaknesses. The sales manager can even use this information to formulate a highly personalized training program for the salesperson that focuses on exactly what needs improvement.

Curbside Meetings

Another important tool for managing seller productivity is the curbside meeting. Termed "curbside" for its flexible nature, this casual and disarming one-on-one meeting with the salesperson can be more productive than a dozen formal meetings. At the heart of the curbside meeting is informality, which allows the manager and seller to talk freely and discuss matters in an open manner without fear of retribution or penalty.

Suppose the seller is having trouble at home—it is unlikely the seller will talk about it in one of the sales meetings in front of all his or her peers, but it may become such a distraction that the salesperson cannot function at work. In such a case, the curbside meeting is the type of atmosphere that will bring the salesperson's guard down enough to have a truly meaningful conversation that will shed light on the situation.

An informal curbside meeting at a local coffee shop, for example, can do wonders for a seller's productivity. Because it is informal, sellers don't feel threatened and are encouraged to talk about the problems they are encountering in the field. In addition, because it takes place away from the office, both seller and manager will dedicate their undivided attention to the conversation, undisturbed by calls and other distractions.

The manager should aim to resolve the issue in the curbside meeting if possible and offer potential solutions. If the seller recognizes an approach that may resolve the situation, then they both agree to try it and see if things improve. It is important for the manager to follow up on this and check back with the seller soon after to see whether the approach did indeed alleviate the problem.

Formal Evaluations

Formal meetings with the salesperson can be used as a tool to improve productivity; however, managers should proceed with caution because most salespeople equate such meetings with the final warnings received before a person is terminated. Having a formal meeting with one of the salespeople can cause a ripple effect of anxiety across the sales force. If it is done improperly, other salespeople can learn about it and wonder if they are next, with the likely result of a general drop in productivity. However, used with discretion and at the right time, the formal meeting can help shake sellers out of their slumps and stir them into action. If it does not, then sales managers must determine whether they need to terminate the salesperson.

Separation

RW Principle

In all cases of dismissal, the manager must study and comply with the company's personnel policies as the first priority. These policies are often enacted to comply with government laws and ignoring these may result in lawsuits and considerable fines for a company. Consult with a human resources manager whenever you are unsure of proper protocol.

When sellers do not perform well, they are doing a disservice not only to their own pocketbooks, but also to the companies at which they work because those companies are depending on them to bring in a certain amount of sales. Obviously, when sellers aren't doing their jobs and all corrective actions have failed, then sales managers are forced to terminate them. While it should be a last resort, dismissal is nonetheless a necessary tool that managers use to steer nonproducing sellers toward another sales field or career. Separation should be done in the presence of a witness, and the manager should show the seller the documentation for all of the corrective actions taken up to the time of dismissal. Following the dismissal, it would be beneficial to explain to the other sellers what the dismissed seller did wrong to dispel notions of broad or whimsical dismissals.

Chapter Summary

+ Productivity can and must be measured on an individual and a group level. The sales manager should formulate guidelines and statistics by which to evaluate not only the performance of each salesperson, but also the overall success of the department as a whole.

+ The task of measuring productivity can be daunting and stressful at times, but managers who shirk their responsibilities in this area will do their company and sales force a great disservice.

+ Creating sales projections and realistic sales goals that are agreed on by both managers and salespeople is the first step to mastering productivity.

+ Sales projections and goals must be distributed with each launch of a new line or at the beginning of each season. The entire sales force should be given their goals and quotas regardless of their ranking in the company because productivity knows no exceptions.

+ It is important to understand that there are high-sales producers and there are others who struggle to achieve their goals. The evaluation process and the weight of the final numbers must include parameters that are fair to all segments of the sales force.

+ In establishing the final goal, the manager must take into account the type of territory, account assignment, previous and current volumes, and trends in the specific marketplace and territory, including the BPI.

+ Setting or creating sales goals is not in itself enough; it is imperative that methods be developed for evaluating the successful achievement of these goals.

+ Combined quantitative and qualitative performance is the standard way to measure productivity.

+ One of the most important duties performed by sales managers is their function as productivity facilitators. The successful sales manager must be proactive in assisting salespeople meet their goals.

+ Improving productivity of the sales force is vital to the success of any business. This can be done by conducting empowerment meetings, boosting morale, and providing the team with additional sales tools.

+ The sales manager must utilize managerial and corrective tools to help the individual salespeople meet these sales goals. These tools include:
  - Salesperson's determination. A sales goal that is set in agreement with the salesperson is a key performance facilitation tool.
  - Shadowing provides the sales manager with direct insight into what the salesperson is actually doing in the field.

- The curbside meeting is a flexible, casual, and disarming one-on-one meeting between the manager and the salesperson.
- Formal evaluations can be used to shake a salesperson out of a deep slump and help him or her to improve, but managers should proceed with caution since this may make everyone in the department nervous.
- When a seller does not perform and all corrective avenues have been exhausted, the sales manager is forced to dismiss the salesperson.

RW CASE STUDY

Chris Kolbe is the president of Original Penguin, a fashion collection of men's and women's apparel, accessories, and footwear. The Penguin originated in 1955 and quickly became known as the original golf shirt brand. During the fifties, sixties, and seventies, the Penguin became a classic U.S. sportswear icon.

Do you set goals and expectations for your sales staff, and if so, how do you go about setting them?

If you don't have goals, it is very unlikely that you will move forward. This is why we set goals for every one of our sales staff. Usually before the season begins we go through a planning cycle where management looks at the very big picture and identifies our expectations for the company in general. Then we take a bottom's up approach and try to work it out from the detail level up to the larger picture and see what we can do in terms of product strategies, retailing strategies, and marketing to help support the sales efforts. In the sales meetings, the sales managers and staff review the territory and major accounts, break down the sales plans, put in their numbers, and strategize how to meet their expectations. It is vital that the salespeople internalize these goals and understand how we arrived at these figures, so they can assume these goals in earnest.

How do you measure productivity and monitor progress?

We have a computerized system [that] keeps track of all orders and generates a weekly report card, if you will, for each salesperson. This report details the salesperson's bookings (orders placed), which of the salesperson's accounts have ordered and which have not. This forces the salespeople to monitor their own progress as the first step, and it also gives the sales managers a tool to monitor performance. If half of the salesperson's accounts have not placed an order and we're well into the season, then we know there's a problem. Productivity is also measured compared to peers. If a third-tier salesperson produces more than a first-tier seller, then it really brings it home that the first-tier seller has a performance problem [that] needs to be addressed.

What avenues do your sales managers take to help their salespeople achieve these goals?

You can draft great and noble plans, but if you can't execute them, then what are they worth? Not much. We stress that performance is key with all of our sales staff. Since sales is commission driven, the more you sell the more you earn and that's enough of a motivation for most salespeople. Our contracted salespeople (not employed directly by Penguin) always have the threat of losing the account and are motivated to perform every season. Our in-house staff is a little less commission-driven, but they have more ownership in the company and have performance reviews and bonuses as incentives. What we generally do though is put the points of the sales goals implementation plans into role-playing scenarios where the salespeople go through these with [one another] before they go out to see any customers. This forces them to think these plans through rather then just sit there and listen to the sales managers. We do not implement sales contests within our company. We do emphasize the superior product and brand name recognition that Original Penguin has. We work to inspire the salespeople to be a part of it. The salespeople have to believe they are "selling a brand, not an item," and they have to believe in the brand. It's a mindset.

What are some of the remedies you utilize to address under-performance?

We stay in constant communication with the salespeople and apply constant pressure to keep them on track. Most of them try hard and know that it's about getting the sale rather than waiting. However, if a salesperson is getting progressively worse and [is] way off [his or her] goals, we will find someone else to do it. Sometimes there are personal issues in the way, and we try to help [salespeople] work through this and assist them to remove the roadblocks in their way. But there comes a point of no return where business-wise, if under-performance persists, the company cannot keep the salesperson on its payroll. What we look for in a salesperson is an unrelenting, determined individual. You cannot be passive in sales. There are ways to be aggressive without being offensive. Those are the guys [who] make it in the long run.

Questions to Consider

1. Why do you think it is important for salespeople to "internalize their sales goals"? What do you think happens if they don't?

2. What part does believing in the product play in Original Penguin's salespeople's motivation? Do you think it is effective? Which would you prefer—inspiration or contests? Why?

3. What according to Kolbe is the "point of no return?" How should a manager deal with someone who has reached that point? Why?

RW EXERCISES

1. In your opinion, why are sales goals set, and what do you think would happen if sales managers did not set goals for their sales forces?

2. Give an example of a realistic goal and an unrealistic goal. Explain why it is realistic and what effects each goal will have on a seller's performance.

3. Explain in your own words the factors that a sales manager needs to take into consideration when adjusting goals for change and why each is important.

4. Pair up with another student so one of you acts as the sales manager and the other acts as the salesperson, either in retail or B2B. In the first scenario, the manager should simply give the seller goals without consulting the seller and ignoring any objections the seller may have. Note down the outcome of the meeting and how you think it would affect the seller's performance. In the second scenario, the manager should consult the seller, review any changes in the territory, and adjust sales projections accordingly and get agreement from the seller on the goals. Write down how each approach affected the process and outcome of the presentation. Switch roles for a different perspective, and note the new responses.

5. Based on your own conclusions from the readings in this section, how would you conduct a performance evaluation if you were a sales manager? Which of the quantitative and qualitative factors would be most important to you and why?

6. Why do you think a successful sales manager should be a productivity facilitator? Give an example of how productivity facilitation by the manager may work to improve salespeople's performances.

7. Pair up with another student so one of you acts as the sales manager and the other acts as the salesperson, either in retail or B2B. Go through each of the five managerial and corrective actions discussed on pages 202–206 (salesperson's agreement, shadowing,

curbside meetings, formal evaluations, and separation), and note down the outcome of each action and how you think it would affect the seller's performance. Write down how each approach affected the process and outcome of the presentation. Switch roles for a different perspective, and note the new responses.

8. Review the scenario from exercise 6, and write what managerial and corrective steps, if any, you would take as a sales manager as a result of the evaluation. Explain your reasoning and why you feel these actions will improve the seller's performance.

END NOTES

1. American Marketing Association dictionary. Online at www.marketingpower.com.
2. Drucker, Peter. *The Practice of Management*, New York: Harper & Row Publishers, Inc., 1954.

CHAPTER 12

Objectives

+ Learn the broad framework and dynamics of the fashion sales industry.
+ Understand the typical structure for a fashion sales force.
+ Explore the roles and responsibilities that salespeople and managers have within that structure.
+ Learn the differences between retail and B2B structures.
+ Comprehend the typical structure for a fashion sales buyer.
+ Examine the do's and don'ts in organizational interaction.

ORGANIZATIONAL STRUCTURE AND INTERACTION

Overview

It is important for salespeople to understand the organizational framework within which they are working to facilitate interaction and productivity. Salespeople who do not know with whom to speak about customer credit matters, delivery dates, or even bureaucratic matters will have difficulty servicing their accounts and doing their jobs. Proper knowledge of the organization and the methods to interact with others are vital to any salesperson's—and indeed sales manager's—success.

Introduction

No salesperson is an island. All salespeople must interact with their prospective and existing buyers every day. This book has covered at length the principles, methods, and caveats that salespeople should follow to develop business relationships with their customers. Selling to buyers and keeping them happy is essential not only for generating repeat orders, but also for preserving the reputation of the salesperson and the company.

But what about the other people with which a salesperson must interact? What about the employees in a buyer's firm who answer the phones, receive orders, or write out checks? Salespeople will have to deal with one of these employees at some point and the way they interact with these employees can make or break a relationship with a client. Remember these are employees on the buyer's payroll and their allegiance is with the buyer first. Be rude to a receptionist, say something negative about the buyer to the loading dock manager, joke about the company's payment history with the bookkeeper, and word may reach your buyer's ear quickly. Next thing you know, the client stops buying from you. It behooves a salesperson to develop relationships with a buyer's employees but to know how to properly interact with them.

The production manager, accounting staff, and delivery team who work with the salesperson at the same company are important allies. Expedited production, quick processing of a client's credit, and speedy delivery are all in their hands. It is worth the salesperson's time to learn who in the company performs what job and develop good working relationships with each person. This chapter discusses organizational framework, the role of the salesperson or sales manager as it relates to the company, and a few general rules to observe when interacting with staffs.

Know Your Organizational Chart

The primary people in the fashion sales industry with whom salespeople should be familiar include the manufacturer, reseller, salesperson's manufacturing representative, retailer, sales manager, production manager, controller (accounting manager), shipping department manager, and end user. Each person plays an important role within the industry and helps the product move along from its origin to the consumer (Figure 12.1).

Manufacturers

The fashion product is conceived by the manufacturer. Manufacturers design, produce, and assemble—either domestically or by outsourcing—raw materials into a finished product. They sell the finished product to

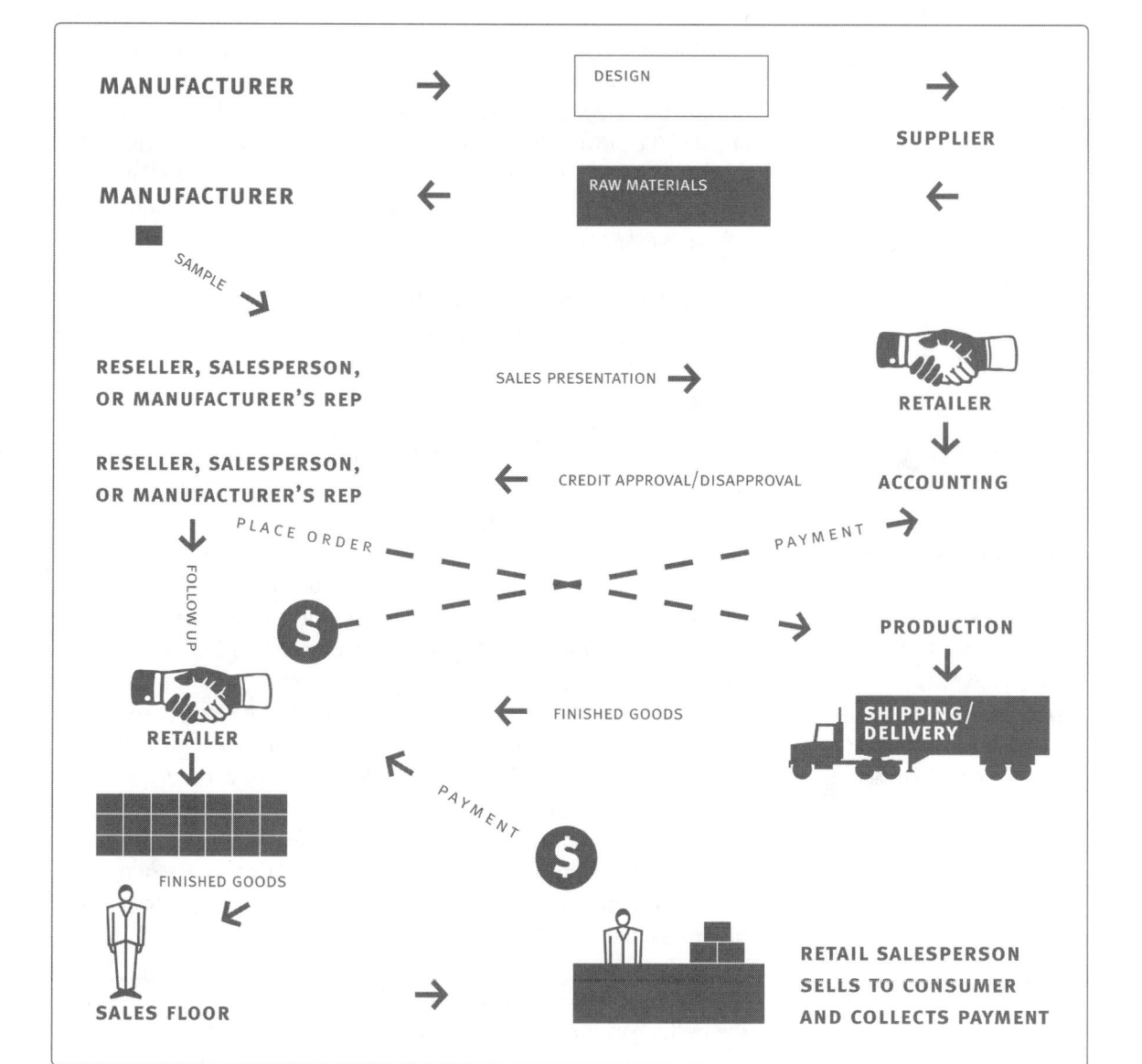

(figure contents)

MANUFACTURER   →   DESIGN   →

                                                                SUPPLIER

MANUFACTURER   ←   RAW MATERIALS   ←

     SAMPLE   ↘

RESELLER, SALESPERSON,   SALES PRESENTATION →   RETAILER
OR MANUFACTURER'S REP

RESELLER, SALESPERSON,   ← CREDIT APPROVAL/DISAPPROVAL   ACCOUNTING
OR MANUFACTURER'S REP

                PLACE ORDER - - -   PAYMENT →

FOLLOW UP   PRODUCTION

RETAILER   ← FINISHED GOODS   SHIPPING/
                                                                DELIVERY

                        PAYMENT
FINISHED GOODS ↙

                                                    RETAIL SALESPERSON
SALES FLOOR   →   SELLS TO CONSUMER
                                                    AND COLLECTS PAYMENT

FIGURE 12.1

**The fashion industry supply chain
at a glance**

A broad view of the typical product and
information flow within the average fashion sales structure.

the many markets of the world. Manufacturers must have salespeople
who are able to communicate the manufacturer's message to their target
markets. To reach the retailer or end consumer, manufacturers utilize
different types of sales forces—the most prominent fashion manufacturers may have a direct, captive sales force, while other manufacturers may
engage the services of independent manufacturers' representatives who
work on commission.

Many designer brands do not manufacture their own products, but
have them produced by contractors who have the machinery and labor

to make the products. Most well-known designer-name products are manufactured overseas by contractors who are given the fabrics, designs, patterns, and labels to do so. The lower labor costs have enabled the most well-known brands to keep a competitive edge in the market place by offering their customers value. The merchandise is shipped in bulk to the U.S. company and marketed by the manufacturer's sales network.

Outside Salespeople Versus Inside Salespeople

Manufacturers may work with a direct sales force employed by the same companies for which they work or represent, independent or outside sales representatives, or a combination of the two.

Outside salespeople are typically assigned a geographic territory or specific major accounts referred to as **key accounts**. These salespeople normally reside in their respective territories and are in direct contact with the retailers and resellers within those territories. For example, an outside salesperson whose territory is in the Southeast would likely live in that territory and would travel within that territory to call on accounts. The territory consists either of several counties, the entire state, or even several states in the region depending on the sales volume and the company. For example, the southeast region usually consists of the states of Florida, Georgia, and Alabama. Territory assignments are based on the present sales volume, projected volume, and number of active accounts. A nationally advertised branded fashion line with consumer demand would require extensive coverage in a smaller concentrated area. Compensation of outside salespeople depends on their type, but they are usually paid by commission only. In some cases, they are issued draws against commissions. They do not receive salaries or bonuses, nor are they reimbursed for their selling expenses.

The direct sales force that works in the same company as the manufacturer are employees of that company and are therefore reimbursed for their selling expenses. They represent the company's products only and are compensated with salary, salary plus commission/bonuses, and even, in some cases, weekly draws (advance payments against future commissions).

Inside salespeople are physically located at a company's headquarters or in one of the regional offices throughout the country. They are mostly salaried, though some work on salaries plus commissions or bonuses. Inside salespeople rarely travel for sales calls but typically work with buyers who visit the office directly, with or without the solicitation of an outside salesperson. They also work with company accounts that are referred to as **house accounts**.

House accounts are those that are assigned to inside salespeople or

---

RW Dictionary

Outside Salespeople Independent sale representatives who reside in their home territories and meet up with buyers within those territories to sell product lines.

Key Accounts High-volume and/or highly profitable accounts that form the backbone of the company's client roster.

RW Dictionary

Inside Salespeople Handle orders that come into the office directly, with or without the solicitation of outside salespeople, and work at the company's headquarters or in one of the regional offices.

House Account A major account with high volume that is assigned to a dedicated inside salesperson or sales executive because it requires considerable time, attention, and support. These accounts are major and may receive additional services based on their huge volume, leaving little room for compensation to a straight-commission or outside sales-person. The inside salesperson/account executive responsible for this major account is usually salaried and may receive a bonus or commission based on increases in sales volume.

executives in sales management. Commissions are usually not paid to anyone on these accounts. In essence, the company sees fit to sell directly to these major customers. Typically, house accounts, because of their high volume, necessitate management to spend more time, energy, and funding to maintain and increase their business.

Manufacturers' Representatives or Independent Reps

The manufacturer's representative can either be an individual or a business. As a representative, he or she is not part of the manufacturer's payroll and falls into the same category as outside salespeoeple. In fact, the typical manufacturer's representative can and does represent several noncompetitive manufacturers. Much like the matchmaker of old days, the representative brings and cultivates buyers, matching the buyer with the manufacturer of given products that are for sale. Representatives normally receive a straight commission on their sales without ever obtaining ownership of the goods. The commission rate varies with companies and can range from 6 to 10 percent on merchandise shipped. These commission rates fluctuate depending on consumer demand for the product. Manufacturer's representatives and commissioned salespeople are paid on shipments, not on initial bookings, less any trade discounts, returns, and allowances to customers such as advertising and markdowns. Payment is usually monthly, and most companies make payment on the tenth of the month following receipt of shipments.

Resellers

Resellers do not manufacture a product; they purchase finished goods from producers in large quantities at discount prices (usually). They take title of the merchandise, and market, warehouse, and ship it to their customers. The resellers' channels are very flexible; their customers can consist of any or all of the following: other resellers, other manufacturers, retailers, government agencies, institutions, and/or other businesses.

The Retailer

The retailer can be a department store, a chain of fashion shops, or an individual boutique. The retailer sells directly to consumers. Salespeople in retail stores interact with shoppers to assist them in finding the items that best fit their needs and prompt the sale. In high-ticket departments and in expensive boutiques, the retail salesperson has the chance to form a relationship with the customer; in the low-ticket departments, sales are normally quick and impersonal. The rate for straight commissioned retail salespeople can start at 5 percent, although *some* high-ticket departments pay a greater commission rate. Some stores will pay lower commission rates on sale goods. Many retail stores pay commissions weekly, and others pay monthly. Statements are usually issued monthly to the selling staff and deductions are included for returns.

The Sales Manager

The sales manager is the executive in charge of the salespeople within a specific territory or entire sales force. Sales managers hire, direct, train, and motivate salespeople. They are responsible for setting sales goals, supervising salespeople's progress toward those goals, and solving problems that hinder productivity. They are also the go-to person when salespeople need assistance addressing a price, production, or delivery issue. Sales managers attend design, marketing, and merchandising meetings and provide important feedback to these entities as to what's happening in the marketplace as reported by their sales forces. They also work in close proximity with the marketing, accounting, production, and shipping department managers to coordinate sales with promised delivery dates.

The Marketing Manager

In smaller and independently owned companies, we find the role of the **marketing manager** is usually in the hands of the owner or the sales manager. If both positions exist within one company, then the sales manager works closely with the marketing manager, as he or she does with design, product development, and the other major departments. Sales and marketing go together like bread and butter: One really cannot work successfully without the other. The two functions must be put into play for a product to succeed.

Briefly, marketing functions are distinctively different from sales because market orientation focuses on demographics and psychographics and therefore involve gathering information about consumers or end users. They are always asking, "What do they want, and how can we satisfy their needs?" To facilitate the design and sale of a company's products, marketing management is also involved in fashion market trends and the company's competition. Without feedback from the sales department, marketing cannot fully achieve its goals. One of marketing management's main concern is conducting research of the target customers' wants and needs and instituting promotional efforts to reach them. Therefore, the flow of information from the sales department back to the marketing department is, to a large degree, what enables a company to adapt to shifts in the market and respond to changes in consumer preferences.

The Production Manager

Besides working closely with the design, piecegoods purchasing, shipping, marketing, and sales departments, **production managers** are principally involved in overseeing the manufacturing of goods, setting priorities for cutting, sewing, and packaging of the goods and do so by agreed-on deadlines. Solving production and lead-time issues are also main responsibilities of production managers.

The Controller

The controller is the executive responsible for approving or disapproving the extension of credit to customers and managing the financial end of the business. Credit lines are allocated to customers based on information from credit-rating agencies such as Dun & Bradstreet. They can also generate reports on the paying history of any existing customer, which can be quite insightful.

The Shipping Department Manager

Shipping department managers work in closely with production, sales, and marketing managers to schedule the shipment dates for initial orders and delivery dates for reorders. They are also responsible for working with the various transportation companies to ensure timely deliveries to the customer.

Once a product is ready, it gets packaged as necessary. Shipping department managers adhere to the delivery schedule of the product, and, as mentioned, they assign the orders to be shipped to the customer following the customer's shipping instructions. Clients who do not have credit lines must pay the balance of the order on delivery with predetermined terms of COD (Collect on Delivery). Delivery drivers (or the shipping company, such as UPS) must receive payment of the shipment before beginning to unload the merchandise to the customer. A great many companies will not accept COD orders because it may not be cost effective. Customers refuse COD orders for a number of reasons, one of them being that they may not have the funds at that time to pay for the shipment. The merchandise returns to the manufacturer at the manufacturer's expense.

The End User

As the name suggests, this is the person who actually buys the fashion item to wear, use, or give as a gift. The needs and wants of the end user should always be kept in mind as a point of reference during any type of a sales transaction.

Where Does the Salesperson Fit?

The supply structure of a particular fashion manufacturer can be as complex as the one illustrated in the preceding pages or as simple as the manufacturer selling directly to the end user. Structures often vary from one manufacturer to the next, but there is always a need for salespeople, be it on a B2B or retail level.

B2B

Let's look at the typical sales force structure within a B2B organization. As covered in Chapter 4, the B2B salesperson sells not to a consumer, but to the corporate buyer of a reseller or retailer fashion company. The corporate buyer acts not only on his or her own needs and likes, but also on the requests and directions of the executives and marketing and sales staff of the company they represent. So when the buyer considers purchasing a particular line, he or she probably wants to like it personally. However, buyers make purchases primarily to satisfy the needs and wants of the target customer. They also depend heavily on input from marketing about what they feel is marketable, what the salespeople deem a product worth selling, and what the buyer considers will make or save money for the business.

Most companies have a vice president of sales or of sales and marketing; they oversee all of the sales and marketing efforts of the organization. The vice president of sales may also serve as the sales manager, or there may be a regional and/or district sales manager position under him or her, depending on the volume of sales and size of the sales force (Figure 12.2).

Generally speaking, the sales force is divided into geographical territories and in many companies also by key accounts. Depending on the size

FIGURE 12.2

Organizational Flow Chart for a Large Company

A typical fashion management and sales force structure in a B2B environment.

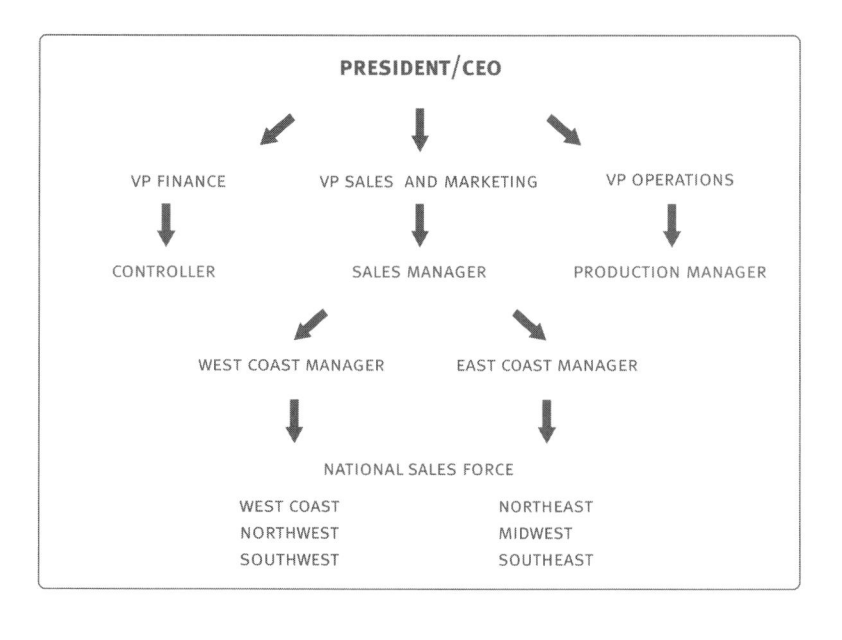

PRESIDENT/CEO

VP FINANCE   VP SALES AND MARKETING   VP OPERATIONS

CONTROLLER   SALES MANAGER   PRODUCTION MANAGER

WEST COAST MANAGER   EAST COAST MANAGER

NATIONAL SALES FORCE

WEST COAST	NORTHEAST
NORTHWEST	MIDWEST
SOUTHWEST	SOUTHEAST

of the company, territory management can be managed by one, any, or all of the following: the vice president of sales, national sales manager, regional sales managers, and district sales managers. Larger companies will have intensive management coverage and can incorporate the many different levels of sales managers.

If a company manufactures products for distinctly different target markets, such as womenswear, menswear, and childrenswear, they will usually employ a separate sales force to cover these individual markets. Companies have tried using the same sales force to sell to different markets, and the results were in many cases unsuccessful. It can only work if the geographic territories are very small and concentrated. Fashion selling is fast paced—the seasons are short and selling several unlike products to different buyers requires more time to cover these accounts. In this time-sensitive business, this approach is just not cost-effective. To achieve full effectiveness, it is advisable to have the salesperson concentrate on a specific market, catering to its target customers. For example, having the same salesperson sell womenswear, menswear, and childrenswear will tend to dilute the seller's product knowledge because of the many different styles and types of merchandise in these different product lines. In addition, attempting to offer unrelated product types through the same sales force may disrupt the proper account coverage and prevent the salesperson from paying adequate attention to each account.

Look at the example outlined in Figure 12.2. The West Coast manager manages all of the salespeople in her territory: the West Coast, the Northwest, and Southwest. The West Coast manager carries out all of the responsibilities, functions, and duties described in chapter 9, as they relate to her territory: She sets sales quotas for her salespeople, supervises them, trains them, and facilitates their production.

The California sales rep answers to his direct boss, the West Coast manager, but also to any of the managers above her. Typically, if the California sales rep encounters a delivery problem, he will inform his West Coast manager first. Depending on the company's policies, she then either addresses the issue directly with the production manager or refers it to the sales manager. In larger companies, regional managers and/or district managers will be part of the table of organization, and the respective sellers in these areas will report to their specific superiors with the reporting procedure going up the line.

Retail

A little more than four million retail salespeople are currently employed in the United States.[1] Retail establishments continue to make up the brick-and-mortar environment; while mail order catalogs and the Internet have encroached on this environment somewhat, most people still want to see, feel, and try on a piece of clothing or goods before buying it, and no one can predict the likelihood of this changing.

The typical retail sales structure is integrated into the vertical management channel of the department store chain. Here again, depending on the management structure, we may have a district manager who is responsible for all aspects of business in all of the stores under him or her, including sales, visual displays, promotions, merchandising, customer service, and hiring.

Each store is headed by a store manager, who often has an assistant manager and department managers to assist with the operation of the store. Obviously, since the department store's business is to sell items, one of the manager's key concerns is the volume of sales. In larger stores, there may be a supervisor, department/section manager, or head salesperson within some departments who assists the store manager in managing the salespeople on the floor. The salesperson is answerable to either these people in the supervisory role or to the store manager, and any customer service issues the salesperson cannot easily handle are referred to them (Figure 12.3).

The retail salesperson is the eyes and ears of the retail business—by being in direct contact with the end users, the salesperson has first-hand knowledge of a consumer's wants and needs. In addition to selling, the role of the retail salesperson is also to represent the store—they are the ones who communicate the culture and personality of the store to the end users.

FIGURE 12.3

Organizational Flow Chart for a Large Department Store

A typical fashion sales force structure in a department store environment.

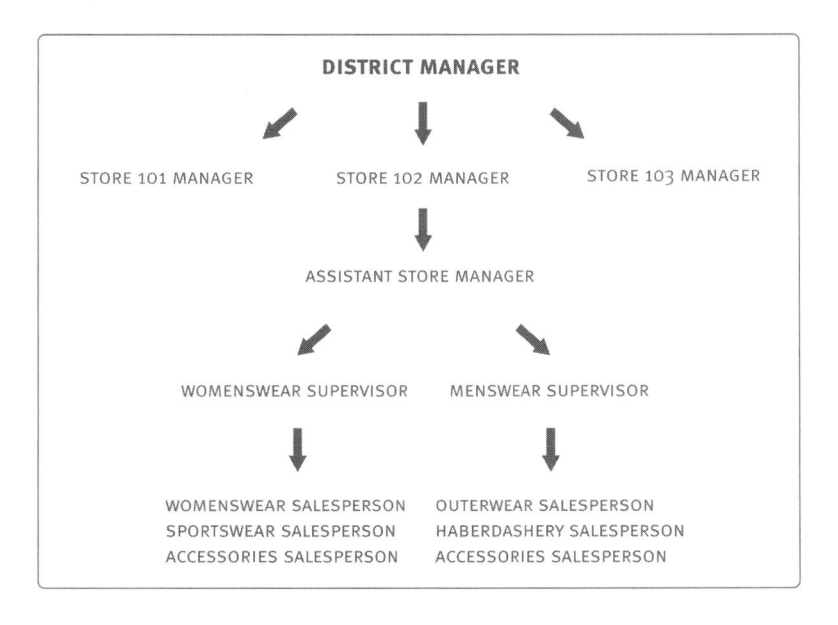

DISTRICT MANAGER

STORE 101 MANAGER   STORE 102 MANAGER   STORE 103 MANAGER

ASSISTANT STORE MANAGER

WOMENSWEAR SUPERVISOR   MENSWEAR SUPERVISOR

WOMENSWEAR SALESPERSON   OUTERWEAR SALESPERSON
SPORTSWEAR SALESPERSON   HABERDASHERY SALESPERSON
ACCESSORIES SALESPERSON   ACCESSORIES SALESPERSON

Whatever the salesperson does or says will have tremendous impact not only on the sale, but also on the retailer's image.

The salesperson is also the one on the floor who is responsible for maintaining an orderly area. Although stores have stock personnel whose job it is to maintain stock and keep it uncluttered, it is in the salesperson's best interests to maintain their areas neat. After all, the state of the department directly affects the number of sales he or she will be making.

Organizational Interaction: Do's and Don'ts

Now that we've inspected the organizational framework of the fashion sales environment and the various ways that the salesperson can fit into it, it is important to note several guidelines that can assist the salesperson to better interact with those around him or her. The following do's and don'ts outlined here are meant to provide a broad and general direction on how to approach organizational interaction. However, it is up to the salesperson not only to follow these sensibly, but also to constantly evaluate the actual environmental conditions around him or her to determine how to best apply them.

Do's

+ Do make certain you know your RFDs.
+ Do make it your business to understand the chain of command in your company. Become knowledgeable as to the company's table of organization.
+ Do go to your immediate superior when confronted with a problem that you earnestly attempted to solve within your resources.
+ Do make certain you understand company policy, and when in doubt, check with your immediate supervisor for clarification.
+ Do follow company policy.
+ Do relay any problems as soon as they occur to your immediate superior.
+ Do make it a point to indicate to your superiors that you would like an evaluation of the job you are performing semiannually if it's not offered.
+ Do try to get along with your fellow workers. If someone in the organization does something that is annoying to you, try to discuss this first with the individual before taking it to your immediate superior.

Don'ts

+ Don't wait to learn your RFDs if you are uncertain.

+ Don't take it on yourself to decide where to take the problem or question you may have.
+ Don't go over your immediate superior's head unless he or she is not available or if you have been told you can do so when the situation demands immediate attention.
+ Don't assume you are doing a great job without first having a conversation with your boss.
+ Don't rush to report an incident to a superior without talking to the person first, unless it is one of sexual harassment, discrimination, or any other abuse. These acts should not be tolerated.
+ Don't procrastinate in reporting the problem—if you do, the problem will only get worse.
+ Don't make any decisions that are contrary to the written company policy even if the customer demands immediate action.

The Client's Office

Sooner or later in a business relationship, the salesperson must interact with the client's office or administrative staff. Most times the salesperson may have to speak with people who do not have direct authority over the purchasing decisions, but who are nonetheless important.

Secretaries, bookkeepers, and the sales manager within the buyer's organization may each be able to influence the buyer. Alienate the assistant, and you may not get another appointment with your buyer. "Talk tough" with the bookkeeper, and you may lose the whole account. The point is that those who work in the buyer's office are on the buyer's payroll and are looking not only for their own interests but also for the buyer's. Their word may have a significant effect on the buyer's decision. Often, the gatekeeper may hold the key to a meeting with the buyer. However, it's best to limit conversations with personnel who are not decision makers to show that you value their time as well as your own. In other words, give assistants only the facts they need to know.

Remember that the person who's taking messages today may be the buyer tomorrow—respect that person and any other person on the buyer's staff. It is a good idea to learn the names of the key personnel in the buyer's office. Being nice to the front desk receptionist and inquiring about how he or she is doing each time you visit the buyer can help you gain an edge over the competition. When the competition knocks on the door, the receptionist may never let them in because he or she prefers to keep dealing with you.

If any of the buyer's office's staff calls with a question, make sure you get the information and return the call promptly. Just because they are below the buyer on the buyer's organizational chart does not mean their question is not important; in fact, their question may affect the buyer's entire company, and not responding can have dire consequences. At the same time, make sure not to step on the buyer's toes by accepting instructions on a specific order from the buyer's staff. Always check with the buyer first to ensure these instructions are valid prior to modifying any details on a sales order.

Your job as a salesperson begins in earnest once the buyer signs on the dotted line, and caring for the buyer and his or her office staff post-sale is the best way to keep that customer happy and coming back for repeat orders.

Chapter Summary

+ All salespeople must interact with coworkers and superiors within the companies at which they work, as well as their buyers' companies. Whether this interaction is professional or unpleasant can greatly contribute to or detract from the seller's success.
+ A salesperson should be familiar with the following key players in the industry: manufacturer, reseller, salesperson, manufacturer's representative, retailer, sales manager, production manager, controller (accounting manager), shipping department manager, and end user.
+ While organizational structures often vary from one fashion company to the next, there is always a need for a salesperson, be it on a B2B or retail level.
+ Marketing functions are distinctively different from sales. Marketing focuses on gathering information about customers and prospective customers, fashion market trends, and the company's competition to facilitate the design and sale of the company's products. But without the feedback from the sales department, the marketing department cannot achieve its goals fully.
+ Most B2B companies have a vice president for sales and marketing who oversees all of the sales and marketing efforts of the organization. There may be regional and/or district sales manager positions under him or her, depending on the volume of sales and size of the sales force.
+ Generally speaking, a B2B sales force is divided into geographical territories and often also by key accounts.
+ The typical retail sales structure is integrated into the vertical management channel of the department store chain. The store manager is responsible for all aspects of business in all of the stores under him or her, including merchandising, customer service, and hiring.

The store's assistant manager may help in managing the sales force. In larger stores, a supervisor or head salesperson may assist in sales management as well.

+ Knowing and adhering to the do's and don'ts of organizational interaction can assist the salesperson to better interact with those around him or her and significantly improve performance.

+ Sooner or later, the salesperson must speak with administrative people at their buyers' offices who may not have direct authority over purchasing decisions but are important nonetheless. Treat them all with respect and strive to assist them in the same manner you would assist the buyer.

RW CASE STUDY

Erv Magram is the former president and CEO of the fashion catalog company Lew Magram, Ltd. and the current managing director of the catalog division at CCT Marketing LLC. He has more than thirty years of experience in the fashion sales industry.

How important is it for the salesperson to develop a relationship with the administrative staff at the buyer's office?

It is important in sales to be well liked; it really is. The personal relationship of the manufacturer's salespeople with the buying organization or retailer in the fashion example is critical. If the relationship is strong, there will be greater trust. Trust is of tremendous importance because the buyer's job depends upon the success of his or her purchasing decisions. If the salesperson is dishonest, the buyer will likely make a disastrous buying decision, which may very well result in the buyer's unemployment.

The buyer or retailer will visit the salesperson that is trusted and liked more often. More visits usually mean more sales. But most important, once a fashion trend is set, manufacturers and wholesalers quickly catch on and supply virtually the same goods to the retailers. Within this context, relationships become very important because it is what, in many cases, sets you apart from the competition. I'm not only talking about the relationship with the buyer, but indeed with others in the buying organization. If you treat assistants poorly, you will pay a heavy price. The great actor and comedian Jackie Gleason used to say, "Treat people well on the way up because you meet the same people on the way down." An enduring lesson in business is that you never know who will be working for whom in the future or who this or that person might know, who might be in a position to affect your income—and thus your life.

To what degree can a salesperson's relationships with people in the industry affect his or her career?

Since I sold my catalog business several years ago, many of my former employees have kept up their relationships with me. I know, of course, it is due to their loyalty, genuine friendship, and my inescapable charm! But I also am well aware that most of them understand that at some point I might be able to help them with a reference or might simply know someone who they might like to get closer to. There is nothing wrong with this, and it is simply a smart business thing to do. Now that I am in sales myself, I, too, have gone out of my way to keep up certain friendships and relationships because I never know who one of my former employees might be employed by in the future—possibly a large firm that would be very interested in my product.

What information can the seller provide the buyer within the framework of their business relationship?

By cultivating a strong relationship with salespeople, the buyer will get the inside and early word on new trends and may be shown items before other retailers get to see them. The salesperson will alert the buyer to important fashion changes since every day the salesperson may see several buyers and merchandise managers from all types of retail organizations and will therefore have a feeling for what is going on at all price points and in all age groups.

What about the management in the buyer's company? Should the seller try to get to know the managers above the buyer as well?

It is a good idea for the salesperson to seek to build relationships with those in the retailing organization other than the buyer. Why not ask the buyer to bring the merchandise manager to the next meeting so he or she can meet your VP of sales or company president. This works for all participants—not only does it help the sales organization by developing a relationship with the "higher ups," but it also creates a greater mutual importance to the relationship. When I was CEO at the Lew Magram catalog, I would very often spend a day with the buyers in the market. The manufacturer was thrilled I was there and would attach a new importance to the relationship due to that visit.

In addition, if the salesperson has a relationship with an individual high up in the buyer's organization, that person who presumably carries considerable weight in the overall purchasing of the company will naturally be less likely to diminish the purchasing relationship in favor of another firm [that] has developed such a relationship. He or she is more likely to okay a strong steady buying stream, and let's face it, who in the organization will have the power or intestinal fortitude to want to lessen it with such a relationship in effect—certainly not the buyer on the front lines.

Questions to Consider

1. According to Magram, how important is it for the seller to get to know the staff in the buyer's office?
2. How do you think you would treat the office staff at a potential client? Why?
3. Why do you think it is vital for the seller to become acquainted with office staff?
4. Why do you think it is vital for the seller to become acquainted with management in the buyer's company?

RW EXERCISES

1. What is the difference between a direct sales force (employed by the manufacturer) and the reseller or manufacturer's representative? Give an example.
2. How do outside salespeople differ from inside salespeople? When will a potential buyer be approached by either one? Give an example.
3. Which sales position do you find most interesting or challenging? Why?
4. Create a fictitious scenario where you are the vice president of sales for a fashion manufacturer. Explain the type of product you are manufacturing, the target market, and the end user. Set up the organizational chart you think would be most productive for your company, and explain the important advantages of your organizational structure.
5. Pair up with another student, so one of you acts as the salesperson and the other acts as a coworker or superior. Set up three scenarios that require the manager to practice one of the do's and don'ts discussed in this chapter. Write down how each principle affects the seller's relationship with the coworker or superior and what you think its effect would be on productivity. Switch roles for a different perspective, and note the new responses.

END NOTES

1. U.S. Department of Labor Statistics. www.bls.gov/oes/current/oes412031.htm.

CHAPTER 13

RW

Objectives

+ Understand that change is an inevitable and leading force in the fashion industry.

+ Define change and how it applies to the field of fashion sales.

+ Inspect the three categories of change and how each manifests itself within the working environment.

+ Survey the various sources of information that predict upcoming change.

+ Learn the steps a salesperson or executive can take to utilize changes to their advantage.

+ Explore the various methods used to formulate plans of adaptation.

ADAPTING TO CHANGE IN THE FASHION MARKETS

Overview

Today's fast-paced environment has placed an enormous amount of pressure on fashion companies to keep up with change. Demographics, social and political events, and competition contribute to the volatile shifts in the market. How can salespeople and managers keep up with these changes? How can they learn to anticipate why and when changes occur? What are some of the strategies they use to stay ahead of these changes? This chapter answers these questions so you can achieve success in the ever-changing world of fashion sales.

Introduction

By definition, fashion *is* change. To be fashionable, a person must dress according to what's in vogue, in style. What was "in" yesterday is often not what's "in" today. Therefore, change has always been an intrinsic shaping force within the fashion industry. Today's fashion industry is in a state of constant change not only in terms of styles, colors, and consumer taste, but also in terms of retail strategies, innovations in manufacturing, and improvements in selling methodologies and marketing efforts. Sales managers and the salespeople who report to them adjust their approaches to management, sales, and business relationships so they can stay ahead of their competition.

Of course, the inevitable variations in styles that take place at least annually, if not every season, are significantly important changes that the acute salespeople follow carefully as well to maintain their edge. No field or industry is free from change. Many businesses aspire to remain in a magical comfort zone where things always stay the same. They don't want things to change. However, there are two major forces that cause changes and are outside their control—consumer demand and competition. Change is not only a natural process in the business world, but also one that is necessary for a company's existence. The seemingly whimsical oscillations in designer choices and consumer preferences simply exacerbate the process in the fashion sphere. This chapter discusses how salespeople can recognize these changes when they take place and the various ways they can use them to their advantage.

The Market Is Shifting!

Change is a very broad term that can encompass virtually anything that ever happens. Since the passage of time in itself constitutes change, it could be argued that anything that ever happens in the sales office is change. Within this framework, the office copier breaking down or the sales manager getting married could both be categorized as change. For the purpose of this chapter, however, we use a definition of change that is better suited for the analysis and evaluation of the sales environment conditions. Essentially, what we are interested in is what we call the **market shift**, a significant change that can potentially affect sales.

But what exactly constitutes a market shift? Can any change in the industry, regardless of its importance or consequence, qualify as a market shift? To be considered a market shift, does change have to be so vast in scope that it affects each and every facet of the industry? Is a change in style also a market shift? These are important questions that must be

RW Dictionary

Market Shift A significant change that can potentially affect sales.

answered before we can fully understand what the term means and how it applies to a seller at any level of the fashion industry. There are three types of market shifts: product-oriented, people-oriented, and structure-oriented. By evaluating a particular market shift along these categories, we can then determine its importance, significance, and the appropriate adjustment methods.

The Product-Oriented Market Shift

Bell-bottoms, miniskirts, torn jeans, and flip-flops are all examples of a **product-oriented market shift**. These market shifts typically follow one of the following two models or a combination thereof: creative design and consumer demand.

The **creative design model** of the product-oriented market shift occurs when a label or a specific designer creates a unique style or feature that becomes popular with the consumer market or some of its segments. This could also be called the **top-down model** because the design originates at the top of the manufacturing hierarchy and is resold down the value chain until it is purchased by the consumer. It should be noted that many well-known designers who created their own original designs when they started out and are publicly traded companies today rely on a team of designers to come up with new innovations of style and color. Other designers, especially high-end specialty designers like Giorgio Sharoubim, of Giorgio's of Palm Beach, Florida, remain the chief creative talent for the label, utilizing other designers only to assist in the development process after a concept is born.

RW Dictionary

Product-Oriented Market Shift A significant change in a product—in style, color, size, or any other feature of the actual fashion item—that can potentially affect sales.

RW Dictionary

Creative-Design or **Top-Down Model** Top-down model styles are created solely at the designer's drawing table based on the designer's own inspiration (Figure 13.1).

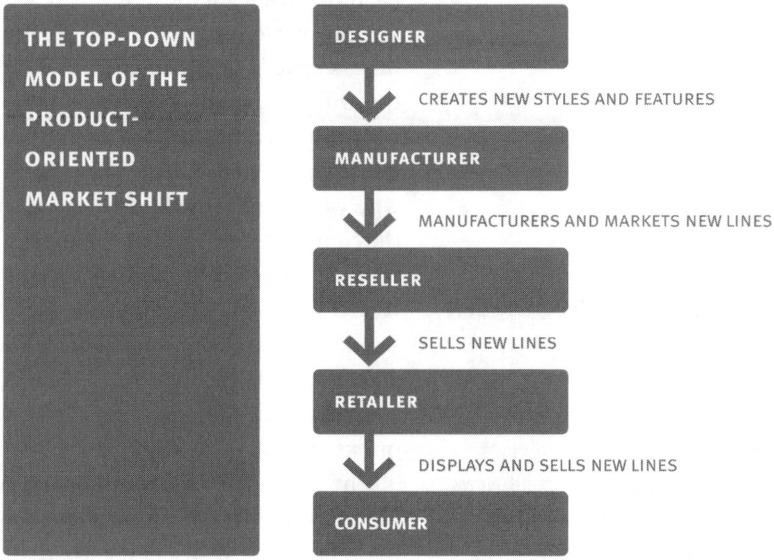

FIGURE 13.1
The Top-Down Design Model

Styles are created solely by the designer and staff.

THE TOP-DOWN MODEL OF THE PRODUCT-ORIENTED MARKET SHIFT

DESIGNER
↓ CREATES NEW STYLES AND FEATURES
MANUFACTURER
↓ MANUFACTURERS AND MARKETS NEW LINES
RESELLER
↓ SELLS NEW LINES
RETAILER
↓ DISPLAYS AND SELLS NEW LINES
CONSUMER

RW Concept

More than ever before, today's media is highly influential in forming and communicating fashion trends and, therefore, is an important factor in the product-driven market shift.

Within nondesigner-named companies such as Juicy Couture, Diesel, Lacoste, XoXo, Ecko, Akademiks, Rampage, Guess, Dockers, Levis, and Nike, the creative process takes place within the merchandising and design departments, typically made up of a group of designers led by a head designer and merchandising executive.

Top-down model styles are created solely at a designer's drawing table based on the designer's own inspiration. However, a large number of new styles essentially reflect consumer needs that are the result of lifestyle changes, market research, and trends and competitive information from sales and marketing. The top-down model is therefore intrinsically and intimately linked to the second model of consumer demand.

Sonia Rykiel is a Parisian designer who personifies the top-down model. She is one of the true innovators of design who for many decades created new fashions and is still doing so. Rykiel became known for one of her first creations: the poorboy knitted sweater. It was a drop jeweled neckline, cropped and slim-fitting, and had the seams on the outside of the garment. The drop jeweled neckline has been copied by many designers and is still popular in today's global market. She was one of the first designers to print sayings on her sweaters. The poorboy sweater was featured on the cover of *Elle* magazine more than forty years ago. Its modern-day version is still selling in France and other retail stores globally.

Rykiel's creativity and the success of her sweater created a consumer demand, from the top-down, throughout the international fashion industry. The poorboy design also started a dramatic fashion shift. The silhouette of knitted tops would undergo a change in many markets. The consequences of this change could come about by this type of scenario. Fashion media got the news out about the success of the poorboy. Industry leaders were alerted to this fashion change. Retail merchandisers and buyers talked to their suppliers about this. Alert suppliers communicated this information to their sales, marketing, and merchandising management who in turn would decide if the sweater was right for their markets. They would then transfer the information to the appropriate personnel who would make the final decision on whether this change could fit into the companies' image. If it did, the design staff would soon present prototypes of the poorboy in many different fabrications and colors. Copies of Rykiel's look would then be marketed to different and lower-priced markets. Sellers and sales managers whose companies were involved in this trend were called on to play active roles in selling the versions of their poorboy knitted tops to their buyers. This is an example of a product-oriented shift.

The **consumer demand** or **bottom-up model** is a result of a synchronous demand by enough consumers to justify a response from the manufacturer. Such a demand can be spurred by a number of factors or

RW Dictionary

Consumer Demand or **Bottom-Up Model** The change in the product is initiated by consumer demand. News of the public's need travels up the fashion sales hierarchy (Figure 13.2).

FIGURE 13.2

The Bottom-Up Design Model

Product design initiated by consumer demand.

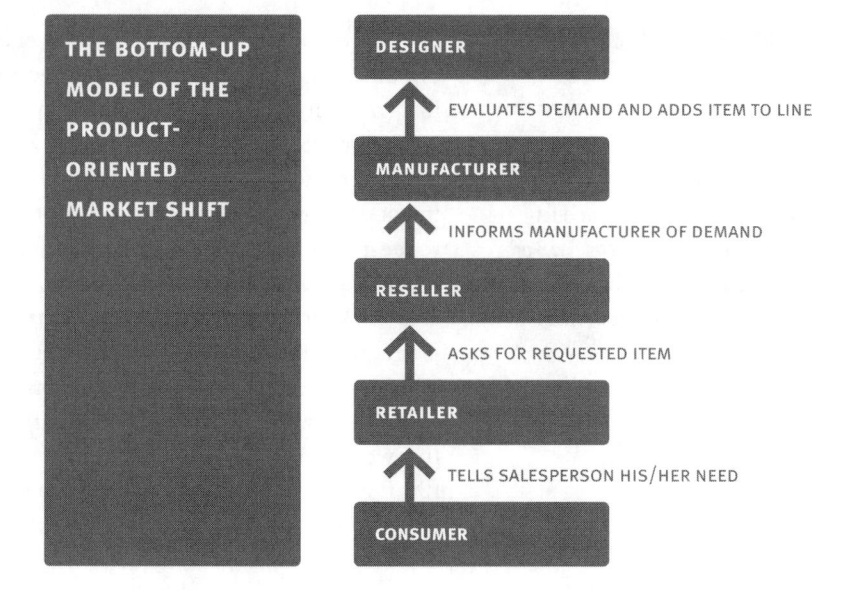

events. A large portion of the global fashion consumer population watches a celebrity's every move. The publication of photographs or video clips of a movie star sporting a specific blouse can cause a deluge of demands for that item or color. In the same way, columnists in leading fashion publications can prompt a demand for a specific fashion feature as well.

We also find that financial times can dictate the tastes of consumers and, therefore, the direction of consumer demand. The length of skirts and dresses could be called a barometer of sorts for the state of the U.S. economy. It has been said, as the economy improves, the public's taste for shorter skirts increases as well. Miniskirts and hot pants made their appearance in the 1960s. The U.S. economy in the 1960s was strong, and people felt secure in this prosperous environment. In 1960 inflation was at 1.4 percent. Mary Quant, a well-known designer in England, originated the mini look, and it was soon adopted by young U.S. consumers. In the 1970s, we had a tumbling economy; in 1975, inflation was 14.1 percent, and skirt lengths got longer. One can make a case that in a poor economy the lengths of skirts and dresses are longer.[1]

In this model, news of the consumer demand travels up the fashion sales hierarchy. This often leads the manufacturer to evaluate the potential for the item, and if it seems profitable, to add the requested item to the line. Most retailers and fashion boutiques institute a system for keeping track of consumer demand. The typical system utilizes want slips—a form that the retail salesperson fills in when a customer requests an item that is not available. The want slip details the item, colors, styles, or price that the consumer requested and is turned in to the department manager. Depending on the size of the store, the information goes up the management line and ends up on the buyer's desk. The buyer and merchandise management decide whether the information they received is "nice" or "necessary." Nice information regarding want slips can be requests for merchandise that accommodates a few consumers such as merchandise that is a fad (short-lived shelf life) or merchandise that is on a downward trend and will not impact future sales. Necessary information regarding want slips are requests that are made by a large number of customers. Does this item/s reflect the image of the store/department? Will the item/s have a reasonable stock turn? Can we stock this item in a timely manner? Obviously, if it is a request that is deemed necessary, the buying end of the organization will scour the market to find sources that will satisfy its customers.

Let's see how this may play out in the real world. The latest trend in footwear is that preteens and teenagers are asking for more fashionable flip-flops. They are now wearing them for all occasions. Retailers are getting calls for flip-flops in different fabrications, textures, and fashion colors. Prices seem to be no object.

Recently a female athletic team visited the White House, and they were all wearing flip-flops with their dresses. This shift is a sign of changing times—it appears as if this may be the start of something big. Buyers may look at it and regard it as merely a trendy item that will come and go and may not allocate it much shelf space. But what if they are wrong? Suppose flip-flops are here to stay, claiming a larger share of the lucrative footwear market. Then flip-flops become a necessary item. We can see those want slips reaching the buyer's desk in great numbers and going up the chain of command. Footwear sellers are seeing brisk sales in the marketplace by the increase of fashionable flip-flops, which may just replace the casual sneaker. Athletic footwear suppliers must be shaking in their shoes (pardon the pun). What if this trend takes hold? Salespeople will be able to see firsthand what's happening and report their findings to their companies. The footwear market may be witnessing a major market shift. It looks as if the flip-flop can become an even hotter item for the younger market of preteens and teens. Footwear designers are working fast to bring different designs to the market. The use of trim and other accessories is now being offered in retail prices exceeding $100. This is another example of a product-oriented market shift.

The People-Oriented Market Shift

In addition to the market shift that results from changes in style, the fashion industry is also subject to another type of market shift, which is common to many other industries—the **people-oriented market shift**, which is the result of a change in demographics and psychographics.

Demographics are traditionally made up of a series of surveys providing a breakdown of the target market according to age, gender, race, education level, household size, and household income. In an ideal demographic study, a seller can see what percentage of the population in his or her territory is middle-age, retired, male, female, or college-educated. This information offers statistical facts that identify end consumers, as well as invaluable guidance as to which of the seller's lines may be most popular. Clearly, a leather miniskirt will not do as well in a territory where people are mostly middle-age, have families of two kids or more, are conservative, and live in rural settings, as it would in a large city.

Demographics are not only important in establishing the initial line of products, but also in predicting market shifts so buyers and sellers can adapt. If a significant change in the population within a specific territory takes place, it's only a matter of time before a seller begins to feel the effects of these population shifts. The fashion industry is extremely sensitive to demographics since, barring the ubiquitous T-shirt perhaps, fashion products are always targeted at specific markets. A dress shirt is either for men or women, for businesspeople or party people, for the young crowd or the old. It is unlikely that a fifty-year-old male accountant will wear the same shirt as a twenty-five-year-old woman and vice versa. Therefore, if a seller's product targets fifty-year-old male business professionals, and these business professionals are for some reason moving en masse to the next county, then the seller must be able to adapt to this change or be out of business.

Psychographics is another component of the people-oriented market shift. By looking at the cultural behaviors, social trends, and attitudes of specific segments with a certain geographic boundary, psychographics can provide a seller with significant information about the mindset of the potential consumers as to their employment, way of life, and uniqueness. The old adage of "people who are alike each other, like each other" applies to psychographics segmentation, where the population is divided into groups of people who share related psychological characteristics. These characteristics can be similar lifestyles, needs, ways of thinking, attitudes, views, and perceptions. Psychographic research is essential to learn what consumers in different demographics want and need.

The Structure-Oriented Market Shift

Finally, market shifts can be the result of changes in the industry's structure itself, such as the reorganization of the dynamics among manufacturer, reseller, retailer, and consumer. The **structure-oriented market shift** is typically a broad change of the industry itself whose transformation spans years or even decades.

The United States has experienced many market changes. The apparel and textile industry has seen dramatic changes in terms of jobs and pro-

RW Dictionary

Structure-Oriented Market Shift A significant change in the structure of the industry—the way product is designed, manufactured, distributed, or sold—that can potentially affect sales.

duction facilities. In years past, the "Made in America" label in clothing was a given, since design and production took place inside the country. Today, apparel, with the exception of selective lines, is primarily produced off-shore. Textile production in the United States is at its lowest productive capacity today because it cannot match the low wages of the competition in the global market.[2]

In a U.S. Department of Agriculture report titled "The Changing World Network of Trade in Textiles and Apparel," authors Thomas Vollrath, Mark Gehlhar, and Stephen MacDonald discuss the effects of policy reforms stemming from the 1995 Uruguay Round of the World Trade Organization.[3] The reforms reduced tariffs on textile and apparel products to typical levels, effectively shifting the global textile manufacturing market dramatically. The report states, "Collectively, these reforms should stimulate growth in textile trade, which already outpaces trade in other sectors of the world economy. For example, trade in textiles and apparel in the last decade nearly doubled to $334 billion. These reforms also promise to significantly alter the location of production and the direction of fiber and textile trade."

Therefore, apparel and textile manufacturing have pretty much entirely left the United States. It has become easier for foreign companies to invade U.S. markets, and there are indications that they will continue to dominate the production end of fashion and other markets. Here again the smaller apparel and textile mills will not be able to compete with the low costs of production that overseas mills can offer. We must point out that the loss of most of our productive capacity in fashion goods should not be blamed on the other countries in the global market. Due to our standard of living and the increasing cost of labor, we were vulnerable to these competitive forces whose standard of living is much less than ours.

Over the past two decades, this market shift has transformed the structure of the fashion industry, and the ripple effects of this transformation have been felt throughout the fashion sales circles. This leaves us with other areas in which we can compete. Sales, marketing, merchandising, and design are the areas where the United States can keep its leadership. The fashion industry can't exist without these areas. "You may be able to make it, but can you create it and sell it?"

Another example of a structure-oriented market shift is the move from smaller retailers and manufacturing businesses toward large discount retailers featuring designer apparel and private labels. To survive, smaller boutiques must specialize in specific markets, offer better personal service, and be able to fulfill the needs of their customers in ways that department store behemoths cannot.

While bigger businesses are getting bigger, offering better price values, they are also in most cases less service-oriented and more restricted in flexibility. Megaretailers typically take a longer time to adapt to change because the implementation of the adaptation steps must clear through many levels of middle and top management and must fit within the strict corporate guidelines. In this respect, smaller guys can gain the advantage by understanding and responding to the changing markets quickly since they can be more flexible than the bigger stores.

Putting It All Together

Salespeople and managers must be able to recognize when a market shift is taking place and take steps to adapt to it with the aim of taking advantage of any opportunities the shift presents while losing the least amount of business possible. Ignoring a market shift or failing to take the steps necessary to adapt to it can bring about drastic negative consequences to a company's survival. Ideally, salespeople and managers should have in place a reliable network for sources of information through which they may be alerted to potential market shifts; then it is a matter of processing the information, realizing when a shift is taking place, identifying its type (e.g., whether it is product-oriented, people-oriented, or structure-oriented), and formulating a strategy of adaptation.

Unfortunately, there is no rule prohibiting market shifts of a different type or several market shifts of the same type from coexisting. Therefore, in the hectic RW of business and fashion sales, it is not uncommon for multiple market shifts of different types to be taking place simultaneously. The product-oriented market shift is ubiquitous in the fashion business, both temporally as well as geographically, as there is always some sort of change in style, color, or features happening somewhere in the fashion world. Therefore, any demographic shift would usually take place on top of the continuous shifts in style. When that occurs, the effects of change grow exponentially, since the company has to deal not only with the shifts themselves, but also with the results of their coexistence.

Recognizing and properly adapting to market shifts is a must if people are to stay in business, says Erv Magram, former president and CEO of the fashion catalog company Lew Magram, Ltd. The company's history is a prime example of the variety and complexity of the market shifts fashion businesses have to face. The catalog company, which, at it's peak grossed $85 million, began in 1948 with only a counter inside a Manhattan-area barber shop. There, Magram's father, Lew Magram, started selling ties and cuff links, and when a small store became available next door, Lew opened his own store, offering old-fashioned custom-tailoring, complete with individual measurements, paper designs, and final fittings. One of Lew's satisfied customers was Jack Haley, who played the Tin Man in the original *Wizard of Oz*. Haley told his friends in show business about Lew's store, and soon Magram sold custom shirts to Dean Martin, Sammy Davis Jr., Frank Sinatra, Johnny Carson, and other famous names, making a name for himself as the "Shirtmaker to the Stars."

A few years later, many celebrities moved to Los Angeles to follow the film industry's transfer to Hollywood, and Lew faced a people-oriented market shift—some of his top clients were now thousands of miles away. Lew's solution was to launch a mailing to his West Coast clientele, which he called "Shirtales," where he wrote not only about his product but also about Who's Who gossip heard around town in New York City. By the mid-1960s, the mailer developed into a sixty-four-page, full-color catalog. Magram, who started working in the company in 1971, still remembers the success of the catalog's flamboyant fashion during the wild 1970s, when polka-dot pants, ruffled shirts, and velvet bow ties were trendy items.

"In the late 1970s, American taste was becoming more conservative, to the point where we had trouble getting a list to mail the catalog to," explains Magram. The company was faced with a serious product-oriented market shift—consumers' tastes were changing. "We saw what products were being dropped, what others were selling, saw the trends around us. L.L. Bean and Lands' End were growing rapidly at that time; they were 180 degrees opposite of Magram. We saw that flamboyant was on its way out. And in business, you have to understand that if a good thing is over, then you can bang your head against a wall all you want, it's still going to end, and you better figure something out or you'd be out of business."[4]

In trying to figure out a solution, Magram spoke with a number of colleagues and listened to their take on the situation. One friend who was a mailing list broker and had the finger on the industry's pulse told Magram that the catalog should switch to featuring womenswear, since that was the hottest segment of the industry in terms of growth. Magram consulted other friends and verified that indeed womenswear was taking off. "We started testing a few women's items by including them in the [catalog] book, and they sold. We were surprised since the catalog was for men—we guessed that in many of the target households, the women were shopping for the men. If they hadn't responded to the women's items, we would have been dead," Magram recalls.

Two years later, the catalog was made up of virtually nothing but women's items; and sales figures were increasing healthily. Magram was able to adapt to another market shift, one which was serious enough to wipe the company out. "Soon after, we closed the men's store and simply focused on the women's catalog and built it up to where it is today," Magram says.

Staying Informed

There is no systematic, scientific formula that can be used to accurately recognize market shifts. This is not a cold, hard science subject. There are no litmus tests or market shift-o-meters. Each market shift is a unique case of its own, and while two shifts can be comparable or nearly identical, there are always variables within the framework that separate one shift from another. In other words, no two market shifts are the same. However, the general guidelines and broad principles discussed herein, as well as learning from past experiences, can help one fare better in detecting market shifts.

We have defined the three types of market shifts and discussed their differences; now let's explore how to stay aware and ahead of the market and gather information that will alert you to significant changes in the industry. The key is being in touch with the market. It takes a great deal of legwork and research to remain up-to-date on what's happening in the real world of fashion sales, but it is a necessary task if you want to deal successfully with market shifts. The following sections discuss key methods and strategies about how to accomplish this.

Carefully Listening to Buyers

Buyers are an excellent source of market information, since they are often in close contact with the salespeople on the front lines and know in great detail what is selling and what isn't. Being on the scene with your buyers and finding out what they are buying and why they are buying certain items can usually tip you off to upcoming market shifts.

Networking Within the Industry

Developing relationships with knowledgeable, reliable people in all levels of the industry sets up an extremely important network for sharing information from which all participants benefit. It pays for a manufacturer to routinely talk to a few managers in local department stores to find out which items are hot and which are collecting dust. Just as the mail-order broker told Magram what segment of the population to go after to revitalize the business, so do people in the industry rely on one another to provide feedback and information.

"You can tell some lines or items sell while others don't sell anymore; in this industry, people talk," says Magram. "Comments like 'I heard this is the future' or 'this is over' can be very helpful. Salespeople need to be networked, they need to develop a group of mentors or colleagues in the industry and cultivate friendships with them so [they] can exchange information with them."

He cautions against jumping to conclusions based on one credible source's opinion though. "Just because one person tells you something, doesn't automatically make it true. I wouldn't bet the farm on it. If what the person is saying makes sense, I'd check with other people and research industry publications, and then use my own judgment," Magram explains.

Reading Trade and Fashion Magazines

Subscriptions to some of the leading trade publications in your line of fashion—such as *DNR*, and *Women's Wear Daily*, are musts for keeping up with current industry and fashion changes. Many such publications routinely publish broad evaluations of the market, complete with statistics and comparisons, which can point to upcoming market shifts. Additionally, these publications also typically include a "news" section, where significant events or changes are written up and sometimes explained as well. Consumer fashion magazines, such as *Allure, Cosmopolitan, Glamour, GQ, Harpers Bazaar, Vogue*, and *W* magazine, are also important sources for what's happening in the fashion industry.

Shopping the Competition

The competition is not stupid, and therefore, it is worth the time to routinely survey what they are offering, which of their lines are selling well and which are not. As a seller, it pays to spend some time walking the aisles of the local department store or boutique and surveying which items are on display. This can often reveal clues to market shifts in the making. Suppose that in the course of walking the aisles every month, you begin to notice an increase in newer hip items targeting teenagers. Let's say that up to this point your buyer has been reluctant in picking up your newer styles. This would be good information to present when meeting with your buyer next time and could very well result in a sale.

Magram says that in the catalog business, most everyone made sure to sign up and receive their competition's catalogs in the mail. "We would study each issue of each catalog inside out, keep the back issues, and cross-compare them. We would see which items were dropped, which items stayed in. We had a whole system for scoring items; if it ran twice it was a winner, and if it got more space and lasted more than three or four issues, then we knew it was a very successful item. Not to mention we would price-check our competition while we were at it," he says. Successful salespeople or managers must be able to learn from their competition, rather than resent it.

Visiting trade shows to see what other companies are showing and selling is also an integral part of this strategy. The styles and colors you see in the various booths, the information others in the trade exchange with you, and the networking contacts you make there can be of invaluable help in determining what other companies are featuring and make you more aware of what the market is featuring. This market knowledge will help your buyers gain confidence in your knowledge of what's going on.

Best Laid Plans

As the Lew Magram, Ltd. case demonstrates, recognizing the problem is not enough; according to Magram, people must also be willing to do something effective about it and, above all, be flexible. But how can one know what avenue to take to adapt to current market shifts?

Many market shifts can be dealt with by conducting a survey of resources in relation to the market shift and brainstorming ideas that can be potential solutions. If Taylor, a reseller of women's fashion in ABC County, finds that a flood of young families is moving into her territory, then she must study up on the resources her company offers for young mothers, expecting mothers, female toddlers, and young girls. Then, she should present her buyers with the demographic information that documents this market shift, plus show them the styles that could help them adapt to it. In this way, Taylor is staying ahead of the market shift and will likely benefit from it sales-wise.

Oftentimes, the very sources that inform sellers of market shifts can also provide information about what seems to work for others in the industry dealing with the same types of shifts. If they cannot be of help, then it is wise to chat with other members of your network or research the topic in trade and other publications. As mentioned earlier, acting on only one recommendation or piece advice is very risky and can bring about the demise of the company. You must fact-check any recommendation before implementing it and discuss the matter with other sources to establish its universality. You must also evaluate whether the solution is doable and practical and holds potential for profit.

Let's look at some of the steps salespeople and sales managers can take to adjust to market shifts in the fashion industry.

+ Keep informed as to new developments in your market by making certain that you receive credible information regarding these changes.

+ Ask yourself and your superiors if these changes are important.
+ Find out how your bosses think it will impact your market and your job.
+ Examine what opportunities these changes will offer.
+ Figure out what problems they will present.
+ Research new opportunities that may result from these market changes.
+ Choose the best method for communicating these changes to your buyers.

Being proactive is another way for a fashion company to counteract the damage caused by market shifts. Having an ongoing program that strives to constantly improve design and marketing and sales strategies is an important tool in balancing the scales of change. In essence, by routinely reviewing operations and instituting improvements whenever possible, companies can proactively enact calculated changes that are under their control; these smaller-scale changes keep companies in tune with the market and improve the organizations' abilities to be flexible. Fashion companies are also wise to train their younger employees to be better sellers, marketers, and designers and also introduce them to the many opportunities that selling and sales management jobs have to offer.

However, even the best laid plans can falter or fail. This is unfortunately an integral part of business. The first important thing to remember is that if a plan doesn't work after you give it your best efforts, there is no point in hammering it to the ground; recognize when a plan is not working and find an alternative. Second, don't take it personally—this is business. Last but not least, never ever give up. Giving up is the one change no company or sales team can recover from; don't dwell on your failures—find an alternate solution and get on with it. As mentioned in chapter 1, "Nothing happens unless someone sells something." Every fashion company depends on its sales personnel and sales management to be the pioneers on the frontier of change, capably recognizing and dealing with market shifts to help guide the companies for which they work—and themselves—toward a better and brighter future.

Chapter Summary

+ Fashion *is* change. Change has always been an intrinsic shaping force within the fashion industry.
+ Sales managers and the salespeople who report to them must adjust their approaches to management, sales, and business relationships to stay ahead of their competition.

+ For the purposes of this chapter, we need a focused definition for change: What we are interested in is what we call the market shift, a significant change that can potentially affect sales. There are three types of market shifts: product-oriented, people-oriented, and structure-oriented.

+ The product-oriented market shift is a significant change in the product—in style, color, size, or any other feature of the actual fashion item—that can potentially affect sales.

+ The people-oriented market shift is a significant change in demographics and psychographics that can potentially affect sales.

+ The structure-oriented market shift is a significant change in the structure of the industry—the way product is designed, manufactured, distributed, or sold—that can potentially affect sales.

+ A seller should have in place a reliable network for sources of information through which he or she may be alerted to potential market shifts; then it is just a matter of processing the information, realizing when a shift is taking place, identifying its type, and formulating a strategy for adaptation.

+ There is no systematic, scientific formula that can be used to accurately recognize market shifts. Each market shift is a unique case of its own.

+ There are several key methods and strategies to stay in touch with the market: listening to buyers carefully, networking within the industry, reading trade and fashion magazines, and shopping the competition.

+ Recognizing a market shift is not enough; you must also be willing to do something effective about it and, above all, be flexible in adapting to it.

RW CASE STUDY

George Feldenkreis is chairman and CEO of Perry Ellis International (per the company's annual report, the net sales for the fiscal period ending January 31, 2005 was $633,774,000). In the 1960s, he founded Supreme International, a company known for manufacturing school uniforms and guayaberas, a four-pocket, tropical-inspired shirt. Supreme International went public in 1993 and became Perry Ellis International with the acquisition of the well-known fashion line in 1999. Feldenkreis founded the Universal National Bank of Miami and currently serves on the Board of Trustees for both the Jewish Federation and the University of Miami. He also supports numerous health and social organizations in the Miami community. Feldenkreis received the Lincoln-Marti award for his role in the Cuban Refugee Program and has also been honored with the "David Ben-Gurion" award. He shares his life-long experience in dealing with changes in the marketplace.

What are some of the major changes in the fashion industry that you've seen over the years?

The fashion retail business has changed tremendously in the last forty years, especially since 1990 because of the proliferation of the megastore. The policies that Wal-Mart has instituted in recent years have changed the ways we retail, and these changes were followed by the disappearance of U.S. manufacturing into Asia. Many retailers today buy directly from manufacturers in Asia and sell it in the U.S. Some of them have gone into private brands. There's been a lot of consolidation, creating "vertical" retailers. We've seen retailers becoming bigger and bigger, requiring resources—such as financing and logistics—that can supply in these volumes. One order from a Wal-Mart or Target can total $10 million; the sheer size of such an order is mind-boggling. Today, all major retailers are public companies, whereas twenty years ago, there were many privately-held retailers. Public companies have a lot of pressure on them to grow the 10 to 12 percent a year that's expected.

How has Perry Ellis International adjusted to those changes that affected your business?

We adapt every month by looking over our sales figures and making adjustments. We also review sales plans on a quarterly basis and survey what customers like and what they don't like. We have R & D [research and development] groups in Los Angeles and New York and 350 people in design. We send people to Europe and Asia to research the market and look at what ideas they bring back with them. Our sellers are instructed to work closely with the retail stores to find out what they need so we can supply these items as early as possible. We design new products constantly.

Has the role of the salesperson changed as well?

The traditional sales methods are still around, but from a sales perspective, the qualifications of the seller have changed. A seller can go out and have a round of golf with the buyer and know the names of the buyer's wife and children; however, if the seller doesn't also have the information, knowledge, and expertise, then they don't have a future. Today's salesperson has to be familiar with production, logistics, turn-arounds, in addition to the product itself. The salesperson today has to know more about his [or] her product than the buyer—particularly on the logistic side. For example, in the old days, you would sell a sweater at $20.00, and it would sell for $40.00 retail. Now, for example, you sell an item for $20.00, and it's marked up to retail at $39.00 for three weeks, and then it's marked down to $25.00, and after eight weeks it goes for $20.00. You have to have what is called a "ladder plan." Every time you sell a program it includes a "ladder plan," which indicates to the buyer at what point prices are to be reduced and when to take the mark down in order to maintain an average profit for the buyer. Otherwise, we are obligated to pay for excessive markdowns. Department stores today require a 42 percent markup, and if it's less, the vendor has to pay the difference. The ladder plan indicates at what point to take the markdown, so the merchandise moves to help maintain the required markup. Today, a salesperson must know how to plan the sales regardless of how good she or he is at selling. If they don't know how to present the ladder plan or understand the mechanics of presenting the plan or how to follow through and implement the plan, they will not be successful. We have another group added to our sales team called "marketing coordinators" who are responsible for how the merchandise is displayed in the stores, but they are also responsible that the ladder plan is implemented at store level and the markdowns are taken as planned so we do not have to be responsible for excessive markdowns. There is a saying that, "the first mark down is the best mark down." Our accounts are retail partners, and we are held to the agreed upon percentage—so we must perform.

What can a salesperson or sales manager do to stay ahead of and adjust to changes in their markets?

You have to be ahead and focus from your viewpoint where the fashion world is going to be five, ten, and twenty years away. Today, the salesperson must know the product better than the customer and has to be constantly looking at what the competition is selling. In addition, the salesperson should be always looking for new opportunities to sell additional products to his customers. A vital role of the salesperson is to understand the company's plans and to serve as a bridge between the customer's needs and the company plans for new products. Also, you have to keep up with changes in demographics; for example, Hispanics is the fastest growing demographic group in the U.S today. You have to adjust continuously.

Questions to Consider

1. What are your thoughts about Perry Ellis International's practice of reviewing sales plans quarterly? Do you think it gives them an advantage? Why?

2. Why do you think a salesperson should be familiar with logistics of the "ladder plan" and production details in today's sales environment?

3. Do you agree with Mr. Feldenkreis that "Today, the salesperson must know the product better than the customer"? Why?

4. Mr. Feldenkreis mentions in that a significant change of demographics is taking place in the United States today. What is this change, and what type of market shift would you classify it under?

RW EXERCISES

1. Describe in your own words the three types of market shifts, and give an example for each.

2. Why do you think it is important for sellers and managers to be able to recognize and adapt to a market shift? What do you think would happen when they do not adapt to it? Give an example.

3. Research your library, Internet resources, and trade publications, and identify a market shift that took place in the fashion industry during the twentieth century. Describe the market shift and the circumstances around it, and determine which type of a market shift it was (product-, people-, or structure-oriented).

4. How can a market shift offer new opportunities to a fashion company? Give an example.

5. Analyze your personal life: Make a list of those people who make up your reliable network of information sources? Why do you listen to them as opposed to other people? Do you exchange information with each, or is it a one-way flow? How would you make decisions in your life if you weren't able to consult with your network on a regular basis?

6. Research your library, Internet resources, and trade publications and identify a fashion company that experienced a market shift. Describe the company, the market shift and its type (product-, people-, or structure-oriented), the circumstances around it, whether or not the company adapted to it, and how. Also, note down your thoughts about the case: Do you think the company could have done better in adapting to the market shift. If so, how could they have achieved that?

7. Pair up with another student so one of you acts as the salesperson and the other acts as the buyer. As the salesperson, chat with the buyer and gather some information that relates to a market shift. Note the information gathered, how it affects you as a salesperson, and how you went about gathering it. Switch roles for a different perspective, and note the new responses.

8. Assume you are a sales manager in a fashion company that is facing one or more market shifts. Write down the scenario details (e.g., what type of company it is, what product lines it specializes in, the market shift), and recommend a strategy to adapt to each market shift and your reasoning behind it.

END NOTES

1. The Federal Reserve Bank of New York Web site. http://search.newyorkfed.org/search/ frbny.jsp?querybox=inflation+1960=and1970&sear.

2. Sargent, T. J., N. Williams, and T. Zha. "Shock and Government Beliefs: The Rise and Fall of American Inflation." NBER working paper w10764, 2004.

3. United States Department of Agriculture, Economic Research Service. The Changing World Network of Trade in Textiles and Apparel. Online. www.ers.usda.gov/AmberWaves/scripts/print.asp?page=/ september04/DataFeature/.

4. Phone interview. August 14, 2005.

CHAPTER 14

THE GLOBAL MARKETPLACE

Objectives

+ Realize the importance of the global perspective in selling.

+ Recognize how the concept of cultural divide can exist between sellers and buyers from different countries and how to overcome it.

+ Understand the importance of culture in selling.

+ Explore the various aspects and issues that the seller faces in a global market.

+ Look at several proven strategies for entering a foreign market, and review their pros and cons.

Overview

The fashion industry has always been intrinsically related to the global marketplace, but it is increasingly more so today. It draws on trends and styles from many different countries and repeatedly crosses both political and cultural borders to effectively export its fashion items and products. Ralph Lauren is not just an American label: It is known worldwide, as are Tommy Hilfiger, Perry Ellis, Kimora Lee Simmons for Baby Phat, Donna Karan, Calvin Klein, and Marc Jacobs. Likewise, Louis Vuitton is not just a European label, as it too is known worldwide, as are Dolce & Gabbana, Gucci, Armani, Hugo Boss, Gianni Versace, Chanel, Christian Dior, Yves Saint Laurent, Lanvin. Japanese labels, such as Issey Miyake, Kenzo, and Hanae Mori, are sought after not only in France, Italy, Germany, and Japan but also in the United States, Canada, Argentina, Australia, and other international markets. Karen Walker, the New Zealand fashion designer featured on pages 108–111 of this text, has an international reputation. The Karen Walker brand is represented in more than 130 stores throughout the world. In today's global and highly diverse world, fashion salespeople and sales managers are often expected to be adept not only in sales methodology as it relates to their home towns, but also within an international as well as intercultural framework.

Introduction

The fashion world is more global today than it has ever been before. Fashion lines that are sold in New York will most likely be in demand in London, Madrid, and Tokyo. Styles that debut in Paris and Rome are likely to be in demand in Los Angeles and Rio de Janeiro. Fashion manufacturers should not and cannot afford to ignore the significant potential revenues from selling their products abroad. Foreign markets should be explored and evaluated for entry and distribution opportunities, style and product compatibility, and pricing structures.

To successfully sell in a foreign market, the manufacturer is wise to conduct surveys, market research, and product testing to determine consumer tastes in matters of styles, sizes, colors, and seasonal changes. Salespeople and sales managers today find themselves increasingly involved in transactions across borders. Since Florida is a gateway to the South American and Caribbean markets, it is not uncommon today for the Southeast sales territory to include the Bahamas or Colombia. The Southwest territory may often cover Mexico in addition to California, Arizona, and Texas. As a result, today's successful seller must be familiar with a variety of different cultures and be capable of adjusting his or her sales methods to accommodate for the cultures' values and norms.

The Cultural Divide

Since the global marketplace operates across borders, continents, and oceans, there is often a set of cultural differences between sellers and buyers, which this text prefers to call the cultural divide and which affects the sales process. In *Cultural Anthropology*, Serena Nanda and Richard L. Warms define culture as the "learned behaviors and symbols that allow people to live together in groups" and as the way people adapt to the environment, organize society, and give meaning to their lives.[1] While culture is a very intricate and complex topic, what this book is most concerned with are the norms and values that govern interpersonal relationships.

When comparing people from the United States with the Trobriander tribe of Papua, New Guinea, for example, the first noticeable difference is appearance—some Americans dress in the stereotypical jeans and T-shirt, while some Trobrianders dress in their traditional indigenous garbs. Next, we find that the language is different. It would be difficult for an American to try to sell anything to a Trobriander because their cultural divide is so wide they cannot even communicate.

But that is an extreme example. A moderate, but perhaps more difficult example, would be to compare an American with a Canadian. Both are culturally similar in the way they dress, behave, and even talk, since most Canadians speak English. However, Canadians live in a much colder climate, their population density is significantly lower than that of the United States, and their political system is in general more socialistic. While these differences may not seem significant, they are still differences. Sellers who ignore these differences may lose their chance to close a sale; all it can take is one comment about how horrible cold climate is for the seller to completely alienate the buyer and lose the sale.

The idea of cultural divide is directly associated with the concept of empathy discussed in chapter 1. Recall that empathy is when a person listens to another attentively; understands the other person's thoughts, emotions, and feelings; and adjusts his or her own moods and behavior accordingly. Within the context of this definition, cultural understanding can be broken into three parts. First, a seller must learn about the other culture, either directly from the buyer, from others who are familiar with the culture, or from authoritative books. Next, a seller must truly understand the culture and fully understand the buyer's thoughts, emotions, and feelings within the context of that buyer's culture. A key part to this step is the removal of bias and avoidance of ethnocentrism; *ethnocentrism* is an anthropological term denoting the skewed judgment of other cultures and the belief that one's culture is superior to all others. In other words, the seller perceives U.S. culture to be superior to Canadian culture, which establishes a cultural divide that cannot be surmounted. The only way to get past the cultural divide is for the seller to properly and genuinely be empathetic to the buyer. Finally, the seller must adjust, within reason and integrity, his or her own moods and behavior to the buyer's. If a seller is meeting a client in Thailand and the seller knows that touching someone's head is considered bad manners in Thailand, then it follows that the seller should make an effort to show respect and avoid touching anybody's head while he or she is there.

Similarly, it is considered rude in Japan for people to write on business cards or to put them in their pockets without studying them first. Such rules are fairly simple to follow, and a seller who must travel to Japan is wise to do so. That said, a sellers should never feel that they have to do something against their own beliefs just to please their buyers; no reasonable buyer will ever expect a seller to abandon his or her own culture. Sellers are entitled to their own principles even while visiting a different country.

Often, merely taking the time to learn about the buyer's culture and acknowledging its importance in conversation is sufficient to form empathy with the buyer. There's no need for the seller to become an absolute expert on every facet of the buyer's culture or to "convert" to it

RW Story

In Japan, bowing is the usual greeting. Japanese etiquette requires the individual to bow lower when meeting people of higher rank, be it companies or otherwise. I [Sherman] noticed when I arrived in Japan and met the folks at the airport that the driver bowed very low when he met the top executive who was in charge of the seminar, but when he greeted middle management, he would not bow as low. As an American doing business in Japan, I didn't think it appropriate for me to bow when I met Japanese sponsors. Instead, I nodded on meeting them, and they responded accordingly.

and follow all of its values and norms. A basic knowledge and understanding of the culture, an exhibition of respect for that culture, and a genuine attempt to bridge the cultural divide is often all that a seller needs to do to succeed.

Ethnicity & Selling

The cultural divide is evident not only in the traditional sense across borders, but also in the sense that within U.S. borders, in particular, the cultural and ethnic makeup is seen as significantly more diverse than ever before. For example, according to the U.S. Census Bureau 2000 report, a full fourth of the U.S. population is now made up of a minority population. Hispanics and African Americans each account for 12 percent of the population, and other nonwhite populations accounts for the remaining 1 percent.[2]

Thus, it is statistically plausible to assume that even in the United States, three out of every ten buyers will be members of some minority group who may have a wholly or partially different set of cultural values than the seller. Spanish speakers are often quite formal in their dealings with one another in business settings. It is expected of men to offer a firm handshake when they meet and when saying good-bye, while a hug and a light kiss on a cheek is a common greeting among Spanish-speaking women. Formality can also be distinguished by what one says; in the Spanish language, there are several formal and informal forms of address that are used in different situations. For example, while both *usted* and *tu* mean the pronoun "you," one is expected to use *usted* in formal settings and *tu* in informal settings.

Similarly, many Hispanics dress in formal business attire when in business settings. A seller who shows up to a meeting with a Hispanic corporate buyer wearing sneakers and jeans is sure to leave a long-lasting unfavorable impression.

However, salespeople should note that it is quite socially acceptable for most Spaniards and select South/Central Americans and Caribbeans to be half an hour late to a meeting. Therefore, the seller should be prepared and not get upset if the buyer is late.

Selling to Other Cultures

There are many misconceptions about the mechanics of selling in the global environment. When salespeople need to work in an international market, they must spend time learning about the customs, cultures, atti-

RW Story

A few decades ago, I [Sherman] organized and conducted several fashion selling seminars in Tokyo, Japan, for the Fashion Institute of Technology of New York City. It was sponsored by Asahi Kasei/Dow Chemical Co., Ltd. Tokyo, Japan. The participants were sales, marketing, and management people from Japanese apparel and textile companies. We did role-playing and set up scripts and situations. I was overwhelmed with how willing the audience was to participate. We communicated through the help of interpreters. The group reacted just as any group did in the United States. What a learning experience! This exercise proved that some of the basic selling methods are universal except for the language and methods of communication and cultural differences. Personal selling language is universal as long as the proper methods are employed.

I introduced the various sales practices used in the United States, including discussing presentations, answering objec- tions, and asking for the order. My good friend, Max Hugel, former president of Brothers, U.S., advised me that the participants wanted to know how sales-people in the United States work with their buyers because they wanted to Americanize their methods. Although I obviously knew that Japanese translators were communicating my message to the audience, I was not aware of how much time it took to translate what I was saying. So I went on and on, told what I thought was a funny story about selling, and did-n't receive any reaction from the group. Oops, I said, and went onto some serious business things and guess what? Moments later the audience let out a burst of laughter. I soon realized that it took longer to translate my comments than I imagined. In a business situation, this lack of understanding can be awk- ward.

My first trip to Japan taught me the dif- ferences in cultures and ground rules for doing business. For example, Japanese manufacturers give gifts to their buyers and other business associates; it's not considered bribery as we would interpret it in the United States. Gift giving is part of the culture in Asia. After completing this seminar, I was given several gifts: one was a replica of a samurai helmet, and another was Japanese artwork. I soon learned that gift giving in the com- mercial environment was a normal act. I was embarrassed for not knowing this, for had I been told, I certainly would have had gifts for my Japanese friends. The next seminar, I was well prepared and brought plenty of Johnny Walker Black Label scotch (a favorite among the spon- sors). The whole approach to selling in this culture is based on understanding the methods of doing business that is based on relationships and trust. When selling to other cultures in the global marketplace, it is quite apparent that employees in management and nonman- agement positions must be part of that culture.

tudes, and values of the people in the respective countries to which they want to sell. Sellers who don't do their research may unintentionally make mistakes that others perceive as offensive, insensitive, or ignorant. Such research should result in information that allows sellers to figure out ways to communicate their messages in manners that will be easy for buyers to accept.

As with domestic selling, salespeople who sell their products globally need to develop an appropriate approach and strategy for reaching their customers. Selling is selling no matter where you go, but you've got to know the territory. The principles of personal selling are a great topic for discus- sion in this chapter because, as we will explain, despite notable differences, most of the major selling principles are the same the world over. To be suc- cessful in the global market, we have to be concerned with and sensitive to the different cultures and their methods of doing business and approaching the buyers. We must also be conscious of incorporating the basic principles of personal selling. We cannot eliminate the expertise the seller must have in prospecting, presentations, persuasion, answering objections, and closing methods. In this respect, the basic selling principles remain the same universally. Integrity, relationships, and customer retention are the guideposts in selling anywhere in the world. The difference is in how we approach these sales procedures in the international markets.

Doing business in the global marketplace relies on many of the same people situations as it does within the United States. In a sense, many aspects of the sales principles and methodology are based on a broad, psychological level that applies to all humanity, regardless of cultural or ethnic differences. Concepts such as maintaining high integrity and building a relationship with the customer are universal and work everywhere.

While we all realize that the cultures are different in each of the international areas, the personalities and characteristics of the people involved both on the buying and selling sides remain the same the world over. There are extroverts and introverts, pragmatists and dreamers, honest and dishonest people, and nice people and not so nice people. These distinctions exist regardless of language or geographical location. In addition to knowing about trade agreements and finances, knowing the culture and customs will also make a great difference in achieving success.

Specific Global Issues

While understanding culture plays a major role in improving sales abroad, the seller must also be aware of the economic and political factors involved. Let's review some of the major noncultural issues that global sellers face.

Government and Regulations

In the book *Doing Business in China*, authors Tim Amber and Moran Witzel start off by saying, "Relations, Relations, Relations."[3] They add that if salespeople use American or European methods when working or partnering with Chinese firms, they are destined for failure. Relationships with the government and officials are the major concerns salespeople should have when working in China. Thinking globally and hiring local Chinese people is the only way to have lasting success in China. Doing business in China means always thinking in terms of the Chinese government and historical culture, not in U.S. standards.

Similarly, every country has its unique set of trade. Before embarking on any entry plan into a new market, sellers must research the country's import regulations to ensure compliance. Some countries impose hefty

VAT (Value Added Tax) An indirect sales tax that is added to a product at some of its production and distribution stages, which is typically passed on to the consumer.

duties that make entry nearly impossible; others demand the importer employ a certain number of locals. It is imperative to consult with an American lawyer who specializes in international trade or a local lawyer who deals with international corporations on import matters.

Even after a seller receives an import license, there are many other issues to consider: local law regarding employee benefits, sales tax or **VAT**, and delivery transportation within the country. We will discuss the advantages of partnering with local independent sales agents who are already familiar with the local laws and regulations later in this chapter.

Personnel

Selling in foreign markets can only be successful if the people in that country are part of the process. The methodology of selling has to be tailored to relate to the individual country and its culture. We soon learned that U.S. entrepreneurs and managers had to act as trainers and teachers and try to not be totally involved in the selling transaction. The final result for success would depend on the local home-grown personnel they hired and not alone on their selling expertise.

Language

You can't market to foreign markets unless you understand the language, and by language, we don't mean simply the verbal or written aspect: We are also referring to the culture and way of life in these markets. People like to deal with others who share common bonds with them—hiring a local person, whether as an agent or sales organization will go a long way to ensure that your merchandising message is communicated. It will not only help in marketing the product but also with adjusting to changing needs in those foreign markets. Who best can communicate the happenings than those that "live in the neighborhood"? We must address the culture of the country as it relates to selling the product. The Asian markets approach selling with their unique style. They rely heavily on relationships to do business. Although price and value play important parts, they alone will not always enable a product to make its appearance.

Knowing the language itself can become a powerful advantage in a global selling situation, especially if the seller will be selling in that country often. Being able to converse with the buyer in his or her own language at once puts you within the buyer's trust—you are no longer an outsider, but someone with whom they literally speak the same language. There are many courses and products out in the market to help learn a language, such as cassettes, CDs, and workbooks. The major languages (Spanish, French, Italian, German, and Portuguese) are offered in many community colleges and are typically affordable as well as effective. If one cannot learn the language in full, it can be advantageous to learn

According to Wal-Mart's stockholder's statement 2000, cultural transitions haven't always been smooth for Wal-Mart International.

In Argentina, Wal-Mart didn't anticipate that shoppers would desire a more comfortable environment with wider aisles; they opened the first store with relatively narrow aisles similar to those in the United States. They also underestimated the heavier traffic. Finally, they missed that Argentines wanted simple gold and silver jewelry instead of the ornate jewelry that is sold in the United States. Wal-Mart states, "In Mexico City, we sold tennis balls that wouldn't bounce right in the high altitude." They also built parking lots at some of the stores in Mexico only to realize that many of their customers got there by bus and had to trudge across the large parking lots with bags full of merchandise. They solved the problem by creating bus shuttles to drop customers off at the door. They admitted these mistakes but are now working smarter internationally to avoid cultural and regional problems.

Wal-Mart Stores, Inc. is the world's largest retailer, with $285.2 billion in sales in the 2005 fiscal year. The company employs 1.6 million associates worldwide through more than 3,600 facilities in the United States and more than 1,570 units in the Americas, Europe, and Asia. More than 138 million customers per week visit Wal-Mart stores worldwide.

some key words and phrases. However, this could potentially get the seller into trouble since the buyer may assume the seller speaks the language fluently and misunderstandings can occur. In this situation, it is recommended for the seller to practice key phrases during small talk before or after the meeting and speak English during the crucial parts of the sales presentation.

Sizes, Silhouettes, and Color

We have also found that not only color but also silhouette and size range must be thoroughly researched in foreign markets. Colors and silhouettes play an important role in the various corners of the world. Whether it is in Europe, Asia, or any of the African countries, they all have their own sensitivity to color and silhouette. The following examples indicate the importance of the knowing the culture and customs and how they directly have an effect on decision making regarding color and silhouettes.

U.S. designer lines must adjust their sizing proportions to the consumers in the international marketplace. Many years ago a well-known U.S. company had the experience of presenting a fashion line of merchandise to Takashimaya Department Store in Tokyo, Japan. The size range was small, medium, and large. Realizing that the consumers were smaller in stature in Japan, they offered the product in small and medium only. What they didn't realize was that the size small in the United States was totally different from a small in Japan. They knew the body size was different but did not take into consideration the proportions of arms and legs in relation to the body size. The initial offering was not successful, and from then on, they hired Japanese designers and patternmakers.

We have never forgotten the story of a well-known ladies' fashion designer who was entering the Asian marketplace and was excited about presenting the summer collection. The clothing was sized to accommodate the Asian consumer—smaller portioned sizes and more conservative necklines were offered. The collection was magnificently designed—but when it was presented, it drew a gasp from the buying audience. With all the work and design expertise, why did they receive such a negative reaction? The major part of the collection was called the "Chiaroscuro collection" (*Chiaroscuro* means "the art form of black and white"); all the styles were in black and solid white with trim in the same color. It looked great, but there was one big faux pas—in Asia, the color white is considered a mourning color. Had the proper research been done regarding the culture as they did with the styling, this would never have happened. This was not the only mistake that U.S. manufacturers and retailers have made on entering the global marketplace.

We all agree that color is synonymous with fashion success. The style and silhouettes may be great, but if the color is not accepted, we find the items on the markdown rack. While white stands for purity in the United States, it is used for mourning in Asia and, therefore, is the kiss of death to any fashion line.

The color red is a symbol of success and luck in China and used a great deal in different ceremonies; in India it stands for purity and is common in wedding attire, whereas we in the United States, it is used by Christians during Christmas and many people during Valentine's Day. Yellow in Asia is associated with something holy and regal, and in the Western cultures, it exudes happiness. The dominant colors in the many African countries are green, red, gold, and black, as manifested by the flags of these countries. Green in China is not the choice color for packaging, and a green hat means a man's wife is cheating on him. Green is also the color of Islam in India, while in Ireland, it has significant religious significance—the shamrock and Catholicism. But blue is the dominant color for the global market—the Chinese associate blue with immortality, Hindus with the color of Krishna, and Israelis a symbol of holiness. If you want to play it safe globally, go blue—it's the safest color.

Seasons

Every region has its own distinct seasons—summer, spring, fall, and winter—and the international manufacturer must strictly adhere to merchandise for these seasons. So in entering a foreign market, one has to be conscious of the seasonal changes and block out temperatures and weather conditions that may affect sales. Sending heavier weighted fabric in darker colors in the warmer seasons will not enable the manufacture to hit that home run. We talked about knowing the territory—that's why hiring and training salespeople and management is essential to coordinate the right product at the right time.

Methods to Enter the Global Market

Entry into the global market necessitates the use of various marketing methods, strategies, and planning. We will discuss these different ways such as participating in trade shows, establishing a sales force, or licensing your product. The methods used will depend on the financial strength of the organization, its brand recognition, and its products. Some of these methods can be combined and made to work within the global market framework. For example, the company can participate in trade shows utilizing their sales forces or trading companies. However, in developing a licensee system, we find that the licensor acts as a consultant and usually does not have a major role directing the marketing and sales of the product.

International Trade Shows

Participating in international trade shows can be the first step for companies who wish to enter a foreign market. Trade shows are very important in overseas markets and are an immediate entryway for new products to be introduced. In European and Asian markets, trade shows account for a greater percentage of total sales than trade shows in the United States. Later in this chapter, we will discuss some of the advantages and disadvantages of participating in trade shows.

Trade shows provide an excellent opportunity to market your product and extend your brand name in the specific overseas markets in which you are interested. This book has stressed the importance of trade shows for the U.S. market. It is even more important if you feel your product is right for the global marketplace. The trade show is the most inexpensive way to market your product in the global market. It's the best place to test the response to your merchandise to see if your product is marketable in a specific area. Your expenses are reasonably fixed: air travel, hotel, food and drink, and entertainment, if you are fortunate to meet prospective buyers. Trade shows are conducive for networking due to the informal atmosphere and side-by-side exhibitors booths; you have the opportunity to approach local salespeople, trading companies, or licensees. It becomes an excellent vehicle for recruiting personnel. Initially, you may decide that your product should be marketed at these trade shows without hiring outside salespeople, but you will find that you do need the help of local salespeople. It is important to understand that if you wish to participate in these international trade shows success cannot be achieved in one or two showings. Only by attending consecutive showings throughout the year will the buyers be able to find you—it's all about consistency.

Attendees at these shows are interested in finding new products and also find it a convenient venue to place orders with the companies with which they are currently doing business. So the opportunity is there if your product is right for that market. Before signing up for any trade show, it is important to first research the activity of its past shows and determine if they were successful and who the participating companies were. Are their products compatible with what you want to introduce?

You should know who the organizers of the shows are: their reputations, performance, and experience. Not all trade shows are productive. It will take a bit of research, and the best method is to obtain a list of exhibitors to determine if the exhibitors' products are complementary to the merchandise you are offering. If you have a designer line, you would not want to participate in trade shows that have low-end merchandise.

RW Dictionary

Return on Investment (ROI) Every investment a business makes has an expected return. If the return is less than the investment, then the business loses money. If it is more than the investment, then the business earns a profit.

Look for exhibitors who are well-known (i.e., brand names) and who you feel are competitive—this will help expose your merchandise to the right prospective buyers. Finding a trade show that caters to your customer base is a big step in the right direction. The important thing here is to determine if your product is one that fits into the theme of the trade show. By researching the product mix, you will best know if this trade show is for you. Most show organizers will provide a list of exhibitors on request before you sign up.

You should also be cognizant of the total cost factor. Are there any hidden charges besides payment for the booth? Look for the small print in the contract—do you as an exhibitor have to pay for the shows advertising and promotion costs? Is there a charge for lighting and setup? If so, what are those charges? As in any business investment, you should know all the costs to help determine if you can plan to get a return on your investment (**ROI**). Ask yourself if the show will be cost effective. What are your expectations? Usually, first time appearances in a trade show will not be cost effective. The reason it may not yield a profit is that it takes time for the attendees to know where you are located and the type of merchandise you are showing. The main reason for this is that as a newcomer you are more likely not to get a good location. Those who have participated in past shows are the ones who take the best locations. Most shows assign the locations based on seniority—those who have participated in previous showing get the best locations. Also the best known brands get priority locations. The cost of the show should be looked at as an investment. If you break even in the first few shows, you have made a profit. The organizers of the trade show will advertise and promote the show listing the participants, but you should not depend on their promotions. It is imperative to produce your own attractive mailer and send it directly to the prospective attendees. The mailer is one of the major ways of reaching the list of buyers who attended the previous shows (registered participants receive this mailing list from the organizer before each trade show).

Usually these shows are made up of booths in different sizes. The most important thing that the participant must do is have the area displayed to attract attention and make sure there is proper lighting. Poor lighting will not attract the attendees. The most successful participants prepare brochures, price lists, PR, and advertising material as handouts and do a creative mailing prior to the show dates. Again, it is important to have a salesperson (interpreter) who is able to speak with the people of that country. Show organizers can often help you hire this sales assistant.

Trade Shows Pros and Cons

Typical advantages of participating in these trade shows are the following:

+ Receiving at no cost a list of both past and current attendees

+ Improving your company's prestige
+ Introducing the product to a captive audience
+ Receiving immediate reaction to your line
+ Reducing the cost of introducing your merchandise
+ Showing is less costly than hiring outside sales personnel
+ Gaining exposure to trading companies or independent sales representatives if you are interested in future hiring of outside sales personnel
+ Networking with other participants and buyers
+ Fixed costs
+ Investments similar to advertising or public relations

Disadvantages of participating in trade shows are the following:
+ First-time participants are unknown to the buyers.
+ Immediate results may not be realized.
+ Trade shows may last for only a few days to a week.
+ Limited time is available to obtain orders.
+ Costs may exceed results.
+ You are symbiotic to the total traffic of the attendees.
+ If the show is not well attended, your outcome may not be exciting.
+ First-time participants don't receive good locations.

There are a number of sources for finding international trade shows. Biz Trade Shows (www.biztradeshows.com) is one such directory of trade fairs and business events, which brings you exhaustive coverage of exhibitions, trade shows and expositions, conferences, and seminars for various industries worldwide. You can browse through the most comprehensive information on individual trade events worldwide, along with their event profiles, organizers, exhibitor and visitor profiles, venues, and dates to plan your participation much in advance.

Establishing a Global Sales Force

Many companies in the United States prefer to hire salespeople who understand the local culture of the different areas in their territories. It is even more important in the global market to hire salespeople or trading companies who employ their own salespeople and managers and live in and know the territory. Let's face it: To be successful in the global market, one has to have a full staff of people who know these markets and are the major players, managers, and sellers. They must be able to set policy and establish the strategies for reaching their respective markets. Americans can train their international employees in the product, but the one-on-one communication process has to be their own.

The advantages of having your own sales staff or sales agents are that you can regulate the growth of the product and get faster access to the market with a fixed cost. You also have management control of the hiring and firing and as a result can increase the amount of salespeople or decrease the staff as you see fit. One of the disadvantages in having a global sales force is that because these sellers have to be involved in the decision-making and strategies for reaching their respective markets, they could call on only those markets they are already familiar with, instead of reaching out to better markets that can yield greater results and opportunities for growth. Another disadvantage is the loss of control because they know more about the territory than you, and at times, this can be disastrous.

Using Trading Companies or Independent Sales Agents

In many cases, the best way to facilitate the entry into these international markets and have effective distribution channels is to engage the services of local trading companies or independent sales agents in these countries. This trend is much more effective for many companies than organizing their own sales forces. Trading companies have their own sales forces and are in direct communication with the target customers. It can be easier to deal with the trading company executives and agents than having to deal with the management of a company sales force.

One of the big advantages in hiring these entities is that most are able to speak fluent English and understand the objectives and goals of your company. The other is a financial advantage because payment is usually based on commissions and on performance. The use of trading companies and sales agents has proven to be both cost-effective and efficient in most cases. Another important advantage is that they understand the regulations governing products entering their country—duties, taxes, and the law. The only disadvantage is that if the trading company decides to leave your employment, they can take away many of the company's customers. This can be a temporary problem until you hire a replacement.

Licensing

Taking the route to license your fashion product globally works exceptionally well for designer and other branded lines. Licensing is the fastest growing method for marketing a product and gaining brand name exposure in the United States and the international market.[4]

In the United States, we first witnessed the dramatic growth of licensing in athletic wear with some of the following companies: Nike, Adidas, Champion, Russel Corporation, and Callaway Golf Co. Today, it has spread to all types of clothing, home furnishings, toys, and other branded merchandise. Perry Ellis International is a leading international marketer of apparel, offering a diverse portfolio of brands through multiple distribution channels. They are one of the leading companies engaged in licensing as a licensor and licensee. Perry Ellis International's growth has been phenomenal in apparel markets both in the United States and the global market.[5]

The advantages are simply less expenditures in product development and little or no costs in marketing when the product is released to a licensee to be made and sold by them in their respective countries. The work effort that the company put forth at home in developing the product pays dramatic dividends when the right organization signs on to become a licensee.

Licensors enter into agreements where their organizations permit another to use its intellectual property rights in exchange for payment usually in the form of commission on sales or a specified royalty payment. Getting the proper licensee guarantees the licensor of profits without big investments. Licensors are usually organizations that have brand name recognition.

Licensees have permission to use the licensors' logos, styles, patterns, marketing know-how, and other merchandising aids as their own only without the right of actual ownership of these properties. The licensors maintain ownership. The licensees pay fees depending on the agreements. Fees are usually based on the volume of sales by the licensees. The agreement can be for specific countries and territories and can be for certain time periods.

Ralph Lauren, Donna Karan, Perry Ellis International, and Tommy Hilfiger are just a few of the fashion industry leaders who have licensee agreements in the United States and in the global market. The trend of establishing licensees for U.S. brands in the global market has been strong and is getting stronger . Having a licensee for your brand extends your brand name in these global areas. In essence the licensee pays a percentage of sales for the use of your logo, designs, patterns, and other areas that are needed to market the brand in their country.

For example, Tommy Hilfiger Corporation designs, sources, and markets men's and women's sportswear, jeans wear, and childrenswear through its subsidiaries under the Tommy Hilfiger trademarks. However, through a range of strategic licensing agreements, the company also offers a broad array of related apparel, accessories, footwear, fragrances, and home furnishings. The company's products can be found in leading department and specialty stores throughout the United States, Canada, Europe, Mexico, Central and South America, Japan, Hong Kong, and other countries in the Far East, as well as the company's own network of outlet and specialty stores in the United States, Canada, and Europe.

Polo Ralph Lauren prefers licensing over manufacturing. According

RW Support Organizations

The following organizations and publications will assist companies doing business in Western Europe:

+ The U.S. Department of Commerce
+ The U.S. Chamber of Commerce
+ Europages, The European Business Directory
+ U.S. Export Assistance Centers
+ The Federation of International Trade Associations

Copyright 2000 by Virtual Advisor, Inc. www.va-interactive.com/inbusiness/editorial/bizdev/articles/Europe.html

to Hoover's, the company oversees many of their licensees and about 350 contract manufacturers worldwide. It operates about 275 retail stores and outlet stores in the United States and licenses more than 100 others worldwide.[6]

Perry Ellis International is a leading designer, distributor, and licensor of apparel and accessories for men, women, and children. The company, through its wholly owned subsidiaries, owns or licenses a portfolio of brands that includes 25 of the leading names in fashion such as Perry Ellis, Axis, Savane, Original Penguin, Cubavera, Ping Collection, Nike Swim, Jantzen, Tricots St. Raphael, and Grand Slam.[7]

Chapter Summary

+ The fashion industry is intrinsically related to the global market-place, drawing on trends and styles from many different countries and repeatedly crossing both political and cultural borders to effectively export its fashion items and products.
+ Because the global marketplace operates across borders, continents, and oceans, there is often a set of cultural differences between the seller and the buyer, which we call the cultural divide.
+ Cultural understanding and sensitivity is closely related to the concept of empathy.
+ The cultural divide is evident not only in the traditional sense across borders, but also in the sense that within these borders, the cultural and ethnic makeup is seen as significantly more diverse than ever before.
+ In selling to the international market, you must take the time to learn about the customs, cultures, attitudes, and values of the people in the respective countries to which you want to sell. You must ask yourselves how they differ from your own.
+ To be successful in the global market, we not only have to be concerned and sensitive to the different cultures and their methods of doing business, but also conscious of incorporating the basic principles of personal selling.
+ To be successful internationally, the seller must understand the foreign culture, as well as be aware of the economic and political factors at work in that country.
+ The major noncultural issues that global sellers face include government and regulations, personnel, language, sizes and colors, and seasons.
+ Trade shows are very important in overseas markets and are an immediate entryway for new products to be introduced. Participating in

international trade shows can be the first step for companies who wish to enter a foreign market.

+ Having your own sales staff or sales agents allows you to regulate the growth of the product and get faster access to the market with a fixed cost.

+ In many cases, the best way to facilitate the entry into these international markets and have effective distribution channels is to engage the services of local trading companies or independent sales agents in these countries.

+ Taking the route to license your fashion product globally works exceptionally well for designer and other branded lines.

RW CASE STUDY

George Sharoubim is the owner and founder of Giorgio's of Palm Beach, a designer label that specializes in high-end couture and accessories that is known for its unique designs, using alligator and ostrich skins. It caters to dignitaries, world leaders, and top business executives from around the world.

Is there a major difference between the American taste in fashion and that of consumers in the rest of the world?

Yes, there is. Generally speaking, Americans are very conservative when it comes to fashion. The Europeans like much more classic items, and the cleaner the look of the item, the better it is. Less is more. The less busy an item is, the more elegant and timeless will be its look. In Asia and South America, they usually like items with louder prints, brighter colors, and gold patterns.

How does this manifest itself in the items worn in each country?

Americans can be divided into two categories: 1) conservative at work (i.e., suit and tie) and 2) conservative casual. The latter would apply to a weekend event where one might show up with blue jeans and a button-down or polo shirt. Europeans like to fantasize, and men will wear tight pants versus Americans who most often wear relaxed fit. Americans do not particularly like to show the item's label, while Europeans tend to show it more.

How do you plan your product line so it appeals to such a varied base of clients?

What we do is follow the fashion trends in each particular country or region, but we do so in a classic way so that it retains its international appeal as well. We aim to create something comfortable that doesn't become outdated. We focus on creating elegant designs with today's look in terms of colors and fits, which still keep some classic features.

How do you deal with doing business across borders?

It is extremely important to pay close attention to all legal and official matters and follow them at all times. It has been beneficial for us to hire local experts who can provide advice on the local legal issues. It is also important to understand the culture of the country one is exporting to and respect their customs and values.

Do you adjust your sales methods to fit the global market? If so, how?

We've found that across the world, the selling methods essentially remain the same. Credibility is the top concern for any buyer, be it in America, Europe, or Asia. The taste, design, and approach may differ from culture to culture, but basically the buyer's needs are often similar everywhere you go.

Questions to Consider

1. What are the major fashion differences that exist in the global market according to Sharoubim?
2. Do you think it is indeed important to follow the country's legal regulations as a top priority? Explain your reasoning.
3. Do you agree with Sharoubim that buyer's needs are similar across the globe? Why?

RW EXERCISES

1. In your own words, what is the cultural divide? Have you ever seen a real-life example of it?
2. Write down the positive and/or negative effects you feel a cultural divide can have on a particular sale. Explain.
3. Pair up with another student so one of you acts as the salesperson and the other acts as a buyer of a different culture. Write down how the cultural divide affected the seller's relationship with the buyer and what its effect on the sale was. Switch roles for a different perspective, and note the new responses.
4. Name three parts of the sales methodology you've learned so far in this book that you think are universal. Explain why.
5. Name the parts of the sales methodology you've learned so far in this book that you think are *not* universal and vary according to the buyer's culture. Explain why.

6. Research a particular cultural element in your culture that is viewed differently in the culture of a foreign country. Write down and explain how the difference in culture would affect the sales process if you were the seller and the buyer was from the foreign country. Include your research information and source citations.

7. Pick two of the five noncultural issues covered in this chapter. Write down an example for each issue and include how you think it could affect a company's success in entering a new foreign market.

8. Assume you are a sales manager in a company that is planning to enter a new foreign market. Write down the scenario details (i.e., what type of company it is, what product lines it specializes in, and so on), and then recommend which of the four entry methods should be utilized and your reasoning behind each.

END NOTES

1. Nanda, Serena, and Richard L. Warms. *Cultural Anthropology*, 8th edition. Belmont, CA: Wadsworth Publishing, 2003.

2. U.S. Census Bureau. www.census.gov/population/cen2000/phc-t1/tab01.pdf.

3. Amber, Tim, and Moran Witzel. *Doing Business in China*, 2nd edition. New York: Routledge, 2004.

4. Licensing Magazine. www.licensemag.com/licensemag/data/articlestandard/licensemag/412005/184293/article.pdf. Also: *The Growth of the Corporate Brand*, by Adam Bass. www.goldengoose.uk.com.

5. Perry Ellis Mission Statement. www.pery.com.

6. Hoover's online. www.hoovers.com/free/cp/factsheet.xhtml?&ID=40369&abforward=true.

7. Perry Ellis International. www.pery.com.

RESOURCES FOR THE READER

Publications

Fairchild Publications, www.fairchildpub.com
Fairchild Books, www.fairchildbooks.com
WWD, www.wwd.com
Daily News Record, www.dnrnews.com
Home Furnishings, www.hfnmag.com
Footwear News, www.footwearnews.com
Apparel News, www.apparelnews.com
Elle Magazine, www.elle.com
InStyle Magazine, www.instyle.com
Textile World Magazine, www.textileworld.com

Trade Shows

Atlanta Mart, www.americasmart.com
Bobbin Group, www.bobbin.com
California Mart, www.californiamart.com
Dallas Market Center, www.dallasmarketcenter.com
Igedo International Trade Shows, www.igedo.com
Magic Trade Show, www.magiconline.com
Prêt-à-Porter, www.pretaporter.com
Textile Show, www.textileshow.com
Trade Show Network, www.tssn.com
Interstoff Global Trade Shows, www.interstoff.com
Biz Trade Shows, www.biztradeshows.com

Fiber Bureaus

Cotton Incorporated, www.cottoninc.com
The Wool Bureau, www.woolmark.com

Sales Representatives Organizations

Manufacturers Representatives & Manufacturers Network,
www.manonline.org
Manufacturers Representative Educational Research Foundation,
www.mref.org
Fashion Industry Information Services, sales leads, www.infomat.com
Apparel Search sales employment opportunities,
www.apparelsearch.com

Careers/Internships	A career site for the fashion industry, www.fashioncareercenter.com
	A career site for the fashion industry, www.fashion-jobs.biz
	Internship opportunities in the fashion industry, www.fashioninterns.com
	Jobs and internship opportunities, www.fashion.net/jobs
Demographics and Information Providers	The U.S. Census Bureau, www.census.gov
	Information about population trends and their implications, www.prb.org
	Company financial and industry information, www.hoovers.com
	An online guide to the apparel industry, www.apparelsearch.com
	Fashion industry information search engine, www.infomat.com
	American Marketing Association, www.marketingpower.com

REFERENCES

Chapter 1   Brooks, Bill. "20 Ways to Derail a Successful Sales Career." *The American Salesman*, September 2002.

Cholewka, Kathleen. "Survey Says: Some Sales Execs Are Liars." *Sales & Marketing*, 2001.

Coscia, S. *Customer Service Over the Phone.* San Francisco: Miller Freeman, 1998.

McMaster, Mark. "Online Learning from Scratch." *Sales & Marketing Management*, November 2002.

Swanson, Kristen K., and Judith C. Everett. *Promotion in the Merchandising Environment.* New York: Fairchild Publications, 2000.

Chapter 2   Buzzotta, V. R., R. E. Lefton, and Manuel Sherberg. *Effective Selling Through Psychology*, Cambridge, MA: Ballinger Publishing/Harper & Row, 1982.

Churchill Jr., Gilbert A., Neil M. Ford, and Orville C. Walker. *Sales Force Management,* 2nd edition, Homewood, IL: Richard D. Irwin, 1985.

Maynard, Robert. "Finding the Essence of Good Salespeople: How to Identify the Characteristics that Make Good Salespeople." *Nation's Business*, February 1998.

Ruth, Amanda, and Allen Wysocki. "Top Sellers: Characteristics of a Superior Salesperson." EDIS document SN004, a publication of the Department of Food and Resource Economics, Florida Cooperative Extension Service, Institute of Food and Agricultural Sciences, University of Florida, Gainesville, FL, April 2002, http://edis.ifas.ufl.edu.

Satterfield, Mark. "Selling to the Top: Traits and Characteristics of Senior Level Business Developers." *American Salesman*, December 2001.

Chapter 3   "After All You've Done for Your Customers, Why Are They Still Not Happy?" *Fortune Magazine*, December 11, 1995.

Reicheld, F.F., "Learning from Customer Defections." *Harvard Business Review*, March/April 1996.

Levy, Michael. *Retail Management.* New York: McGraw Hill, 2003.

Schiffman, Leon G., and Leslie Lazar Frank. *Consumer Behavior,* 8th edition. Upper Saddle River, NJ: Prentice Hall, 2003.

Schroeder, Carol L. *Specialty Shop Retailing: How to Run Your Own Store.* Indianapolis, IN: John Wiley & Sons, Inc., 1997, 2002.

Whalin, George. *Retail Success.* Owosso, MI: Willoughby Press, 2001.

Chapter 4 Boone, Louis E., and David L. Kurtz. *Contemporary Marketing,* 11th edition. Mason, OH: South-Western, a division of Thompson Learning, 2004.

Dion, Paul, Debbi Easterling, and Raj Javalgi. "Women in Business-to-Business Salesforce: Some Differences in Performance Factors." *Industrial Marketing Management,* 26, September 1997.

Jackson, Donald, Scott Widmier, Ralph Giacobbe, and Janet E. Keith. "Examining the Use of Team Selling by Manufacturer's Representatives: A Situational Approach." *Industrial Marketing Management,* 28, March 1999.

Vitale, Robert P., and Joseph J. Giglierano. *Business to Business Marketing: Analysis and Practice in a Dynamic Environment.* Mason, OH: South-Western, a division of Thompson Learning, 2002.

Weitz, Barton A., and Kevin D. Bradford. "Personal Selling and Sales Management: A Relationship Marketing Perceptive." *Journal of the Academy of Marketing Science,* 27, 1999.

Chapter 5 Brooks, Bill. "20 Ways to Derail a Successful Sales Career." *The American Salesman,* September 2002.

Hoffman, K. Douglas, Michael R. Czinkota, Peter R. Dickson, Patrick Dunne, and Abbie Griffin. *Marketing Principles & Best Practices,* 2nd edition, Mason, OH: South-Western, a division of Thompson Learning, 2004.

Leone, Patrick. "The Right Way to Get Referrals." *Advisor Today,* October 2002.

Marchetti, Michelle. "What a Sale Costs." *Sales & Marketing Management,* 2001.

Sherman, Jerry, and Eric Hertz. *Woman Power in Textile & Apparel Sales.* New York: Fairchild Publications, 1979.

Weinreb, Michael. "Don't Waste Your Time." *Sales & Marketing Management,* November 2002.

Chapter 6 Garfinkel, David. "Making the Most of IT: How to Squeeze More Profits from the Web." *Sales & Marketing Management.* March 2002.

Girard, Joe, and Robert Casemore. *How to Sell Yourself.* New York: Warner Books, 1992.

Harrow, Susan. *Sell Yourself Without Selling Your Soul: A Woman's Guide to Promoting Herself, Her Business.* New York: HarperCollins Publishers, 2002.

Sherman, Jerry, and Eric Hertz. *Woman Power in Textile & Apparel Sales.* New York: Fairchild Publications, 1979.

Sujan, Harish. "Optimism and Street Smarts: Identifying and Improving Salesperson Intelligence." *Journal of Personal Selling and Sales Management,* 19 1999.

Thull, Jeff, "The End of Solution-Based Selling." www.marketingprofs.com, September 20, 2005.

Chapter 7

Farber, Barry. "Good Show! Sales Presentations." *Entrepreneur Magazine,* November 2004. www.findarticles.com/p/articles, *Journal of Personal Selling & Sales Management.*

Davis, Rick. "Command Performance: To Make Powerful Sales Presentations, You Need a Carefully Prepared and Concise Script." *Journal of Personal Selling & Sales Management,* August 2004.

Leeds, Dorothy. "How to Make Persuasive Sales Presentations." Folio: Special Sourcebook Issue, *The Magazine for Magazine Management,* 1998.

Rackham, Neil. *Spin Selling.* New York: McGraw-Hill, 1988.

Sjodin, Terry L. *New Sales Speak: The 9 Biggest Sales Presentation Mistakes and How to Avoid Them.* Indianapolis, IN: John Wiley & Sons, Inc., 2001.

Tanner Jr., John F. "Adaptive Selling at Trade Shows." *Journal of Personal Selling & Sales Management,* 1994.

Chapter 8

Cannon, Joseph P., and William D. Perreault, Jr. "Buyer-Seller Relationships in Business Markets." *Journal of Marketing,* November 1999.

Levitt, Theodore. *The Marketing Imagination.* New York: Free Press, 1983.

———. "After the Sale Is Over." *Harvard Business Review,* September–October 1983.

Reinartz, Werner J., and V. Kumar. "The Impact of Customer Relationship Characteristics on Profitable Lifetime Duration." *Journal of Marketing,* January 2003.

———. "The Mismanagement of Customer Loyalty." *Harvard Business Review,* July 2002.

Rigby, Darrel K., Frederick F. Reichheld, and Phil Schefter. "Avoid the Four Perils of CRM." *Harvard Business Review,* February 2002.

Sherlock, Paul. *Rethinking Business-to-Business Marketing.* New York: Free Press, 1991.

Sherman, Jerry, and Eric Hertz. *Woman Power in Textile & Apparel Sales.* New York: Fairchild Publications, 1979.

Weitz, Barton A., and Kevin D. Bradford. "Personal Selling and Sales Management: A Relationship Marketing Perceptive." *Journal of the Academy of Marketing Science,* 27, 1999.

Chapter 9   Peter, Laurence J. *The Peter Principle,* New York: William Morrow, 1969.

Deeter-Schmelz, Dawn R., Karen Norman Kennedy, and Daniel J. Goebel. "Understanding Sales Managers Effectiveness: Linking Attributes to Sales Force Values." *Industrial Marketing Management,* 31, October 2002.

Drucker, Peter. *Managing for Results.* New York, NY: Harper & Row, 1964.

———. *The Practice of Management.* New York, NY: Harper & Row, 1954.

———. "Peter Drucker on the Profession of Management." *Harvard Business Review,* 1998.

———. *The Essentential Drucker,* New York, NY: HarperBusiness, 2001.

Grant, Ken, David W. Gravens, George S. Lowe, and William C. Moncrief. "The Role of Satisfaction with Territory Design on Motivation, Attitudes and Work Outcomes of Salespeople." *Journal of the Academy of Marketing Source,* 29, Spring 2001.

———. "Antecedents and Consequences of Salesperson Burnout." *European Journal of Marketing,* 35, 2001.

Kotler, Phillip. *Marketing Management: The Millennium Edition,* 10th edition, Englewood Cliffs, NJ: Prentice Hall, 2000.

Moyers, Bill. "A World of Ideas by Bill Moyers." PBS Video interview with Peter Drucker. New York: WNET, 1988; Chicago: WTTW, 1988.

Sherman, Jerry, and Eric Hertz. *Woman Power in Textile & Apparel Sales.* New York: Fairchild Publications, 1979.

Zoltners, Andris A., and Sally E. Lorimer. "Sales Territory Alignment: An Overlooked Productivity Tool." *Journal of Selling & Sales Management,* 20, Summer 2000.

Chapter 10   Anderson, Rolph, Rajiv Mehra, and James Strong. "Sales Training and Education an Empirical Investigation of Sales Management Training Programs for Sales Managers." *Journal of Personal Selling,* 7, *Sales Management,* 17, 1997.

Cook, S. *Customer Care: How to Create an Effective Customer Focus.* London: Kogan Page, 2000.

Honeycutt, Earl, John B. Ford, Robert Lupton, and Theresa Flaherty. "Selecting and Training the International Sales Force: Comparison of China and Slosvkia." *Industrial Marketing Management*, 28, November 1999.

Karr, R., and D. Blohowiak. *The Complete Idiots Guide to Great Customer Service*. New York: Alpha Books, 1997.

Kulik, Todd. "Forging an Effective Sales Organization." *The Conference Board*, 1999.

Weeks, William A., and Carl Stevens. "National Account Management Sales Training and Directions for Improvement: A Focus on Skills & Abilities." *Industrial Marketing Management*, 36, September 1997.

Chapter 11   Diamond, Ellen. *Fashion Retailing*. Clifton Park, NY: Delmar Publishing, 1993.

Dunne, Patrick M., Robert F. Lusch, and David A. Griffith. *Retailing,* 4th edition. Orlando, FL: Harcourt Brace, 2002.

Dyer, F. Robert, and John F. Tanner. *Business Marketing,* 3rd edition. New York: McGraw-Hill, 2006.

Kaydos, W. J. *Operational Performance Measurement: Increasing Total Productivity*. Boca Raton, FL: CRC Press, LLC, 1998.

Pritchard, Robert D. *Measuring and Improving Organizational Productivity*. Westport, CT: Praeger Publishers, 1990.

Smith, Benson, and Tony Rutigliano. "Building a World-Class Sales Force: Measuring Three Key Factors Is Just the Starting Point." *Gallup Management Journal*, www.gmj.gallup.com, 2001.

Schulman, Peter. "Applying Learned Optimism to Increase Sales Productivity." *Personal Selling & Sales Management*, V19 #1, 1999.

Sujan, Harish., Barton A. Weitz, and Mita Sujan. "Increasing Sales Productivity by Getting Salespeople to Work Smarter." *Personal Selling & Sales Management*, V8 #2, August 1988.

Chapter 12   Anderson, James C., and James A. Narus, *Business Marketing Management,* 2nd edition. Upper Saddle River, NJ: Pearson Education, 2003.

Diamond, Ellen. *Fashion Retailing*. Clifton Park, NY: Delmar Publishing, 1993.

Dyer, F. Robert, and John F. Tanner. *Business Marketing,* 3rd edition. New York: McGraw-Hill, 2006.

Marchetti, Michele. "What a Sale Costs." *Sales & Marketing Management*, 2001.

Sullivan, Malcolm, and Dennis Adcock. *Retail Marketing*. Mason, OH: Thomson Publishing, 2002.

Vitale, Robert P., and Joseph J. Giglierano. *Business to Business Market-ing: Analysis and Practice in a Dynamic Environment.* Mason, OH: South-Western, a division of Thomson Learning, 2002.

Chapter 13   Best, Roger J. *Market-Based Management,* 2nd edition. Englewood Cliffs, NJ: Prentice Hall, 2000.

Kotler, Phillip. *Marketing Management: The Millennium Edition,* 10th edition. Englewood Cliffs, NJ: Prentice Hall, 2000.

Moore, Geoffrey A. *Inside Tornado.* New York: Harper Business, 1995.

Narus, James A., and J. C. Anderson. "Rethinking Distribution Adaptive Channels." *Harvard Business Review,* 1996.

Porter, Michael E. "What is Strategy?" *Harvard Business Review,* 1996.

Rogers, Everett M. *Diffusion of Innovation, 4th edition.* New York: Free Press, 1995.

U.S. Department of Commerce, International Trade Administration. Office of Textiles and Apparel. Online. http://otexa.ita.doc.gov/fr2005/619request.pdf

Vitale, Robert P., and Joseph J. Giglierano. *Business to Business Market-ing: Analysis and Practice in a Dynamic Environment.* Mason, OH: South-Western, a division of Thomson Learning, 2002.

Chapter 14   "What is Culture?" California State Polytechnic University, Pomona, CA, January 23, 2003, p. 34.

Aaker, Joachimsthaler. "The Lure of Global Branding." *Harvard Business Review,* November/December 1999

Adcock, D., A. Halborg, R. Bradfield, and C. Ross. *Marketing Principles and Practice.* London: FT Pittman, 1991.

Dawar, Niraj, and Tony Frost. "Competing with GIANTS: Survival Strategies for Local Companies in Emerging Markets." *Harvard Business Review,* March/April 1999.

Holt, Tomas, O. C. Ferrell, and Robert Hurley. "Global Organizational Learning Effects on Cycle Time Performance." *Journal of Business Research,* 55, 2002.

Nanda, Serena, and Richard L. Warms. *Cultural Anthropology,* 8th edition. Belmont, CA: Wadsworth Publishing, 2003.

Steidlmeir, P. "Gift-Giving, Bribery and Corruption: An Ethical Mea-surement of Business Relationships in China." *Journal of Business Ethics,* 20, June 2000.

Sullivan, Malcolm, and Dennis Adcock. *Retail Marketing.* Mason, OH: Thomson Publishing, 2002.

Trent, Robert T., and Robert M. Monczka. "International Purchasing and Global Sourcing: What Are the Differences?" *Journal of Supply Chain Management,* 39, 2003.

GLOSSARY

80-20 rule States that about 20 percent of the sales force sells about 80 percent of the company's business. These percentages will vary somewhat from company to company.

active account A current customer who buys on a regular basis.

appearance The choice of wardrobe, accessories, and personal style of a salesperson, as compared with the company he or she represents and the clients with whom one meets.

approach The words and physical gestures a salesperson uses to make the first contact with the customer.

assertiveness The need to drum up the maximum amount of business that can be properly handled by the company's manufacturing and distribution set-up.

B2B (Business to Business) Transactions that take place between fashion manufacturers, retailers, or any two business entities.

B2C (Business to Consumer) Sales made by a business to an individual consumer; see also *retail* and *retailing*.

bait-and-switch Luring the customer with a bargain-priced product and trying to switch the customer to a higher-priced product.

big pencil A sales slang term denoting the buyer who represents a major account in the marketplace. This buyer signs large orders, either in volume and/or dollar value.

Buying Power Index (BPI) An index used to determine a specific geographical market's buying power for items purchased usually at popular prices. It is used to forecast demand, and its market can be a region, state, or county.

Customer Retention Management (CRM) Process that identifies and retains customers, creates customer history, builds customer relations, and helps shapes customers' perceptions of the company and its products.

center of influence Someone whose opinion your buyer seeks and respects. Typically, it is someone involved in industry improvement projects through trade associations and industry organizations and who is well respected by peers and colleagues.

closing the sale Asking the client to buy and take the order, thus completing the sales transaction.

clotheshorse A slang term denoting a person who pays much attention to clothes and fashion trends; in other words, a fashion connoisseur.

consumer demand or bottom-up model The change in the product is initiated by consumer demand. News of the public's needs travels up the fashion sales hierarchy.

controller The executive responsible for approving or disapproving the extension of credit to a customer and managing the financial end of the business.

creative-design or top-down model The change in the product is initiated by the manufacturer or its design team.

creativity Taking a thorough look at the existing sales practices of your company and translating them into your own course of action.

cultural divide A set of cultural differences between the seller and the buyer.

demographics A set of characteristics of a certain group that describes its background, economic status, education, and other social factors.

drive for success The power and energy to overcome obstacles or rejection and get things done.

emotional maturity The ability not to lose your cool under pressure.

empathy Listening to another attentively and understanding their thoughts, emotions, and feelings and adjusting your own moods and behavior accordingly.

ethics Moral and behavioral principles that dictate what is right and wrong.

global sales force A team of salespeople who reside abroad, are employed by the company, and understand the local culture of the different areas in their territory.

house account A major account with high volume that is assigned to a dedicated inside salesperson or an executive because it requires considerable time, attention, and support. This type of account may receive additional services based on its huge volume, leaving little room for compensation to a straight commission or outside salesperson. The inside salesperson/account executive responsible for this major account is usually salaried and may receive a bonus or commission based on increases in sales volume.

inactive account A former customer who no longer buys on a regular basis.

inflation An increase in the volume of money and credit relative to available goods and services resulting in a continuing rise in the general price level.

inside salespeople Employees who work in the company's headquarters or in one of the regional offices, and typically handle any orders that come into the office directly, with or without the solicitation of an outside salesperson.

integrity Behaving in an honest manner and according to social and moral principles.

licensee Has permission to use the licensor's logo, styles, patterns, marketing know-how, and other merchandising aids as its own only without the right of actual ownership of these properties.

licensor Allows another to use its intellectual property rights in exchange for payment, usually in the form of commission on sales or a specified royalty payment.

manufacturer A business that turns raw materials into finished, sellable products.

manufacturer's representative An individual or a business that brings manufacturer and buyer together in exchange for a commission, without ever obtaining ownership of the goods.

market The group of individuals who or businesses that within a specific region may have a need for your product and are likely to afford it.

market shift A significant change that can potentially affect sales.

marketing manager The executive who shapes the company's research concerning demographics and psychographics and promotional efforts so that its products can sell based on the target customers' wants and needs.

need A problem the customer wishes to solve or something the customer feels he or she should have.

network In a formal sense, it is a group of business people who agree to meet together or stay in touch regularly and to offer each other support, advice, and business referrals. Informally, it is the group of people with whom the salesperson creates business relationships outside the office through social interaction and community work.

objection The reason a client offers for not buying. Objections are questions or statements that indicate the concerns the buyer has about the product or sales presentation. These must be answered properly before the buyer decides to buy.

open-to-buy Available funding to purchase merchandise.

operational communication The relay and explanation of company policy and proper structure, as well as the provision of needed resources for salespeople to operate.

outside salespeople Members of the direct sales force employed by the company or independent sale reps who may reside in their territories and directly contact retailers and/or resellers within their territories to sell the product lines.

paperwork with a purpose Any form or written notice that documents an order, a customer change, or an employee action and has a meaningful reason for its existence.

people building Developing people to be more productive and more confident in achieving their goals. In the 1970s, before the concept of equal opportunity entered the fashion selling business, traveling or outside saleswomen were very rare. Management, in their efforts to develop their sales forces, coined the expression "manpower development," which became one of the sales managers' key buzz phrases. Fortunately, today our industry has a better representation of women in sales and "manpower development" became "people building."

people problems The range of interpersonal conflicts arising from the competitive nature of the business.

people-oriented market shift A significant change in the demographics and psychographics that can potentially affect sales.

personal selling Developing and maintaining a close business relationship with the customer, where both customer and salesperson trust and respect each other and where the seller interacts for the purpose of continuing the relationship while endeavoring to obtain a sale for the mutual benefit of both buyer and seller.

plus or minus factor A scale from 1 to 10 that indicates the positive or negative approach and attitude of a salesperson.

PMA (Positive Mental Attitude) A positive, optimistic, and enthusiastic approach to the sales presentation.

point of interest Something that is of interest to both seller and buyer, within the business relationship's framework or personally.

preconceived values Benefits or features that make the product desirable to a particular buyer.

product knowledge To know the correct features, benefits, and shortcomings of a product and its compatibility with other products.

production manager The executive who oversees the manufacturing of the goods and the preparation for shipment, coordinates priorities, and solves production and lead-time issues.

productivity facilitation Monitoring and improving the productivity of each salesperson as well as of the sales force as a whole.

product-oriented market shift A significant change in the product (in style, color, size, or any other feature of the actual fashion item) that can potentially affect sales.

prospect A potential buyer; someone who isn't a current customer and who may have the need for and be able to buy your product.

prospecting Locating potential buyers and contacting them with the aim of setting up an appointment for a sales presentation.

psychographics A set of characteristics of a certain group that describes its behavioral and psychological structure.

qualified prospect A prospect who proves to have the need, budget, and ability to buy your product.

qualify The act of determining whether a prospect has the need, budget, and ability to buy your product.

reseller A business that buys goods, typically in volume, and sells smaller quantities to a retailer or another business, also referred to as merchant wholesaler or jobber.

retail To sell a product directly to the individual who will be using it.

retailing The process of selling to the ultimate consumer, also known as the end user.

Return on Investment (ROI) Every investment a business makes has an expected return. If the return is less than the investment, then the business loses money. If it is more than the investment, then the business earns a profit.

sales goal A quantitative target for a sales-related statistic that the salesperson can achieve within a season, year, or other specified time frame.

sales manager The executive in charge of the salespeople within a specific territory or the entire sales force, who hires, directs, trains, and motivates them.

selling An exchange of goods or services designed to deliver a mutual benefit for both buyer and seller, resulting in a continual and positive relationship.

shipping manager The executive who is involved in helping schedule the starting shipment dates for initial orders, as well as the delivery dates for reorders; he or she works with the various transportation companies to assure timely deliveries.

structure-oriented market shift A significant change in the structure of the industry (the way product is designed, manufactured, distributed, or sold) that can potentially affect sales.

supply chain Actions by B2B participants in monitoring the flow of goods through all the steps involved in getting the products to the end user.

suspect A prospect who turns out to be unqualified buyer.

SWOT (Strengths, Weaknesses, Opportunities, and Threats) A marketing term denoting an analysis of these areas, which is essential for strategic planning in any business.

training Programs designed to teach sales methodology, instruct company procedures, and inform about new products.

VAT (Value-added Tax) An indirect sales tax that is added to a product at some of its production and distribution stages, typically passed on to the consumer.

value chain The chain of B2B activities that creates something of value for the targeted buyers.

BIBLIOGRAPHY

Books and Articles

Aaker, Joachimsthaler. "The Lure of Global Branding." *Harvard Business Review*, November/December 1999

Adcock, D., A. Halborg, R. Bradfield, and C. Ross. *Marketing Principles and Practice.* London: FT Pittman, 1991.

"After All You've Done for Your Customers, Why Are They Still Not Happy?" *Fortune Magazine*, December 11, 1995.

Amber, Tim, and Moran Witzel. *Doing Business in China, 2nd edition.* New York: Routledge, 2004.

Anderson, James C., and James A. Narus, *Business Marketing Management,* 2nd edition. Upper Saddle River, NJ: Pearson Education, 2003.

Anderson, Rolph, Rajiv Mehra, and James Strong. "Sales Training and Education an Empirical Investigation of Sales Management Training Programs for Sales Managers." *Journal of Personal Selling* 7, Sales Management 17, 1997.

Best, Roger J. *Market-Based Management 2nd edition.* Upper Saddle River, NJ: Prentice Hall (Division/Pearson), 2000.

Boone, Louis E., and David L. Kurtz. *Contemporary Marketing, 11th edition.* Mason, OH: South-western, a division of Thompson Learning, 2004.

Brooks, Bill. "20 Ways to Derail a Successful Sales Career." *American Salesman*, September 2002.

Buzzotta, V. R., R. E. Lefton, and Manuel Sherberg. *Effective Selling Through Psychology.* Cambridge, MA: Ballinger Publishing/Harper & Row, 1982.

Cannon, Joseph P., and William D. Perreault, Jr. "Buyer-Seller Relationships in Business Markets." *Journal of Marketing*, November 1999.

Cholewka, Kathleen. "Survey Says: Some Sales Execs Are Liars." *Sales & Marketing*, 2001.

Churchill Jr., Gilbert A., Neil M. Ford, and Orville C. Walker. *Sales Force Management 2nd edition.* Homewood, Ill.: Richard D. Irwin, 1985.

Cook, S. *Customer Care: How to Create an Effective Customer Focus.* London: Kogan Page, 2000.

Coscia, S. *Customer Service Over the Phone*. San Francisco: Miller Freeman, 1998.

Davis, Rick. "Command Performance: To Make Powerful Sales Presentations, You Need a Carefully Prepared and Concise Script." *Journal of Personal Selling & Sales Management*, August 2004.

Dawar, Niraj, and Tony Frost, "Competing with GIANTS: Survival Strategies for Local Companies in Emerging Markets," *Harvard Business Review*, March/April 1999.

Deeter-Schmelz, Dawn R., Karen Norman Kennedy, and Daniel J. Goebel. "Understanding Sales Managers Effectiveness: Linking Attributes to Sales Force Values." *Industrial Marketing Management* 31, October 2002.

Diamond, Ellen. *Fashion Retailing*. Clifton Park, NY: Delmar Publishing (Division/Thomson), 1993.

Dion, Paul, Debbi Easterling, and Raj Javalgi. "Women in Business-to-Business Salesforce: Some Differences in Performance Factors." *Industrial Marketing Management* 26, September 1997.

Drucker, Peter. *Managing for Results*. New York: Harper & Row, 1964.

———. *The Practice of Management*. New York: Harper & Row, 1954.

———. "Peter Drucker on the Profession of Management." *Harvard Business Review*, 1998.

———. *The Essentential Drucker*, New York: HarperBusiness, 2001.

Dunne, Patrick M., Robert F. Lusch, and David A. Griffith, *Retailing, 4th edition*. Orlando, FL: Harcourt Brace, 2002.

Dyer, F. Robert, and John F. Tanner. *Business Marketing, 3rd edition*. New York: McGraw-Hill, 2006.

Farber, Barry. "Good Show! Sales Presentations." *Entrepreneur Magazine*, November 2004. www.findarticles.com/p/articles, *Journal of Personal Selling & Sales Management*.

Garfinkel, David. Making the Most of IT: How to Squeeze More Profits from the Web." *Sales & Marketing Management* 154, March 2002.

Girard, Joe, and Robert Casemore. *How to Sell Yourself*. New York: Warner Books, 1992.

Grant, Ken, David W. Gravens, George S. Lowe, and William C. Moncrief. "The Role of Satisfaction with Territory Design on Motivation, Attitudes and Work Outcomes of Salespeople." *Journal of the Academy of Marketing Source* 29, Spring 2001.

———. "Antecedents and Consequences of Salesperson Burnout." *European Journal of Marketing* 35, 2001.

Harrow, Susan. *Sell Yourself Without Selling Your Soul: A Woman's Guide to Promoting Herself, Her Business*. New York: HarperCollins Publishers, 2002.

Hoffman, Czunkota, Griffin Dickson, and Krishman Hutt. *Marketing Principles & Best Practices*, 3rd edition. California: Thomson, 2005.

Holt, Thomas, O. C. Ferrell, and Robert Hurley. "Global Organizational Learning Effects on Cycle Time Performance." *Journal of Business Research,* 55, 2002.

Honeycutt, Earl, John B. Ford, Robert Lupton, and Theresa Flaherty. "Selecting and Training the International Sales Force: Comparison of China and Slosvkia." *Industrial Marketing Management,* 28, November 1999.

Jackson, Donald, Scott Widmier, Ralph Giacobbe, and Janet E. Keith, "Examining the Use of Team Selling by Manufacturer's Representatives: A Situational Approach." *Industrial Marketing Management,* 28, March 1999.

Karr, R., and D. Blohowiak. *The Complete Idiots Guide to Great Customer Service.* New York: Alpha Books, 1997.

Kaydos, W. J. *Operational Performance Measurement: Increasing Total Productivity.* Boca Raton, FL: CRC Press, LLC, 1998.

Kotlor, Phillip. *Marketing Management: The Millennium Edition,* 10th edition. Englewood Cliffs, NJ: Prentice Hall, 2000.

Kulik, Todd. "Forging an Effective Sales Organization." *The Conference Board,* 1999.

Leeds, Dorothy. "How to Make Persuasive Sales Presentations." Folio: Special Sourcebook Issue, *The Magazine for Magazine Management,* 1998.

Leone, Patrick. "The Right Way to Get Referrals." *Advisor Today*, October 2002.

Levitt, Theodore. *The Marketing Imagination.* New York: Free Press, 1983.
———. "After the Sale Is Over." *Harvard Business Review,* September–October 1983.

Levy, Michael. *Retail Management.* New York: McGraw Hill, 2003.

Marchetti, Michele. "What a Sale Costs." *Sales & Marketing Management,* 2001.

Marchetti, Michele. "What a Sales Call Costs." *Sales & Marketing Management,* September 2000.

Marcus, Stanley. *The Viewpoints of Stanley Marcus: A Ten-Year Perceptive.* Denton, TX: University of North Texas Press, 1995.

Maynard, Robert. "Finding the Essence of Good Salespeople: How to Identify the Characteristics That Make Good Salespeople." *Nation's Business,* February 1998.

McMaster, Mark. "Online Learning from Scratch." *Sales & Marketing Management,* November 2002.

Molloy, John T. *Dress for Success.* New York: Warner Books, 1976.
———. *New Dress for Success.* New York: Warner Books, 1988.

————. *The New Woman's Dress for Success.* New York: Warner Books, 1996.

————. *Woman's Dress for Success.* New York: Warner Books, 1984.

Moore, Geoffrey A. *Inside Tornado.* New York: Harper Business, 1995.

Moyers, Bill. "A World of Ideas by Bill Moyers." PBS Video interview with Peter Drucker. New York: WNET, 1988; Chicago: WTTW, 1988.

Nanda, Serena, and Richard L. Warms. *Cultural Anthropology, 8th edition.* Belmont, Cal.: Wadsworth Publishing, 2003.

Narus, James A., and J. C. Anderson, "Rethinking Distribution Adaptive Channels." *Harvard Business Review,* 1996.

Peter, Laurance J. *The Peter Principle.* New York: William Morrow, 1969.

Porter, Michael. "What is Strategy?" *Harvard Business Review,* 1996.

Porter, Michael. *Competitive Advantage Creating and Sustaining Superior Performance.* New York: Free Press, 1985.

Pritchard, Robert D. *Measuring and Improving Organizational Productivity.* Westport, CT: Praeger Publishers, a division of Greenwood Publishing, 1990.

Rackham, Neil. *Spin Selling.* New York: McGraw-Hill, 1988.

Reicheld, F.F. "Learning from Customer Defections." *Harvard Business Review,* March/April 1996.

Reinartz, Werner J., and V. Kumar. "The Impact of Customer Relationship Characteristics on Profitable Lifetime Duration." *Journal of Marketing,* Volume 67, Number 1, January 2003.

————. "The Mismanagement of Customer Loyalty." *Harvard Business Review,* July 2002.

Rigby, Darrel K., Frederick F. Reichheld, and Phil Schefter. "Avoid the Four Perils of CRM." *Harvard Business Review,* February 2002.

Rogers, Everett M. *Diffusion of Innovation,* 4th edition. New York: Free Press, 1995.

Ruth, Amanda, and Allen Wysocki. "Top Sellers: Characteristics of a Superior Salesperson." EDIS document SN004, a publication of the Department of Food and Resource Economics, Florida Cooperative Extension Service, Institute of Food and Agricultural Sciences, University of Florida, Gainesville, FL, April 2002, http://edis.ifas.ufl.edu.

Sargent, T. J., N. Williams, and T. Zha. "Shock and Government Beliefs: The Rise and Fall of American Inflation." NBER working paper w10764, (2004).

Satterfield, Mark. "Selling to the Top: Traits and Characteristics of Senior Level Business Developers." *American Salesman,* December 2001.

Schiffman, Leon G., and Leslie Lazar Frank. *Consumer Behavior,* 8th edition. Upper Saddle River, NJ: Prentice Hall (Division/Pearson), 2003.

Schroeder, Carol L. *Specialty Shop Retailing: How to Run Your Own Store.* New Jersey: John Wiley & Sons, Inc., 1997, 2002.

Schulman, Peter. "Applying Learned Optimism to Increase Sales Productivity." *Personal Selling & Sales Management,* V19 #1, 1999.

Sherlock, Paul. *Rethinking Business to Business Marketing.* New York: Free Press, 1991.

Sherman, Jerry, and Eric Hertz. *Woman Power in Textile & Apparel Sales.* New York: Fairchild Publications, 1979.

Sjodin, Terry L. New Sales Speak: *The 9 Biggest Sales Presentation Mistakes and How to Avoid Them.* New Jersey: John Wiley & Sons, Inc., 2001.

Smith, Benson, and Tony Rutigliano, "Building a World-Class Sales Force: Measuring Three Key Factors Is Just the Starting Point." *Gallup Management Journal,* www.gmj.gallup.com, 2001.

Steidlmeir, P. "Gift-Giving, Bribery and Corruption: An Ethical Measurement of Business Relationships in China." *Journal of Business Ethics,* 20, June 2000.

Sujan, Harish. "Optimism and Street Smarts: Identifying and Improving Salesperson Intelligence." *Journal of Personal Selling and Sales Management,* 19, 1999.

Sujan, Harish., Barton A. Weitz, and Mita Sujan. "Increasing Sales Productivity by Getting Salespeople to Work Smarter." *Personal Selling & Sales Management,* V8 #2, August 1988.

Sullivan, Malcolm, and Dennis Adcock. *Retail Marketing.* London: Thompson High Holborne House, 2002.

Swanson, Kristen K., and Judith C. Everett. *Promotion in the Merchandising Environment.* New York: Fairchild Publications, 2000.

Tanner Jr., John F. "Adaptive Selling at Trade Shows." *Journal of Personal Selling & Sales Management,* 1994.

Thull, Jeff. "The End of Solution-Based Selling." www.marketingprofs.com, September 20, 2005.

Trent, Robert T., and Robert M. Monczka. "International Purchasing and Global Sourcing: What Are the Differences?" *Journal of Supply Chain Management* 39, 2003.

Vitale, Robert P., and Joseph J. Giglierano. *Business to Business Marketing: Analysis and Practice in a Dynamic Environment.* Mason, OH: South-Western, a division of Thomason Learning, 2002.

Weeks, William A., and Carl Stevens. "National Account Management Sales Training and Directions for Improvement: A Focus on Skills & Abilities." *Industrial Marketing Management,* 36, September 1997.

Weinreb, Michael. "Don't Waste Your Time." *Sales & Marketing Management,* November 2002.

Weitz, Barton A., and Kevin D. Bradford. "Personal Selling and Sales Management: A Relationship Marketing Perceptive." *Journal of the Academy of Marketing Science* 27, 1999.

Whalin, George. *Retail Success.* San Marcos, CA: Willoughby Press, 2001.

Zoltners, Andris A., and Sally E. Lorimer. "Sales Territory Alignment: An Overlooked Productivity Tool." *Journal of Selling & Sales Management,* 20, Summer 2000.

Online Sources

About.com, careers section. http://careerplanning.about.com/od/communication/a/email_etiquette.htm

American Apparel & Footwear Association. www.americanapparel.org

American Marketing Association dictionary. www.marketingpower.com

Bass, Adam "The Growth of the Corporate Brand." www.goldengoose.uk.com

Bill Communications, Inc. www.salesandmarketing.com

BizStats.com. Total Number of U.S. Businesses 2000 report. www.bizstats.com/businesses.htm

Dun & Bradstreet. www.dnb.com

Harvard Business School, Institute of Strategy & Competitiveness. Faculty biographies. http://dor.hbs.edu/fi_redirect.jhtml?facInfo=bio&facEmId=mporter&loc=extn

Harvard Business School Web site. Faculty & Research page. http://dor.hbs.edu/fi_redirect.jhtml?facInfo=bio&facEmId=tlevitt&loc=extn

Hoover's online. www.hoovers.com/free/cp/factsheet.xhtml?&ID=40369&abforward=true

Infomat. www.infomat.com

Licensing Magazine. www.licensemag.com/licensemag/data/articlestandard/licensemag/412005/184293/article.pdf

Marketing Pathways. www.marketingpathways.com

National Retail Federation. www.nrf.com

Perry Ellis. www.pery.com

Rotary Club. www.rotary.org/aboutrotary/history/index.html

Testimony before the House Committee on International Relations U.S. House of Representatives Washington, DC, October 21, 2003.

The Federal Reserve Bank of New York Web site. http://search.newyorkfed.org/search/frbny.jsp?querybox=inflation+1960=and1970&sear

Toastmasters International. www.toastmasters.org/about.asp

U.S. Bureau of Census, Statistical Abstract of the United States: 2001, Table No.722. www.census.gov/prod/2002pubs/01statab/business.pdf

U.S. Census Bureau. www.census.gov/population/cen2000/phc-t1/tab01.pdf

U.S. Department of Agriculture, Economic Research Service. The Changing World Network of Trade in Textiles and Apparel. www.ers.usda.gov/AmberWaves/scripts/print.asp?page=/september04/DataFeature/

U.S. Department of Commerce, International Trade Administration. Office of Textiles and Apparel. http://otexa.ita.doc.gov/fr2005/619request.pdf

U.S. Department of Labor, Bureau of Labor Statistics. May 2003. National Occupational Employment and Wage Estimates Sales and Related Occupations. www.bls.gov/oes/2003/may/oes_41Sa.htm

U.S. Department of Labor Statistics. www.bls.gov/oes/current/oes412031.htm

U.S. Small Business Administration. http://app1.sba.gov/faqs/faqIndexAll.cfm?areaid=24

What is Culture? California State Polytechnic University, Pomona, California, 1/23/03, p. 34. www.calpoly.edu/

INDEX